HIGH PUB WALKS
in the
PEAK DISTRICT

Martin Smith

Published by Sigma Leisure – an imprint of
Sigma Press, Stobart House, Pontyclerc, Penybanc Road, Ammanford, Carmarthenshire SA18 3HP.

British Library Cataloguing in Publication Data
A CIP record for this book is available from the British Library.

ISBN: 978-1-85058-979-2

Typesetting and Design by: Sigma Press, Ammanford.

Cover photographs: © Martin Smith; above: The Salt Cellar; below left: The Barrel, Bretton; below right: Butcher's Arms, Reapsmoor

Photographs: © Martin Smith

Maps: contains Ordnance Survey data © Crown copyright and database right 2014

Printed by: TJ International Ltd, Padstow, Cornwall

Disclaimer: the information in this book is given in good faith and is believed to be correct at the time of publication. No responsibility is accepted by either the author or publisher for errors or omissions, or for any loss or injury howsoever caused. Only you can judge your own fitness, competence and experience. Do not reply solely on sketch maps for nagivation: we strongly recommend the use of appropriate Ordnance Survey (or equivalent) maps.

Contents

Part 2: The Circular Walks

Dedication

I would like to dedicate this book to the two people who have been most inspirational to me. The first person is my father, who would have been 100 in 2013 and who first introduced me to walking in the Peak District. He took me over Kinder at the age of 5 and somehow, despite it being a foul day I've never looked back since. Thanks Dad.

The second person is my late wife, Jane. She was a constant companion on my walks for over 40 years, even before we were married. I won't say she always came on walks uncomplainingly, especially tramps over Pennine bogs in grim weather, but she always did come. We climbed mountains throughout the UK, in Ireland, Germany, Austria, Italy and Spain; tramped the North Pennines and the Derbyshire and Yorkshire Dales. Jane was present at The Barrel when this book was first mooted and would undoubtedly have accompanied me on all the walks. Perhaps she did. I never felt alone on any of the walks even though there was no obvious person physically present. Thanks for everything love.

Acknowledgments

First, thanks to everyone who has accompanied me on any of these walks. I'll specially single out my grandchildren who've survived being dragged up and over Kinder, along Derwent Edge and various other places. Incredibly they seem to have enjoyed it. There must be a masochistic gene there somewhere. Thanks especially to Maureen and Margaret who have again proof read this book. It's a thankless task, but a very important one.

Introduction

The origin of this book began as a casual conversation whilst sitting outside the Barrel Inn at Bretton, the highest pub in Derbyshire. Someone asked which was the highest pub in the Peak District National Park. (It's the Cat and Fiddle). The next question was, 'Which is the highest pub in the six counties that make up the Peak District?' From there it was but a short jump to say what a grand walk it would be to link all six. So here goes.

First some ground rules

- The pubs must be within the National Park, or, if there isn't a pub within the Park, then choose the nearest to the boundary irrespective of height.
- The route between the pubs must be as close as possible to a straight line, consistent with minimising road walking and avoiding unnecessary ascent and descent.
- Access land can be used, but rights of way are preferable. (There was a suggestion that the route should be in the National Park all the way. However, it soon became obvious that this would not really be practical, or consistent with the 'straight line' idea, especially around Buxton).

It was also felt to be a good idea to have a circular walk from each of these high pubs. Closer investigation showed that some of them already had such walks in companion books in this Pub Walks series, so there's no point in repeating these here. However, four of the high pubs do not feature in any previous pub walks book, so these now have an individual circular walk in this publication. Some of the distances between the featured county high pubs are so great that it is necessary to split the walk into shorter sections. Inevitably not all these start or finish at one of the high pubs and some don't even start or finish at pubs in the National Park. Any pubs of this nature do not have circular walks of their own in this book. The challenge walk and the circular walks from the high pubs brought the total number of walks to 16.

Inevitably, someone then asked whether that included all the highest pubs in the Peak District. Setting the bar for height at 1000 feet and checking the various maps, I found that there were no fewer than 24 other pubs in the National Park situated at 1000 feet or over. To link all these in a single walk would be a logistical challenge (nightmare?) in itself, so I looked at these extra pubs and found that eight of them featured in either the *Best Dark Peak* or *Best White Peak Pub Walks* books by Sigma, so, again there was not much point in repeating these walks. This left 16 pubs sited at over 1000 feet that had not featured in previous pub walks books. Fortunately, some of these are quite close together – very close in one case, where the distance between the two is measured in yards rather than miles – and so could reasonably be combined into a single walk. I managed to get the number of walks down to 30.

The counties and the pubs

Table 1. The highest pubs in the constituent counties of the National Park

County	Pub	Altitude in feet (metres)
Cheshire	Cat and Fiddle (i)	1690 feet (515 metres)
Derbyshire	The Barrel (Bretton) (i)	1258 feet (383 metres)
Greater Manchester	Cross Keys (Uppermill) Church Inn (Uppermill)	862 feet (263 metres) 789 feet (240 metres)
South Yorkshire	Fox House (Sheffield) (i) The Dog and Partridge (Langsett/Barnsley)	1124 feet (343 metres) 1120 feet (341 metres)
Staffordshire	Travellers' Rest (Flash) (i)	1516 feet (462 metres)
West Yorkshire	The Fleece (Holme)	990 feet (302 metres)

Notes
(i) Circular walks featuring these pubs are described in the companion book *Best Pub Walks in the Dark Peak* also published by Sigma Press.

Table 2. Other pubs in the National Park over 1000 feet above sea level

Pub	Altitude in feet (metres)	Location
New Inn	1516 feet (462 metres)	Flash (Staffs)
Royal Cottage	1480 feet (451 metres)	A53 north of Leek (Staffs)
Winking Man	1464 feet (446 metres)	A53 north of Leek (Staffs)
The Duke of York	1237 feet (377 metres)	Pomeroy (Derbyshire)
The Church Inn (i)	1224 feet (373 metres)	Chelmorton (Derbyshire)
The Wanted Inn	1216 feet (371 metres)	Sparrowpit (Derbyshire)

Pub	Altitude in feet (metres)	Location
Jug and Glass	1189 feet (362 metres)	A515 N of Newhaven (Derbyshire)
The Waterloo	1187 feet (362 metres)	Taddington (Derbyshire)
Stanley Arms	1178 feet (359 metres)	Wildboarclough (Cheshire)
Bull i't'Thorn	1171 feet (357 metres)	A515 N of Monyash X Roads (Derbyshire)
Royal Oak	1126 feet (343 metres)	Hurdlow (Derbyshire)
The Quiet Woman (i)	1084 feet (330 metres)	Earl Sterndale (Derbys)
The Wild Boar	1083 feet (330 metres)	Wincle (Cheshire)
The Grouse	1058 feet (322 metres)	S of Glossop (Derbyshire)
The Snake (ii)	1056 feet (322 metres)	Snake Pass (Derbyshire)
Queen's Arms (i)	1052 feet (321 metres)	Taddington (Derbyshire)
Strines Inn	1044 feet (318 metres)	Strines (S.Yorkshire)
Butcher's Arms	1034 feet (315 metres)	Reapsmoor (Staffs)
Queen Anne (ii)	1024 feet (312 metres)	Gt. Hucklow (Derbyshire)
The Anchor	1019 feet (311 metres)	Tideswell (Derbyshire)
The Devonshire Arms	1016 feet (310 metres)	Peak Forest (Derbyshire)
Peacock	1014 feet (309 metres)	Owler Bar (Derbyshire)
Cock and Pullet (i)	1008 feet (307 metres)	Sheldon (Derbyshire)
Greyhound (i)	1000 feet (305 metres)	Warslow (Staffs)

Notes

(i) Circular walks featuring these pubs are described in the companion book *Best Pub Walks in the White Peak* also published by Sigma Press.

(ii) Circular walks featuring these pubs are described in the companion book *Best Pub Walks in the Dark Peak*, also published by Sigma Press

The pubs and public transport

Details of public transport access to the various pubs are given in the introduction to each walk. All the walks are accessible by public transport, though some of the pubs do not have public transport within a mile of their front door. Timetables for buses and trains throughout this area can be obtained from the East Midlands Travel Line, **www.travelineeastmidlands.co.uk**

The more remote pubs in the Staffordshire Moorlands only have the demand responsive service 'Moorlands Connect' that has to be booked in advance. The service operates on Mondays to Saturdays. Telephone 0300 1118003 for details. The service operates from a number of hubs where it makes connection with mainstream bus services. Of particular interest to this book are the hubs at Flash Bar, Hartington and Longnor.

Accommodation

On the challenge walk, the following pubs have accommodation;
Dog and Partridge (Langsett) **www.dogandpartridgeinn.co.uk**
Ladybower Inn (Ashopton) **www.ladybower-inn.co.uk**
Fox House Inn (Longshaw) **www.vintageinn.co.uk/thefoxhouselongshaw/**
Barrel Inn (Bretton) **www.thebarrelinn.co.uk**
Duke of York (Pomeroy) (camp site only) **www.thedukeofyorkpomeroy.co.uk**
Travellers Rest/Knights Table (Flash Bar) **www.theknightstable.co.uk**
The Quiet Woman (Earl Sterndale) (camp site only)

For accommodation near Uppermill try **www.saddleworthparishcouncil.org.uk**
For accommodation in or near Holme try **www.holmfirth.org**
For accommodation in the Peak District National Park and Buxton try **www.peakdistrictinformation.com**
For accommodation in Whaley Bridge try **www.whaleybridge.com**
For accommodation in Broadbottom try **www.broadbottomvillage.com**

Within the area covered by these walks, there are youth hostels at Bretton, Castleton (Losehill Hall), Crowden in Longdendale, Edale, Eyam, Gradbach, Hartington, Hathersage and Ravenstor (Millers Dale). The are YHA camping barns at Abney, Edale, Gradbach, Nab End (Hollinsclough), Sheen (camping barn and bunkhouse) and Taddington. Contact **www.yha.org.uk** for details.

If you want to do a number of the walks from a single base, then Buxton is the best bet. Of the Challenge Walk, numbers 5-11 can be done from a Buxton base using public transport to the starting and finishing points (without changes of bus or train). Likewise the following Circular Walks can be readily accessed from Buxton; numbers 14,17,19, 22-4, 26,27 and 29. A number of the other walks can be done from Buxton if you are prepared to change buses and trains, but clearly this complicates matters.

The Maps

The following symbols are used on the maps;

.... no obvious path

-.-.-.-. indistinct path

------- obvious path

_____ surfaced track or road

All the walks in this book are on OS maps OL1 (Dark Peak) or OL24 (White Peak).
Walks 1-4, 12, 13, 15, 16, 18, 25 and 28 are on OL1. Walks 5-10, 14, 17, 19, 20, 22-24, 26, 27, 29 and 30 are on OL24. Walks 11 and 21 need both maps.

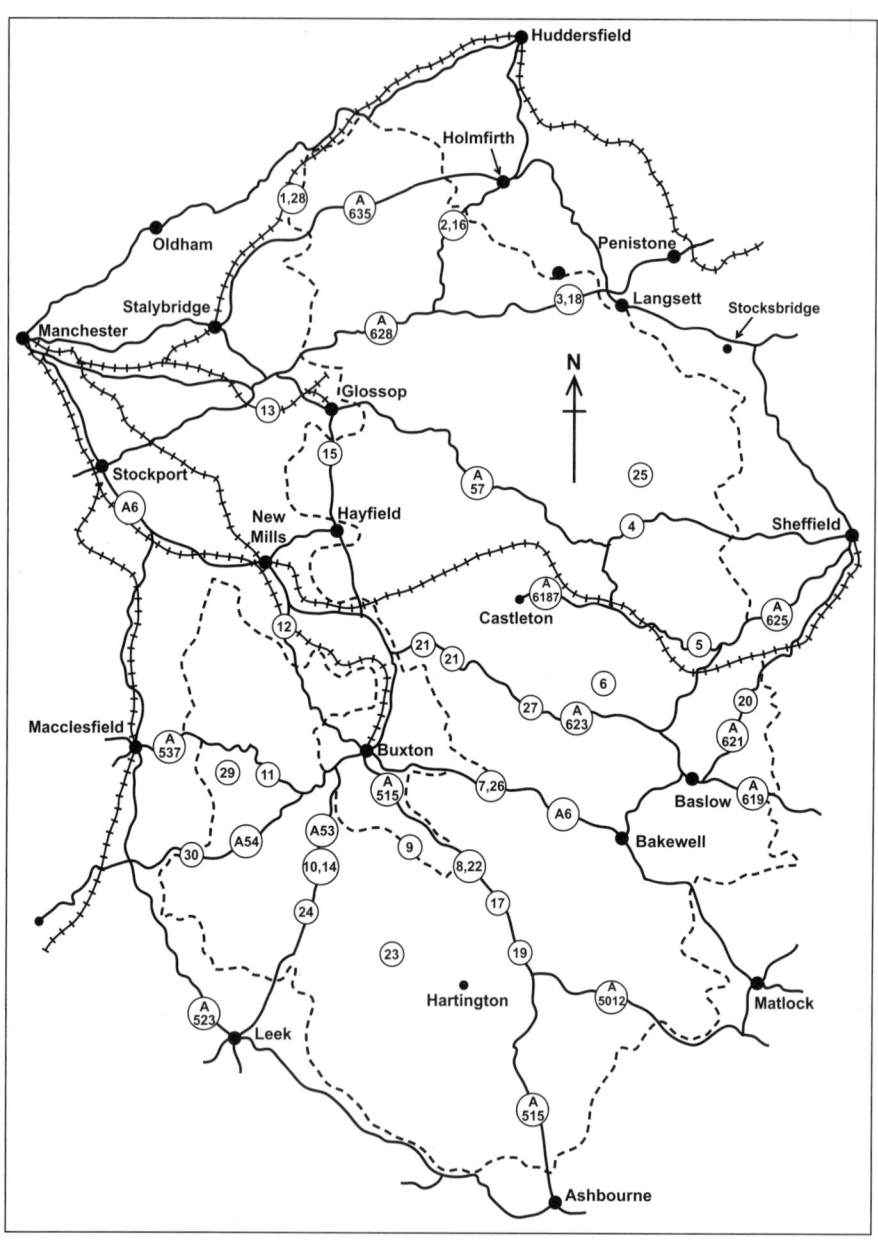

Walks locations

Part 1: The High Pubs Challenge Walk

Introduction

The total route length as the crow flies is about 68 miles (111 km), but this of course hides a multitude of sins. The actual map distance is just over 100 miles (161.27 km) and the total amount of ascent is 17863 feet (5444 metres). The walk splits into six sections of widely varying length. Starting at the northernmost pubs (The Cross Keys and Church Inns at Uppermill), the sections are:

1. Uppermill to Holme, 7.84 miles (12.6 km) 1158 ft (353 metres) of ascent

2. Holme to Langsett (The Dog and Partridge), 8.57 miles (13.8 km), 1850 ft (564 metres) of ascent

3. Langsett to Fox House, 22.26 miles (35.81 km), 3562 ft (1085 metres) of ascent

4. Fox House to Bretton (The Barrel), 6.82 miles (11 km), 1388 ft (423 metres) of ascent.

5. Bretton to Flash (Travellers Rest/Knights' Table), 19.08 miles (30.73 km), 3631 ft (1107 metres) of ascent.

6. Flash to Cat and Fiddle, 4.32 miles (7 km), 817 ft (249 metres) of ascent.

7. Cat and Fiddle to Uppermill (The Cross Keys Inn), 31.28 miles (50.33 km), 5457 ft (1663 metres) of ascent.

The third, fifth and seventh sections are split into shorter pieces because of their length, making a total of 13 walks in all.

Walk 1: Uppermill (Cross Keys or The Church Inn) to Holme (The Fleece)

Start	Cross Keys Inn (Uppermill). GR. SE008062
Finish	The Fleece Inn, Holme. GR. SE107058
The route	Cross Keys/Church Inn, Running Hill Gate, Running Hill Pits, 'Cotton Famine Road', Blake Gate, Dean Head Moss, Black Hill, Pennine Way, Issues Road, Holme
Length	7.84 miles (12.6 km)
Ascent	1158 feet (353 metres)
Time	3¾ to 4½ hours (exclusive of stops)
Map	OS OL1 (Dark Peak)

Getting there
By bus. Nearest bus service is in Uppermill where there are daily services to Ashton, Oldham, Manchester and Huddersfield. It is a ¾ mile (1.2 km) uphill walk (290 ft/88 metres of ascent) from the bus stop
By train. Nearest station, Greenfield, roughly 1.7 miles (2.7 km) from the Cross Keys. Daily trains to Greenfield from Manchester and Huddersfield.
By car. A670 to Uppermill. Then turn up Church Road (signed to Saddleworth church) and follow this road up for about ¾ mile (1.2 km) to a crossroads. The Church Inn lies to the left and The Cross Keys straight ahead. There's roadside parking near both pubs, but that near the Church is better.

The walk

The Cross Keys, 862 ft/263 metres and The Church Inn, 789 ft/240 metres
Oldham Borough is the only one of the Peak Park's constituent authorities that does not have a pub within the Park boundary. However, the Cross Keys and

The Church are within spitting distance of the boundary and The Church even has its own brewery, so to miss these out would be criminal.

Cross Keys to Black Hill

From the Cross Keys, turn left up Running Hill Gate and follow this steadily uphill until you reach a cross roads where the tarmacked road goes left and rough tracks go right and straight ahead. Go straight ahead. The track runs between drystone walls and is deeply sunken, cutting out the views down into the valley. However, you soon reach a gate that gives access into the tumbled remains of Running Hill Pits, a former sandstone quarry. This place deserves fuller exploration, but if time is not on your side, bear left on a sketchy path, which skirts the old workings and curves gently round towards a ruined building.

The OS map shows a curious water feature beyond this point; two straight blue lines across the moor. Sure enough, you'll find two ditches with a path on a raised bank in between. The ditches are far from level and slope down to the site of the pits from the top of the moor. The ditches don't come from any reservoir or serve any obvious purpose at the quarries. It's only when you look

View over Uppermill from Running Hill Pits

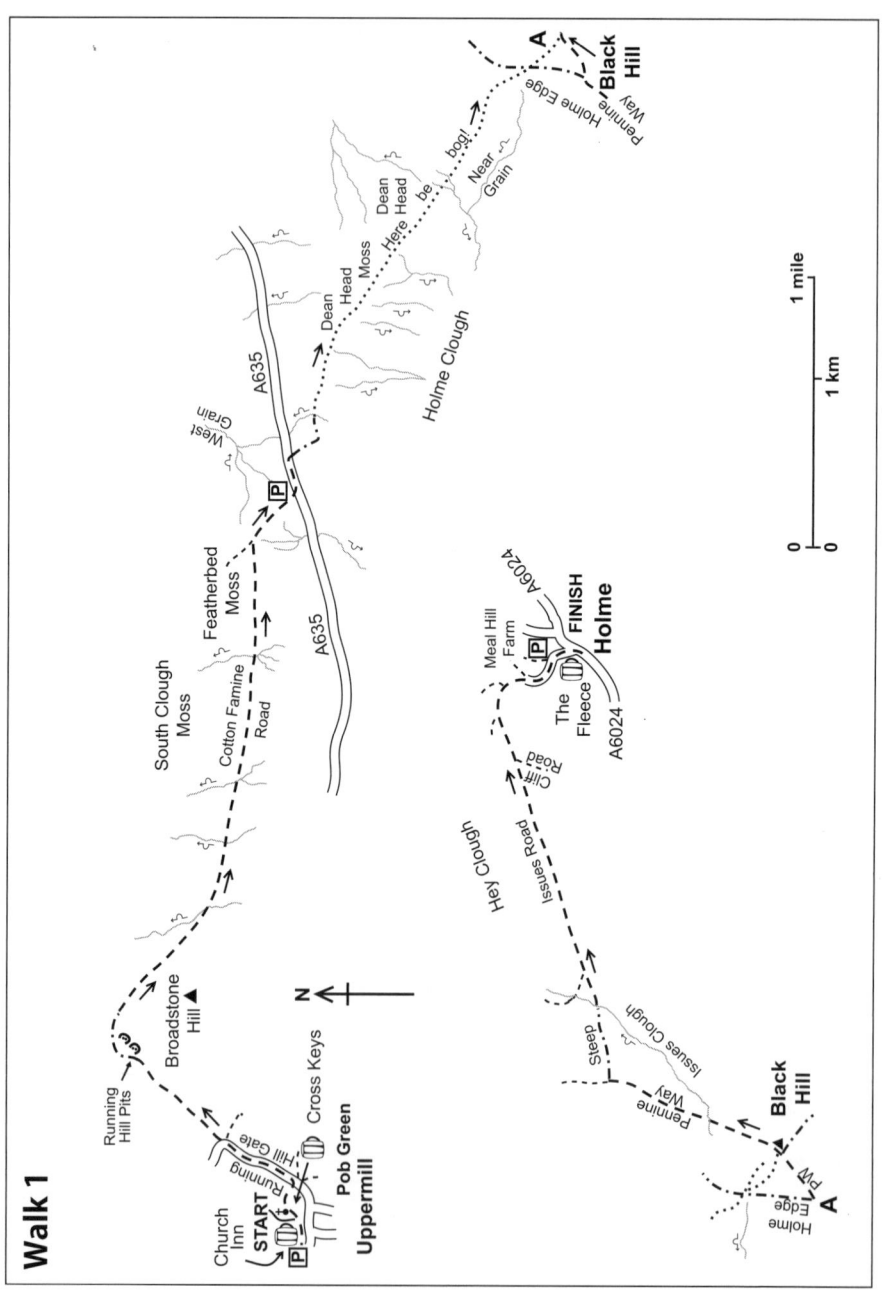

Walk 1

16

at early large scale OS maps that you realise that the ditches are not there to channel water to the quarry, but to act as drainage for the intervening bank. The bank is actually an uncompleted road from the quarries, up and over the moor to join what is now the A635. The 1854 map includes the little word 'ford' at various places along the line of the bank and when you get on top of the moor you'll see that the ditches could not have been used to channel water to the quarry as they slope in the opposite direction. It has been claimed that this was a 'Cotton Famine' road, constructed in the 1860s to alleviate the unemployment in the cotton industry during the American Civil War. However, as the ditches appear on the 1854 OS map, this explanation is unlikely. Another suggestion is that it is an unfinished road from Saddleworth village to Blake Gate. Just such a road was proposed early in the 19th century.

Follow the twin ditches up and over the moor. They form a very useful guide in mist, because otherwise the moor is pretty featureless. The right hand ditch is very obvious throughout, the left hand one, less so. On the first section you'll cross a number of stone arched culverts, now in the last stages of collapse. Be careful, you could easily break a leg here. At one point the ditches make a pronounced turn to the left and then continue over the moor. As you reach the top of the moor the ditches and the bank dip to cross a number of northward running streams. *Some of these drops are more than two metres and it is at this point you realise that the road was never completed as there is no evidence of culvert at these points and they would certainly have been needed.* The path, such as it is, makes its way down one side and up the other, with no difficulties crossing the streams, even in wet weather. The ditches and the bank remain distinct, pursuing an unerring straight line across the moor. The Romans couldn't have done better and indeed the road construction technique seems to bear a strong resemblance to Roman methods.

To the right you'll now see the A635 and Black Hill. The A635 post dates the 'road' you are on, having been constructed in the 1830s. It achieved notoriety in 1832 when there was a double murder at The Moorcock Inn, a mile or so to the west of where you are now. Irish labourers engaged in building the road were suspected, but nothing was ever proved. Dates are something of a moveable feast where these roads and events are concerned, because another source states that the A635 Saddleworth-Holmfirth road, was constructed for the Greenfield-Shepley Lane Head Turnpike Trust between 1821-30. The road reached Blake Gate (the present Oldham/Kirklees boundary) in 1824, and was completed by 1830. This doesn't tally with either the murder of 1832 or the Act incorporating the turnpike, which was only passed in 1823. (Act 1823 4 Geo4 c58). The surveyor for the road was a Thomas Dinsley of Huddersfield, the survey being carried out in 1819 (another date).

You now come across a paved path, cutting across your line of route. Turn right, following the paved path across the moor to reach the A635 at Blake Gate. *This path was the original main route of the Pennine Way, now superseded by the Wessenden route. From this point to the summit of Black Hill you are following the main English watershed, though the amount of water you'll encounter will cause you to doubt how much is actually shed and how much remains.*

The map shows a path continuing on the opposite side of the A635, but there's a fence, no stile and no evidence that anyone has ventured to cross what looks like a rather inhospitable moor. This is despite it being the former route of the Pennine Way. Turn left along the A635 for about 100 yards/metres until you reach a small abandoned quarry on the right. Go through this to a stile in the fence to try to locate a path leading towards the summit of Black Hill.

The way to Black Hill is best described as 'interesting'. The route heads in a generally south-easterly direction and on a clear day the television mast at Holme Moss is an unfailing guide. In mist it's best not attempted, unless you've some skill with the compass. Initially, after the stile, there's a path of sorts alongside a fence. The Pennine Way route bears left at a small cairn, but there's no obvious path. Best to carry on to the end of the fence. About half a dozen isolated posts continue the alignment of the fence. Use these as a guide. At the last big post, with the ground ahead now obviously dipping into Holme Clough, bear left across the moor, making for a small post and what looks like a path. The little post has the acorn symbol and marks the Pennine way route. Bear right here, along a sketchy path. The route is marked by more of these little posts. If you stray off the path, you are on pathless moor, the consistency of which is, at times, only marginally more solid than water. Even on the path it's tricky because of the constant deviations round semi-liquid peat and incipient streams. Off the path, the terrain is ankle-turning tussock grass, sometimes hiding glutinous peaty holes, sometimes merely masking water. Bright green vegetation is not nice turf but *sphagnum* moss and therefore wet. You cross two deep and steep-sided groughs before labouring up the northern flanks of Black Hill, passing a ruined shack as you ascend. At the top there's a good, well cairned path, which leads unerringly towards the summit, only to be confounded by more waterlogged peat. Reaching the trig point on Black Hill will come as a merciful release.

Black Hill. 1908 feet/582 metres

The trig point is perched on an artificial mound and on a good day (which it wasn't when I did the recce') the view is extensive. The actual summit is named

Soldiers Lump on the 1:25000 map, commemorating the original army surveyors who did the first triangulation from this spot. According to Wainwright's Pennine Way Companion, excavations at the summit in 1841 revealed the timber frame base of the original 18th century theodolite. What a god-forsaken spot it must have been then.

Until the major local government reorganisation in 1974, Black Hill was the highest point in Cheshire. Derbyshire annexed the Cheshire portion in that year and Yorkshire retained the rest. Presumably Lancashire, having annexed Saddleworth from the West Riding, declined the opportunity to acquire a stake in Black Hill. Very wise. Black Hill is the highest point reached on the High Pubs Challenge walk, but it's not downhill all the way from here on. Far from it.

Black Hill to Holme

Turn north now, along the paved path that is the Pennine Way. At least this is obvious, though the paving stones can be decidedly slippery in icy or wet conditions. *To your right there's a view down towards the Holme Valley, with Emley Moor mast prominent.* The paved path reaches the edge of Black Hill and descends steeply for a while before levelling out again. To your right is the deep cleft of Issues Clough. Do not attempt a descent here, but continue along the Pennine Way. There are a couple of stretches where there's no paving, but the path is still obvious. You cross an eastward running stream descending into Issues Clough, and then, after another short stretch, the Pennine Way path begins to descend again. Keep a sharp lookout on your right for a narrow, indistinct path, which makes a beeline for Issues Road, which you can (hopefully) see below.

This path descends very steeply over grass to join the western end of the Issues Road (which is no more than a rough track). Follow the track, soon reaching a junction of paths and then passing through a gate into a rough, walled lane. *Salvation is not quite in sight yet, but you do have the feeling that the worst is behind you. Indeed, it is worth looking back to see the slope you have just descended, which looks quite forbidding. The top of the hill was completely shrouded in low cloud when I did the recce', so I was very glad to get down to Issues Road, especially as I'd got a lunch date at The Fleece!*

Go through another gate and continue along the lane. Cliff Road trails in from the right. Like Issues Road, it's no more than a track. You'll soon reach a point where the lane opens out somewhat and there's a lovely view to the left over Digley Reservoir. There's a seat here too if you want to rest and enjoy the view. The lane now bends to the right and joins another rough track, trailing in from the left. Thereafter the lane begins to descend, passing Meal Hill Farm on the left and soon reaching the outskirts of Holme village. *Holme*

Digley Reservoir from Issues Road

Moss mast can be seen to the right, whilst straight ahead you are looking up Ramsden Clough – the next part of this walk, and you catch a glimpse of Riding Wood Reservoir.

Go past the school and carry on down the lane to the centre of the village. There's a small parking area in the Square and frequent buses down the valley to Holmfirth and Huddersfield. The Fleece lies just to the right, along the main road. A very welcome sight it is too. The first pint of Jennings Cocker Hoop went down wonderfully well and the food was excellent too.

The Fleece Inn. Holme. 990 ft/302 metres
Telephone 01484 683449. www.fleeceinnholme.co.uk

The Fleece prides itself on being a traditional country pub. It is the only (and therefore the highest) pub in the Kirklees part of the Peak District National Park, so it is included in this book despite not quite making the magic 1000-foot height. It is also a fine restaurant, serving high quality traditional food, all of which is sourced from local suppliers. It is popular with walkers, many of whom come to enjoy the paths around the local reservoirs. Not surprisingly a goodly proportion of them end up for a jar and a meal at The Fleece. Unlike a lot of pubs nowadays, muddy boots don't seem to be a problem! In any case, there's seating outside.

The pub serves a selection of cask-conditioned beers. Bank's Bitter, Jennings Cocker Hoop and Cumberland were on offer at the time of the recce'.

Opening times

Monday: closed all day (except bank holidays); Tuesday to Thursday: 1200 to 1500, 1800 to 2230; Friday and Saturday: 1200 to 2330; Sunday: 1200 to 1800. Food serving times are: Tuesday to Thursday: 1200 to 1400 and 1800 to 2100; Friday and Saturday: 1200 to 2130; Sunday: 1200 to 1700.

The Fleece Inn, Holme

Walk 2: Holme (The Fleece) to the Dog and Partridge

Start	The Fleece Inn, Holme. GR. SE107058
Finish	The Dog and Partridge, Langsett. GR. SE178011
The route	Holme, Rake Dike, Ramsden Reservoir, Ramsden Clough, Ruddle Clough, Snailsden Pike, Great Grains Clough, Winscar Reservoir, Windle Edge Road, Goddard Lane, Windleden Carr, Fiddlers Green, South Nab, Dog and Partridge
Length	8.57 miles (13.8 km)
Ascent	1850 feet (564 metres)
Time	Allow 4½ to 5¼ hours (exclusive of stops)
Map	OS OL1 (Dark Peak)

Getting there

By bus. There is a good daily service to Holme from Huddersfield and Holmfirth and a seasonal weekend service from Glossop. As far as the Dog and Partridge is concerned, despite being on one of the busiest roads in the Peak District, the only bus to use the road is National Express's daily service between Sheffield and Liverpool. It doesn't stop at the pub, but it does serve Langsett three times a day. You have to pre-book tickets. Nearest ordinary bus service is the daily Barnsley-Penistone-Langsett route, which stops at The Flouch, a mile down the A628 from the Dog and Partridge.

By train. Neither Holme nor Langsett can be reached by train. The nearest station to Holme is Brockholes on the Penistone-Huddersfield line, but Huddersfield station would be a better bet as it's served by a much greater variety of routes and is handy for the connecting bus services. The nearest station to the Dog and Partridge is in Penistone. However, given that the two stations are both on the Huddersfield-Sheffield line and both have bus services that get you nearer the start/finish, you could use the train and bus, but you'd need to be sure of your timings.

By car. Holme village is on the A6024 Holme Moss Road from Huddersfield over to Glossop. There is a small car park in the village square just east of the pub. There's a lay-by on the north side of the A628 just west of the Dog and Partridge and the pub has a large car park that you could use if the landlord gives you permission.

The Walk

Holme to Snailsden Moor

From The Fleece, walk down through Holme village towards Holmbridge. Just past the castellated house on the right, look out for a footpath sign on the right, just beyond the house called Underhill. Go down this path with a wall to your left and a fence/hedge to your right. Go through the gate at the end of the path and into a field. Keep down the left hand side of the field to a gate in the wall. *Ahead you can see across the upper reaches of the Holme valley, up Ramsden Clough to Riding Wood Reservoir. Look back at this point to see the house called Underhill (shades of 'The Hobbit'). This caused some controversy when it was built, as it bears no relationship to other houses in the village, being constructed partly underground – hence the name, a precursor amongst energy saving houses.*

Go through the gate and down the narrow path, hemmed in by the wall on your right and a fence on your left. At the bottom of this path you come to an unusual double stile at the corner of a wood and here you go right, into a field. Bear left down the field to another stile, way-marked as the Kirklees Way, one of a number you'll come across on this walk. Follow the path down through oak and birch woodland, with the ravine of Rake Dike to your left. It wouldn't do to miss your footing here.

At the bottom of the slope there's a bridge over the river and an attractive waterfall. Beyond the bridge, the path climbs away from the river up rocky steps. Where the path levels out, there's a lovely view to the left down this arm of Brownhill Reservoir, with Emley Moor television mast in the distance. The path now swings right and descends again to cross the spillway from Ramsden Reservoir before running across the face of the dam, just below the parapet. The path is securely fenced on either side and at the far end there's a flight of awkward steps. *You know the type; too wide to be taken in one stride and too short for two, so you always end up going up with the same leg.* Once across the dam, the path joins the dam access track and swings left, rising to reach Brownhill Lane.

Go right here, until you reach a gate and stile on the left, signposted as a footpath. *There's a picnic site here too and a car park, but you've scarcely started so you shouldn't need a stop just yet.*

Go over the stile and up the track, which rises steadily, keeping company with a stream and crossing it on culverts on a couple of occasions. The track makes a sharp turn to the right. Ignore the tempting stile in the wall ahead as it is of no help to you and continue on the track, through a gateway. Bear left just past the gateway and go up a grassy slope to join a steep and very badly eroded track. The

Rake Dike Bridge and waterfall

combined efforts of 4-wheel drive vehicles, motorcycles and water have done their worst here. I've climbed 3000 ft mountains with less rough surfaces. As you climb you come to a cattle grid that uses an old tram rail, presumably from Huddersfield tramways, that being the nearest system. Just past the cattle grid there's a T-junction. The main track goes left and is even more badly eroded than the bit you've just climbed. Your route lies to the right, signposted to an Access Point.

(Note that from hereon, the route lies over access land. If for any reason the access land is closed, go left and follow Ramsden Road to its junction with White Gate Road. Turn right there and carry on along White Gate Road and Linshaws Road, until you come to a bridleway sign on the right. Go along the bridleway, through old quarry workings to another road at Harden. Again go right and go down the hill to the Winscar reservoir access road. Right here, following the road across the dam, so reaching the access to the sailing club, where the main route is rejoined.)

Go along the narrow walled track to a gate and stile, noting the sign on the stile that says that no dogs are allowed on this access moor in order to prevent disturbance to birds. The track is rutted, though not as badly as the earlier one. However, as this track is almost level, the water collects in the ruts so you could get quite wet. You may find it easier and drier to go through the wall on the right and walk between the wall and the forest fence. *There are occasional glimpses through the trees down to Riding Wood Reservoir, far below.* Every now and then you'll have to return to the track.

Where the plantation ends, you find yourself well up into Ramsden Clough. The track forks. Your route is to the left, gently rising and heading towards the orange-topped post that marks the course of a gas pipeline. To your right is a ruined building, whilst ahead you can see the remains of other buildings and old quarry workings.

The track soon reaches the quarry workings. *The quarry tips are to your right, huge lumps of stone, tumbled down the hillside into Ramsden Clough. Looking back you can see down the valley to Riding Wood Reservoir and Holme village.* Go through the quarry workings on the track. It ceases abruptly at the furthest quarry face, but a rough path carries on, more or less on the same level, until it is forced up to the left by a fence. Continue by the fence, still heading up Ramsden Clough, which looks increasingly impressive as you climb. Soon the fence bears away to the right, heading downhill and now the path bears left, heading uphill and swinging into Ruddle Clough.

Once you are in Ruddle Clough, you'll spot a stile in the fence on the horizon. The path keeps on the north side of the clough, climbing steadily, soon reaching the first shooting butt. *This one is a very poor example, merely a close-boarded single fence panel and 'the second is like unto it'.* Just beyond the second shooting butt you reach the fence you saw earlier. There's a gate here – the stile you saw previously is some way to the right and not on your route. Go through the gate and just ahead of you is a real shooting butt, well made and camouflaged, with four walls, properly turfed, a real work of art. *On a previous winter visit to this moor we were very glad to find this structure as it had begun to snow. It would be quite possible to rig up a temporary roof over a shooting butt like this if you were unfortunate enough to be benighted on this moor.*

Follow the path up and over the moor passing the various shooting butts and with glimpses over to Snailsden Reservoir to the left. *It has to be said that the crossing of the moor was far easier than I had anticipated, largely because of the number of paths and tracks used for grouse shooting purposes.* The track seems to have been paved at one time, but the stones have sunk into the peat and now alternative routes have developed. The path forks and here anyone doing Walk 16 will leave you.

Snailsden Moor to Windleden Edge

Bear right at the fork in the track and go down to the bridge. Cross the bridge and carry on past the next few shooting butts. When you reach butt number

Walk 2

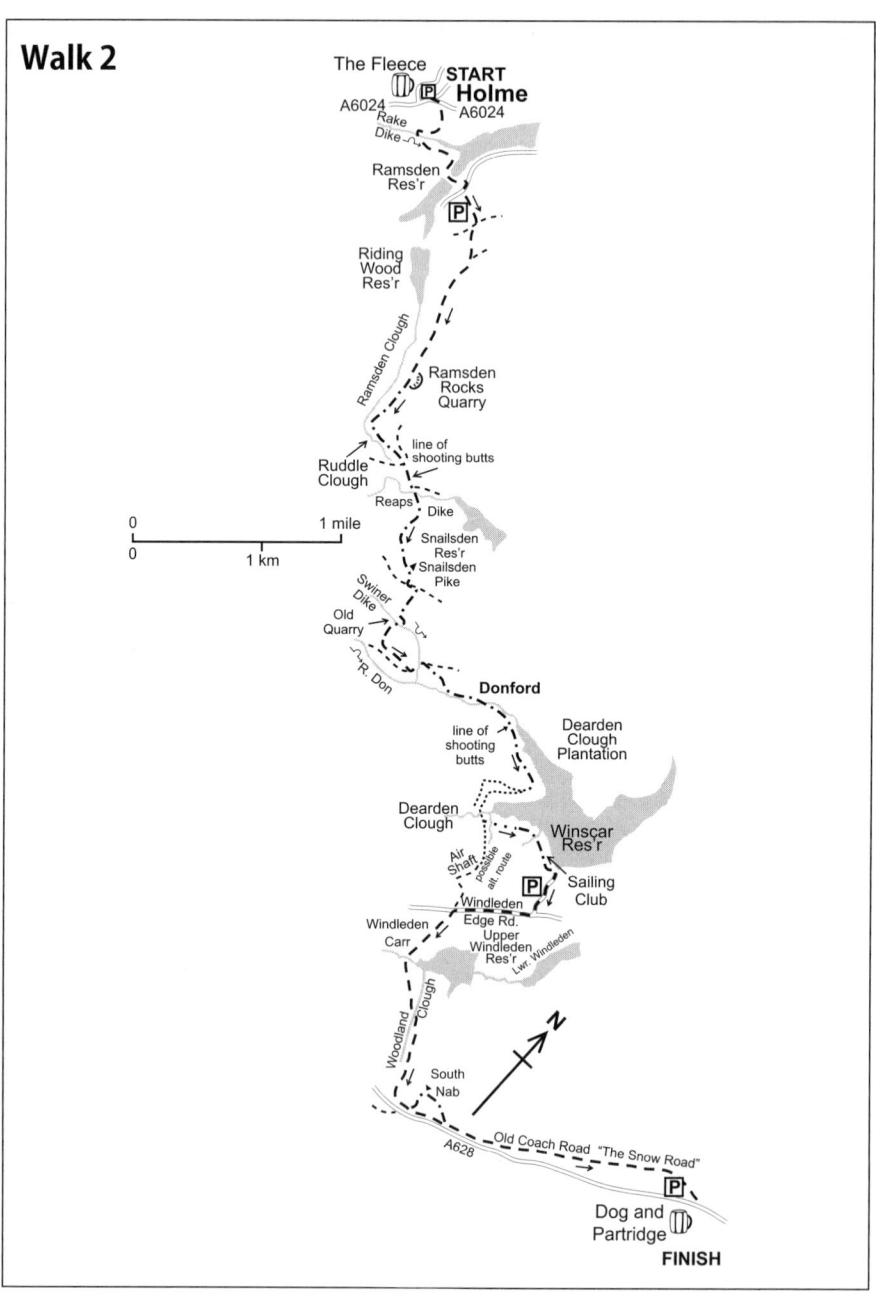

The Fleece

START
Holme

A6024
Rake
Dike

A6024

Ramsden
Res'r

Riding
Wood
Res'r

Ramsden Clough

Ramsden
Rocks
Quarry

line of
shooting butts

Ruddle
Clough

Reaps Dike

0 _____ 1 mile

0 _____ 1 km

Snailsden
Res'r
Snailsden
Pike

Swiner
Dike

Old
Quarry

R. Don

Donford

line of
shooting
butts

Dearden
Clough
Plantation

Dearden
Clough

Winscar
Res'r

Air
Shaft

possible
alt. route

Windleden

Sailing
Club

Windleden
Carr

Edge Rd.
Upper
Windleden
Res'r

Lwr. Windleden

Woodland Clough

South
Nab

N

Old Coach Road "The Snow Road"

A628

Dog and
Partridge

FINISH

11, bear right up a more indistinct track, heading up towards Snailsden Pike. You soon join a more pronounced track and carry on upwards to the flat top of the moor. *Snailsden Reservoir is now well in view to your left.* A myriad of tracks wander across the moor, but the trig point is now in view ahead, so you can choose whichever track you feel will get you there most efficiently. *When I recce'd this walk there had been a keen frost and the moor was hard. The numerous patches of frozen water gave a clear indication that in warmer conditions, this could be a damp and spongy section to the walk.*

Snailsden Pike

The view from the trig point is worth the effort. Despite its modest elevation 1560 ft/475 metres, Snailsden Pike commands a 360 degree view. Black Hill and Holme Moss mast dominate the western vista. To the north the view stretches well beyond Saddleworth moors. Eastwards the view takes in the entire Vale of York, with Emley Moor mast looking like a Tolkien tower and numerous plumes of steam rising from the various power stations like Drax and Ferrybridge. Far away, on the edge of sight there are more hills, probably the Yorkshire Wolds. To the south you can see Winscar Reservoir, the Derwent Moors and the tiny lorries sky-lining over the A628. It would be an interesting exercise to try and count all the wind turbines that are visible from this vantage point; there are plenty of them.

Leave the trig point by one of the many narrow paths heading south-east towards Winscar Reservoir. You'll cross a couple of vehicle tracks and, just as the slope steepens, you'll reach a third one. This is actually shown on the 1:25000 map. Go left here for a short way until you reach a small abandoned quarry. Another vehicle track diverges right at this point, making for a ruined wall. Go down this track, pass through the wall and follow it down until you reach the edge of Swiner Clough. The vehicle track swings left and then right to drop into the bottom of the clough, but it is possible to make a more direct descent. *In the bottom of the clough there are the remains of yet another gritstone quarry. Oddly these aren't shown on the OS map, nor on any of the earlier maps, but there are some interesting features, not least being the stone lined water course, the substantial culvert and some ruined buildings. Don't investigate the watercourse and culvert too closely as some of the stonework is clearly unstable.* Cross the culvert and go up the steep path to rejoin the wall. Parts of the wall have been made into shooting butts and there's a reasonable path alongside them. In front of you now are Great Grains Clough and the River Don, which you have to cross to get to the south bank of Winscar Reservoir.

Where the wall begins to descend towards the river, there's a vehicle track going off to the left. Follow this towards the reservoir. The track descends

Winscar Reservoir from Swiner Clough Moss

gently and soon joins another track before swinging left and entering what remains of Grains Plantation, a mixture of Scots pine, oak and birch. Cross the culverted stream and go up the other side to a gateway that marks the edge of the plantation. The main track carries straight on, making for Snailsden Farm, which can be seen ahead. An indistinct track bears off to the right, diagonally across the field. Follow this and it soon joins another, much clearer track, where you turn right. This track drops down to a ford over the Don.

There are some slippery stepping stones on the left hand side of the ford, but no footbridge. Just downstream there's a huge slab of stone that looks as if it may have been a clapper bridge at one time, but it's useless now. Go up the track on the far side of the river and turn sharp left at the junction. Follow the track high above the river and reservoir, noting the waymarker posts for the shooting butts. Continue along the track, making for Dearden Foot plantation, the clump of trees that can be seen ahead.

The track takes you right to the trees and then a path follows the unfenced edge of the plantation, until you eventually reach a fenced section. Here you realise to your horror that what seemed like a short and easy stroll to the car park at Winscar, is not so. You have to get round the Dearden Clough arm of the reservoir first.

The plantation fence goes sharp left, down to the reservoir. Don't go this way. There's no path on the reservoir edge. The OS 1:25000 map shows a path keeping well up the hillside and heading into Dearden Clough, but you'll need keen eyes to spot it. From the fence corner a narrow path ploughs its way through waist high bracken to reach Dearden Spring and then descends as a clearer track across marshy ground to the south western tip of the reservoir. The OS map shows a ford at this point, but it's not obvious, though there seem to be the remains of a bridge abutment on the far side of Dearden Clough Brook. Make your way across the brook as best you can and here there's a choice of routes.

If you are heading for Winscar car park and/or Dunford Bridge, you need to keep alongside the reservoir edge and skip the next paragraph.

If you are heading direct to the Dog and Partridge, it is possible to make your way straight up the south side of Dearden Clough, following one of the streams that flow down from Lower Grip Hill. At the top of the hill you should be able to make a beeline southward to the airshaft on the Woodhead tunnel and thus reach a track that drops down to Goddard Lane, right opposite the bridleway that leads to Windleden Carr. Now skip the next three paragraphs.

Despite what the OS map says, there's no obvious path alongside the reservoir and the next 2-300 yards/metres is a struggle through tussock grass until, at last, a reasonable path materialises. Stroll along this path until the sailing club comes into view and with it, another shock. There's a small inlet just before the club perimeter and the maps shows a ford. Fat chance. The stream here has obviously become a raging torrent at some time in the not too distant past and the path has been washed away. Descend gingerly to the water's edge, cross the stream and scramble up the steep, shale bank to the fence surrounding the sailing club. Follow the fence round the back of the sailing club. What seems to be a sunken path beside the fence could just as easily be a ditch. Certainly it's wet underfoot. At the end of the fence, the path drops down to the left to a small gate, leading out onto the reservoir access road, just by the entrance to the sailing club. Go right here and make your way to the public car park. Follow the access road to Windle Edge Road.

(If you want buses back to Holmfirth or Barnsley go left and walk down to Dunford Bridge. The bus stop is in the Trans Pennine Trail car park.)

If you are carrying on to the Dog and Partridge go right here, up the hill for about 660 yards/600 metres, to a bridleway sign on the left and the point where the access track from the Woodhead tunnel air shaft emerges from the moor.

Windleden Edge to the Dog & Partridge

At the bridleway sign go through the gate and onto moorland. An obvious path drops down the hillside of Windleden Carr, through some very boggy patches. *Higher Windleden Reservoir lies to your left. This reservoir and its neighbours, Lower Windleden and Winscar were built for the Dewsbury and Heckwondwike Water Works. Lower Windleden was opened in 1872 and Upper Windleden in 1890. Beyond the reservoirs you can see the array of wind turbines to the north of Penistone.* In the bottom of the clough you cross Carr Bottom Dike.

When this part of the walk was recce'd, the bridge across the stream was broken and the remaining plank looked decidedly unsafe. I forded the stream a little higher up without difficulty. The path then rises and drifts round into Broad Clough with good views over the reservoir. The stream in Broad Clough has a serviceable bridge, beyond which the path climbs steeply up the hillside to a bridle gate. *From this point, both Windleden reservoirs are in view and the three large wind turbines near Carlecotes. You can hear the rumble of traffic on the A628 now, but you can't see the road.* The path now bears right, alongside Woodland Clough, following the remains of a wall. The path, which is now cart width, crosses the stream on a substantial stone culvert, obviously much older than the bridges encountered hitherto on this section. *This part of the path predates the reservoirs and presumably carried on down the valley, thus requiring a diversion when the dams were built.* Climb away from Woodland Clough. *Now to your right you can see the trunk road, with the lorries sky-lining across the moor. The A628 is one of the busiest roads in the National Park and there have been numerous suggestions of upgrading it, though none have ever come to fruition. To your left rises South Nab, which is no more than an insignificant lump, fractionally higher than anywhere else, but sufficiently so to warrant a trig point. You can make the ascent to the trig point anywhere from here, though there are no paths.*

Continue along the path until you almost reach the trunk road. A narrow path bears off to the left, roughly paralleling the road and soon reaching a ruined wall. *Old maps show a building within this walled area, which is now known as Fiddlers Green. An 1850s map describes it as an inn known as the Plough and Harrow. Definitely one of the higher pubs! The trig point on South Nab is in view to your left.* If you are not going onto South Nab, skip the next paragraph.

When you reach the ruined wall, there's a sketchy path to the left through a thicket of reeds, leading up to the trig point. *A visit is not compulsory, but there is an extensive view from the top, that makes the ascent worthwhile.* When you leave the trig point, make your way across the moor along what is little more than a sheep path, heading towards the far corner of the ruined wall. When you reach the snow fence, keep alongside it to the gap and then go through to join the old coach road, which here is immediately alongside the A628.

If you decide not to go onto South Nab, carry on along the path through the walled enclosure, bemoaning the loss of the Plough and Harrow and then join the old coach road, here just a grassy track.

Follow the old road until you reach another gap in the snow fence. Here the old road veers away from the A628 and passes through the gap onto a distinctly different alignment. *A signpost indicates that this section is a public byway, but this doesn't alter the nature of the route, which remains a broad grassy track. Despite the proximity of the trunk road this is a surprisingly pleasant walk, with extensive views to the east and occasional glimpses southwards to the Derwent moors. The main road is partly hidden in a cutting, which not only reduces the visual impact but also the noise, though you are never entirely free of it.* After about a mile/1½km of easy downhill walking, the old road bears right. Now the Dog and Partridge comes into view at last.

View to the east along the old coach road

A final stroll down the old road leads you to a gate onto the A628. *To your right is a lay-by, complete with transport café if you want something other than a pub.* The A628 is three lanes wide here, so take great care when crossing to the Dog and Partridge. Fortunately the visibility is very good, so you should have no difficulty. Just make sure you judge the speed of traffic properly. The vehicles coming down the hill don't hang about! However, the pub is worth the effort.

The Dog and Partridge. 1120 feet/341 metres
Telephone 01226 763173. www.dogandpartridgeinn.co.uk

The Dog and Partridge sits in splendid isolation by the side of the A628 trunk road. Apart from a couple of farms, there's no other human habitation around. It's not the easiest pub for a walker to get to – any approach involves walking along a section of the A628, which is not the most pleasant experience you could hope for. As you know, approaching from the north you've also faced the daunting prospect of crossing the road as well. Once inside the pub it's remarkably quiet with the noise of the traffic cut out. The pub does excellent food and serves a number of local real ales on hand pump, including Acorn Brewery's Barnsley Bitter and Barnsley Gold and Bradfield Brewery's Farmers Blonde.

There's a car park at the pub but there's no public transport nearer than The Flouch, a mile away (1.6km). The National Express Liverpool-Sheffield service passes the pub, but doesn't stop.

Situated on the old medieval salt way route, this isolated Inn has history that can be traced back to the Elizabethan period. Originally known as Border Hill House and owned by the Gothard family, the Inn became known as the Dog and Partridge on receipt of its first licence in 1740.

Since that time it has been under the ownership of many local prominent land-owning families such as the Paynes of Frickley Hall, Bosvilles of Gunthwaite Hall and the Pilkingtons of Chevet Hall who still own the surrounding grouse moors today.

Today the Dog and Partridge is a family run inn and hotel and is open all year round and offers a warm and friendly greeting to all who visit.

Fresh home cooked meals are served daily in the bar with traditional roasts being served on a Sunday. The 'Swinden' room with views over the Langsett moors is ideal for families visiting the pub.

Entertainment is provided most days of the week. The Dog and Partridge has been famous for over 30 years for its traditional sing-a-longs that take place every Saturday and Sunday evening. The resident organist accompanies these and all newcomers are welcome.

Opening times

1200 to 2300 daily.
Food is served Monday to Friday: 1200 to 2100; Saturday: 1200 to 2130
Sunday 1200 to 2000. Bank Holidays: 1200 to 1700.

The Dog and Partridge from Swinden Lane

Walk 3: Dog and Partridge to Ashopton (The Ladybower)

Start	Dog and Partridge Inn. (Langsett) GR. SE 178011
Finish	Ashopton (The Ladybower Inn). GR. SK204865
The route	A628(!) Swinden Lane, Mickleden Edge, Cut Gate, Margery Hill, Back Tor, Dovestone Tor, Salt Cellar, White Tor, the Wheel Stones, Winstone Lee Tor, Ashopton (Ladybower Inn)
Length	12.81 miles (20.6 km)
Ascent	1779 feet (542 metres)
Time	4 hours 20 minutes (exclusive of stops)
Map	OS OL1 (Dark Peak)

Getting there

By bus. As far as the Dog and Partridge is concerned, despite being on one of the busiest roads in the Peak District, the only bus to use the road is National Express's daily service between Sheffield and Liverpool and there is no stop at the pub. It does serve Langsett three times a day. You have to pre-book tickets. Nearest ordinary bus service is the daily Barnsley-Penistone-Langsett route, which stops at The Flouch a mile from the Dog and Partridge. The Ladybower, on the other hand, has a daily bus service from Sheffield and the Hope Valley with a stop right outside the front door.

By train. Neither Ashopton nor Langsett can be reached by train. The nearest station to Ashopton is Bamford and the nearest to the Dog and Partridge is in Penistone. However, given that the two stations are both served by local services from Sheffield line and both have bus services that get you nearer the start/finish, you could use the train and bus, but you'd need to be sure of your timings.

By car. The Dog and Partridge is on the A628 trunk road just west of The Flouch roundabout. There is car parking at the pub by arrangement with the landlord and there's a lay-by on the north side of the road, just west of the pub. The Ladybower is on the A57 Sheffield-Glossop road just east of Ladybower Reservoir. There's parking at the pub by arrangement with the landlord and there's a public car park at Heatherdene on the A6013. If you can't find either of these pubs, you certainly shouldn't be contemplating this walk!

The Walk

Dog and Partridge to Cut Gate Head

Emerging from the quiet and calm of The Dog and Partridge, you are immediately onto the A628 trunk road. Turn right and make your way along the verge.

This is one of the busiest roads in the Peak District and you'll certainly notice it. Fortunately your walk along the verge is short and the verge itself is easily walkable, with even a semblance of a path, but it is not the most pleasant experience.

At the bridleway sign, turn right, leaving the traffic behind and entering a walled green lane. Go through the gate. *You can see the moors rising ahead and you should be able to make out the path along Mickleden Edge as it climbs towards the watershed.*

In about ¼ mile/400 metres by a finger post, the track forks. The more obvious route goes straight ahead, but your route lies to the left, soon passing through another gate and entering Swinden Lane. Again this is no more than a walled grassy track.

Bowl along this lane, which is almost dead straight, ignoring any routes going off left or right. *The only sound was the faint hum from the hidden A628 and the calls of curlew and lapwing.* Eventually you reach another gate at a T-junction and here you go left – clearly marked by a white on blue arrow that would do credit to a motorway intersection. In a very short while the track bears right and widens out. A footpath goes off left, but ignore this and thus reach a wide triangular area. Follow the obvious track as it bears right, with the dense conifer woodland to your left. When you are almost at a semi-derelict barn, look out for a small gate on your left. This takes you onto a path through the forest.

As conifer plantations go, this isn't too bad. There was plenty of sunlight filtering through the trees, plus a lot of birdsong and quite a few deciduous trees amongst the pines. The path drops steadily to reach a bridge over a stream. Cross this and go up the slope, ignoring the tempting path to the right. You reach a major crossing of tracks. Here, you go right and immediately begin to

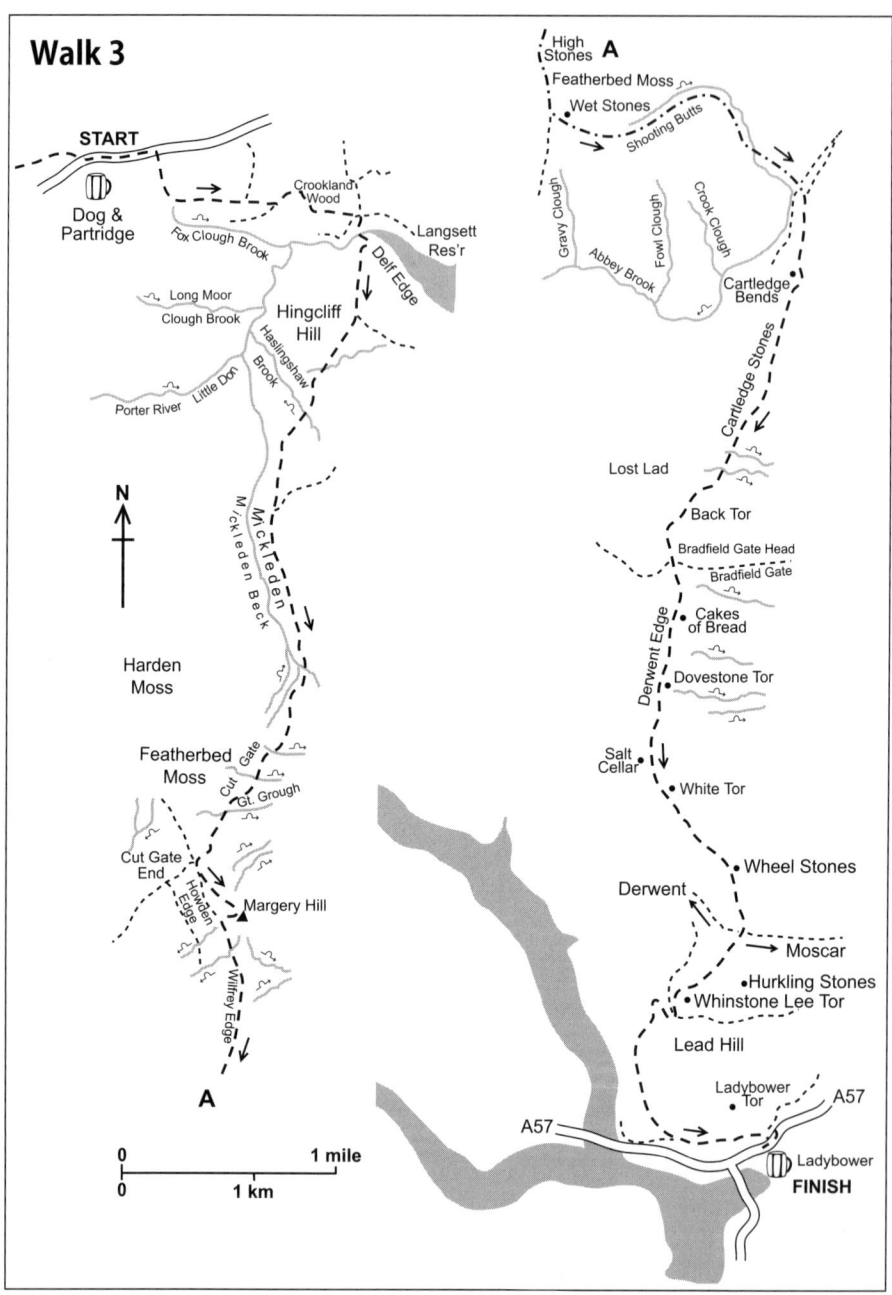

Walk 3

START

Dog & Partridge

Fox Clough Brook

Crookland Wood

Langsett Res'r

Delf Edge

Long Moor Clough Brook

Hingcliff Hill

Haslingshaw Brook

Little Don

Porter River

Mickleden Beck

N

Harden Moss

Featherbed Moss

Cut Gate

Gt. Grough

Cut Gate End

Howden Edge

Margery Hill

Wilfrey Edge

A

High Stones A

Featherbed Moss

Wet Stones

Shooting Butts

Gravy Clough

Abbey Brook

Fowl Clough

Crook Clough

Cartledge Bends

Cartledge Stones

Lost Lad

Back Tor

Bradfield Gate Head

Bradfield Gate

Derwent Edge

Cakes of Bread

Dovestone Tor

Salt Cellar

White Tor

Wheel Stones

Derwent

Moscar

Hurkling Stones

Whinstone Lee Tor

Lead Hill

Ladybower Tor

A57

A57

Ladybower

FINISH

0   1 mile

0   1 km

36

descend again. Ignore the path off to the left and descend to the right along the paved track. This dips quite sharply to a bigger bridge over the main inlet stream for Langsett reservoir, known as The Porter or Little Don River.

At this point you are now in the City of Sheffield. On the far side of the bridge there's a Peak and Northern sign, which proclaims that the route you are on is for the Derwent and Ashop valleys. Follow the track round to the left and begin the climb. There's an interesting information board on the left, giving details about the Langsett Woods restoration project. As you go up the track you'll see that a lot of the fringing conifers have been felled and new deciduous planting has taken place. It'll still be a long time before there's a decent mixed woodland here, but it's a good start. The track climbs quite steeply up a zig-zag, with a glimpse of the western end of Langsett reservoir to your left. You then round a left hand bend alongside the wood and emerge onto open moor.

The moorland stretches away as far as the eye can see with very few distinguishing features, except the prominent cairn on top of Pike Low, away to your left. Fortunately, from a navigational point of view, the path over these moors is well blazed and very easy to follow. Even in thick mist there should be no chance of going astray, though it would then be a tedious walk. In good weather, it's a delightful moorland tramp, never difficult, never steep and with good views all round. To your left you look along Langsett reservoir and over towards Stocksbridge. To the right you are looking up Hordron Clough and back towards the Dog and Partridge.

The track forks just near a ruined stone wall, but keep straight on. *The route to your left will take you to North America!* The view to the right is soon obscured by Hingcliff Hill, which the path skirts and then descends slightly to come into Mickleden.

Mickleden is a steep sided valley and quite a deep one too, thereby living up to its meaning which is 'great (as in big) deep wooded valley'. The stream in the bottom is Mickleden Beck and taken together these names indicate a Norse influence. In the Peak District the use of the word 'beck' for a stream is very unusual. Indeed, this seems to be the only such use of the word in the Park. Most such water courses being referred to as 'brook, grain, sike or sitch'. The last three all have a Scandinavian origin as well.

The path progresses gently along Mickleden Edge, climbing steadily and with increasingly wide views back toward the Woodhead road, Holme Moss mast and hills well beyond that. You pass an isolated Peak and Northern Footpaths Society sign which refers to a route back across the moor to Langsett and Penistone, but this need not concern you, except to reinforce that you are on the correct route (though in truth you'd have to be an exceptionally bad navigator to get lost on this path). *Across Mickleden you will discern a vehicle track descending into the valley bottom. Your route soon encounters this track, coming steeply up and crossing your path. Presumably this is for the purpose of moorland management in connection with grouse shooting, and indeed when this part of the walk was recce'd, the access land surrounding the Cut Gate path was closed to prevent disturbance to nesting birds.* A dint of further steady climbing brings the path up to a cairn.

This cairn doesn't seem to signify anything of note except that there's a great view to the left, stretching well across Yorkshire, with various power stations visible in the distance. The path now tends to the right, skirting round the head of Mickleden, which by this time has lost its depth and has split into numerous streamlets. You pass a small cairn on the left, from which a narrow path goes off to visit Pike Low, but your route carries on, still well defined, over the top of the moor.

This is one of those annoying paths which deludes you into thinking you are at the top, only to reveal another rise ahead. From the first big cairn to the summit of the Cut Gate is about a mile (1.6km). The path twists and turns, crossing numerous small streams and often appearing to run along the bed of the peat groughs. In wet weather this would be a very damp crossing. Gone is the narrow, well-defined path of Mickleden. Now the path sprawls widely to avoid the peat hags. You dip to cross the most significant of these streams, known as Great Grough and then follow the path up in a deep cutting for a further short stretch until suddenly you realise that the hills you are seeing ahead are those on the other side of the Derwent Valley. A final climb and you reach the head of the path where a magnificent panorama unfolds on all sides.

Looking back over Yorkshire you can see that greatest of all waymarks, Emley Moor mast, then round to Black Hill, Holme Moss and onto Bleaklow, Kinder and Mam Tor.

There's a large cairn at the head of the Cut Gate and here you meet the Derwent watershed path. Your route lies to the left, up onto the peat moorland and on to Margery Hill.

If the weather has closed in and is really inclement, you would be well advised to avoid the next stretch and instead descend the well-blazed path down between Cranberry Clough and Bull Clough to Slippery Stones and then take the east bank path down the reservoirs to Fairholmes, where at least there is shelter, food, drink, toilets and even buses. Note that, at weekends the road from Fairholmes to King's Tree (near Slippery Stones) is closed to cars and there is a minibus service operating.

Cut Gate Head to Back Tor

Leave the Cut Gate and follow the broad path across the peat moorland towards Margery Hill. You'll look in vain for an obvious summit, for Margery

Hill only rises a few feet above the rest of the moor. Keep on the path close to the edge overlooking the upper Derwent Valley for the best views. You soon approach a fenced area. *This surrounds a Bronze Age burial mound, at least 3500 years old and, as the fence is designed to ward off unwanted visitors, best leave it alone.* The path skirts to the right of the enclosure, then turns left, across a somewhat damp bit of moor to a stile in another fence. Just beyond is the trig point that tops Margery Hill. *Oddly, this doesn't seem to be the highest point of the hill, an accolade seemingly reserved for the cluster of rocks a little way to the south.*

From these rocks a well-blazed (but muddy) path heads south towards High Stones, the highest point in South Yorkshire. The path has a number of options and again the best view is gained by keeping close to the edge. *You even get the occasional glimpse of Howden Dam far below. From this edge you get a very clear idea of the scale of Cranberry Clough and its tributaries. Like Margery Hill, High Stones is not a remarkable summit, being marked by only a tiny cairn, but it is a commanding view point and one wonders why this site was not chosen for the trig point rather than Margery Hill. To the east stretches Featherbed Moss, a seemingly endless boggy moorland, with no obvious path across it.*

The path you have been following continues along Howden Edge, with Back Tor now in view across the defile of Abbey Brook Clough. The path runs alongside a pronounced heather topped peat bank, and begins to descend. Look out for a post on the left and the start of a line of shooting butts. Turn left at this point. A short scramble up the peat bank by the post takes you onto a track, which leads to the first of the shooting butts.

(In really inclement weather you would be well advised to continue along the descending path, which soon joins the track referred to above and descends to join the 'road' along the east bank of the reservoirs, just south of Howden Dam.)

Assuming you are carrying on, follow the track across the moor with the shooting butts mainly to your right. The track bears right, off the peat and follows the base of another peat bank before continuing in a generally easterly direction, still following the shooting butts and with Abbey Brook Clough to the right. At last the track reaches the end of the shooting butts, just at the head of Foul Clough. *It is possible to descend Foul Clough, cross Abbey Brook and gain Back Tor by ascending Lost Lad, but a glance at the amount of descent and re-ascent is enough to deter most people.*

Decision made, continue along what is now little more than a sheep track, swinging slightly north east and eventually picking up the deep grough containing Cartledge Brook. A sketchy path follows the brook, sometimes on top of the bank, sometimes in the bottom of the grough. A glance at the map will show that the brook describes a graceful arc before heading west to

Ladybower Reservoir from Lost Lad path

become the Abbey Brook. There will be a temptation to cut across this arc, but it is better to stick with the stream in its grough, until the ground levels out and the grough ceases to be a feature. Still stick with the stream. The ground ahead is decidedly boggy, pathless and made up of ankle turning tussock grass and reeds. It is annoying that just across this morass you can see the clear path leading up to Cartledge Bents, Low Tor and on to Back Tor. Where the stream takes a decisive turn to the south-west and begins its real descent into Abbey Brook Clough, a sheep track leads off left, crossing a small subsidiary stream and making its way across the still boggy ground to reach a paved path made up of large blocks of stone. Here turn right.

The 1½ miles (2½km) along this paved way to Back Tor is an absolute delight after the bog trotting near Cartledge Brook, and it can be covered in record time. The gradients are easy apart from the last few yards to Back Tor, where there are steps.

Not so long ago the passage of this moor was a constant struggle to avoid bogs, with the path spreading ever wider as the years went by. The revegetating moorland is ample testimony to the necessity of the paving. It's not just straight forward paving either, because whoever built this path has been practising their basic bridge building skills as well.

Back Tor commands a tremendous view and it is worth scrambling up to the trig point to see it in all its glory. Northwards and westwards the view is dominated by the bulk of Kinder and Bleaklow, but you can usually make out Holme Moss mast on the summit of Black Hill. To the east lie the reservoirs in the Strines/Bradfield valley and Sugworth tower. Southwards you'll see the crags of Stanage, Bamford Edge and to the south-west the Losehill/ Mam Tor ridge.

Ladybower Inn or Moscar?

From Back Tor, follow the broad paved path southwards along Derwent Edge. After only a couple of minutes you come to a standing stone, which marks the route to Bradfield (left) and Derwent (right). *Both places have daily bus services to Sheffield if required. Bradfield has the better service, but is much further.*

Trig point on Back Tor

Continue along the path with extensive views both left and right. *Left you are looking far out across Yorkshire, well beyond Sheffield, whilst to the right you are looking into the heart of the Peak District, with Kinder, the Losehill/Mam Tor ridge and Win Hill being prominent. The curious shaped rocks on the moor on your left are the Cakes of Bread.*

The path rises slightly to reach Dovestone Tor. Here you have a decision to make. The main route of the walk takes you to Ashopton and the Ladybower Inn, but if, for some reason you are not calling at the Ladybower and want to combine Walks 3 and 4, you can head across the moor to Moscar, missing out the Ladybower (and saving yourself a considerable amount of extra ascent and descent). For details of the route to Moscar, **see Walk 25**, Strines. However, if the weather is inclement or if the access moors are closed for any reason, you should take the Ladybower option in any case.

The Ladybower option

Continue along the well-blazed path south from Dovestone Tor, soon passing the Salt Cellar and the Wheel Stones. *It will be an odd person who doesn't want to have a go at ascending the Wheel Stones, but if you do, please take care. They are not as simple as they appear at first sight.* Continue along the path along the edge, ignoring paths off to the left or right until you come to the point where you overlook the main part of Ladybower reservoir. *The view is magnificent, with Win Hill to your right and Bamford Edge to the left. The rocky knoll on the north side of the reservoir is Crook Hill. Derwent and Ashopton viaducts can be seen below, but when the water level is high, you get no impression of their real size as most of the height of the piers is under water.*

A steep and narrow path zig-zags its way down the slope to meet up with the old coach road, still well above the current A57. Here turn left

The Salt Cellar

Scrambling on the Wheel Stones

and follow the old road into the wood and round the back of the Ladybower Inn, which is just below you. Just beyond the pub, a path veers off to the right and drops steeply down to join a rough track, almost at the point where it emerges onto the A57. At the main road, go right and thus reach the Ladybower Inn.

The Ladybower Inn. 763 feet/233 metres
Telephone 01422 651241. www.ladybower-inn.co.uk
The Ladybower is an excellent pub, well patronised by walkers. It is situated alongside the A57 Sheffield-Glossop road and the Sheffield-Castleton bus stops right outside. Muddy boots are no problem here. The range of beers always includes some from local breweries, like Farmers Blonde from Bradfield Brewery. There's usually four 'Real Ales' on tap and a varied selection of other draught beers. The pub was built to serve coaching traffic on the Snake road and it has performed a similar function ever since. The food is invariably good and the portions substantial.

Opening times
Monday to Saturday: 1130 to 2300; Sundays 1100 to 2300.
Bar meals are available daily from 1200 to 2100.

The Ladybower Inn

Walk 4: Ashopton (The Ladybower) to The Fox House

Start	Ladybower Inn, Ashopton GR. SK204865
Finish	Fox House Inn. GR. SK265802
The route	Ashopton, Moscar, Strines Moor, Stanage Edge, Burbage, Fox House Inn
Length	9.45 miles (15.21 km)
Ascent	1783 feet (543 metres)
Time	4¾ to 5½ hours (exclusive of stops)
Map	OS OL1 (Dark Peak)

Getting there

By bus. Daily buses to Ashopton from Sheffield and Castleton. Seasonal service from Glossop. Daily buses to Fox House from Buxton, Castleton, Bakewell, Sheffield and Matlock.

By train. Nearest station to Ashopton is Bamford, which has daily trains to Manchester and Sheffield. Nearest station to Fox House is Grindleford (bottom of Padley Gorge), which has daily trains to Manchester and Sheffield.

By car. The Ladybower Inn is on the A57 Sheffield-Manchester road, just east of Ladybower Reservoir. There is car parking at the pub with the landlord's permission, otherwise there's pay and display parking at Heatherdene alongside Ladybower Reservoir on the A6013. The Fox House Inn is just in the City of Sheffield on the A6187 road from Sheffield to Castleton. There is car parking by the pub, or at the National Trust car park in Longshaw Estate.

The Walk

Ladybower to Moscar

From the pub, go left along the A57 and almost immediately bear left up a rough track. This is the former coach road, which long predates the existing main road. The track climbs steadily and then runs almost parallel to the A57, but at a higher level. The walking is easy until you reach Highshaw Clough Brook. *This was the site of the original Cutthroat Bridge. A highway robbery here in the 18th century gave the bridge its name. A traveller was way-laid, robbed and had his throat cut, but miraculously didn't die of his injuries.* The old bridge has gone, leaving just the remains of the abutments. These necessitate a bit of a scramble, which can be tricky in wet weather, so take care.

Continue along the old road, soon noting a rather fine guide stone on the left, just beyond a gate. See if you can make out the inscriptions and also see if you can discern where the other two roads were. The track now joins a route trailing in from the left, coming from Derwent Edge. Beyond this point the track rises to pass through Moscar House Farm and then continues ahead to reach the Strines road at its junction with the lane to Ughill.

Cross the road and head along the lane signed to Ughill and Dungworth. In about 100 yards/metres, opposite the gas installation, leave the road and go right, through a gate and onto the heavily rutted Moscar Cross Road. Avoiding the worst of the ruts, make your way up the hill, following the 'road' round to the right when you reach the trees. Soon you come to a T-junction where there is a very fine example of a stone guide stoop. You want the Hathersage 'road'.

Bear right, passing through a gate and then down a broad, walled green lane that takes you past Moscar Lodge. Note the 1872 date stone over the door. The green lane becomes a tarred lane that emerges onto the A57 road.

Moscar to Fox House

Cross the road with care, because this is a fast stretch. You'll undoubtedly have heard motorbikes and cars whizzing past as you approached the main road, so you can't say you haven't been warned. Turn right and then at the Peak and Northern Footpath Society's sign, go left, onto the path leading to Stanage Edge.

The path rises gently across the moor, sometimes in quite a deep

Guide stoop at Moscar Cross

45

Walk 4

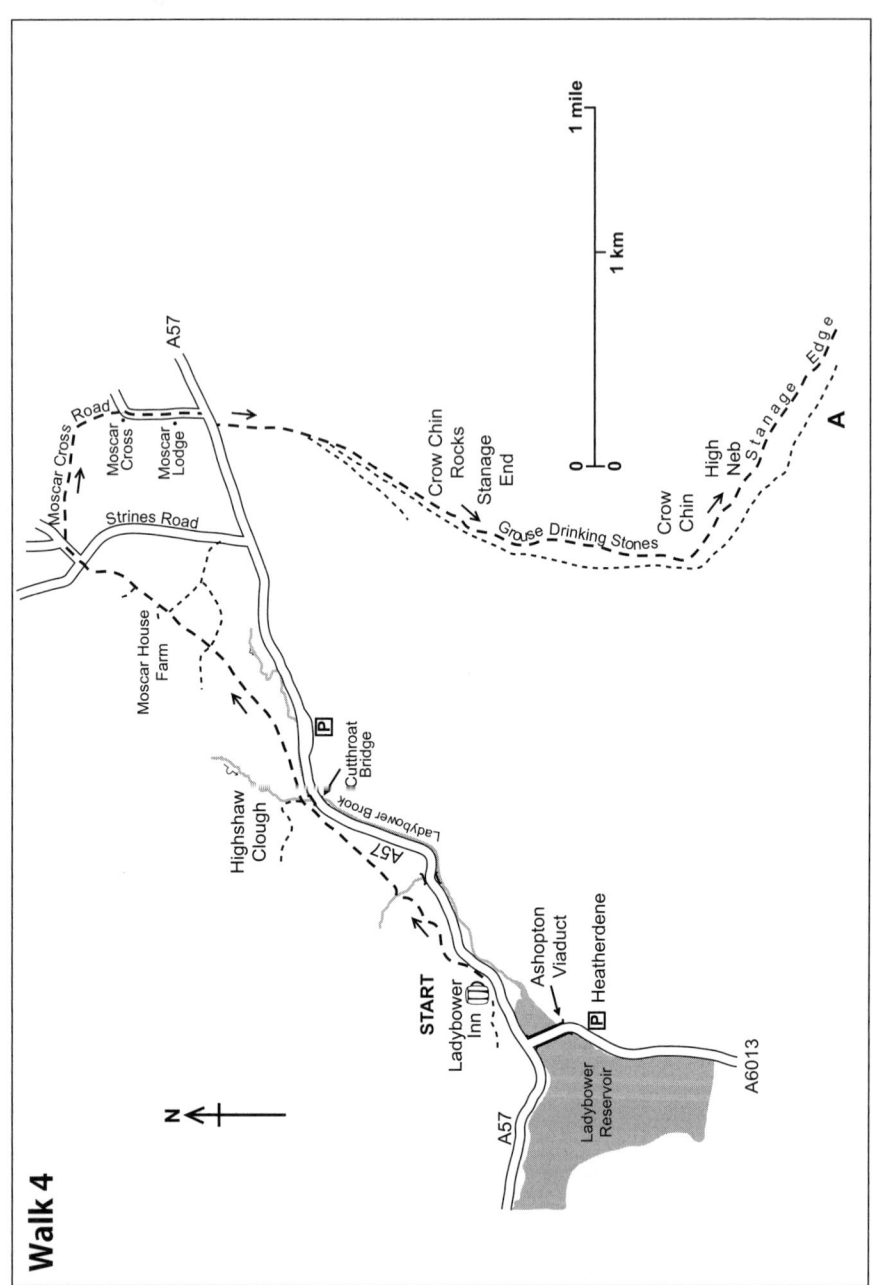

N

Moscar Cross Road

Moscar Cross Road

Moscar Cross

Moscar Lodge

A57

Strines Road

Moscar House Farm

Highshaw Clough

Ladybower Brook

Cutthroat Bridge

A57

START

Ladybower Inn

Ashopton Viaduct

Heatherdene

A57

Ladybower Reservoir

A6013

Crow Chin Rocks

Stanage End

Grouse Drinking Stones

Crow Chin

High Neb

Stanage Edge

A

0   1 km

0   1 mile

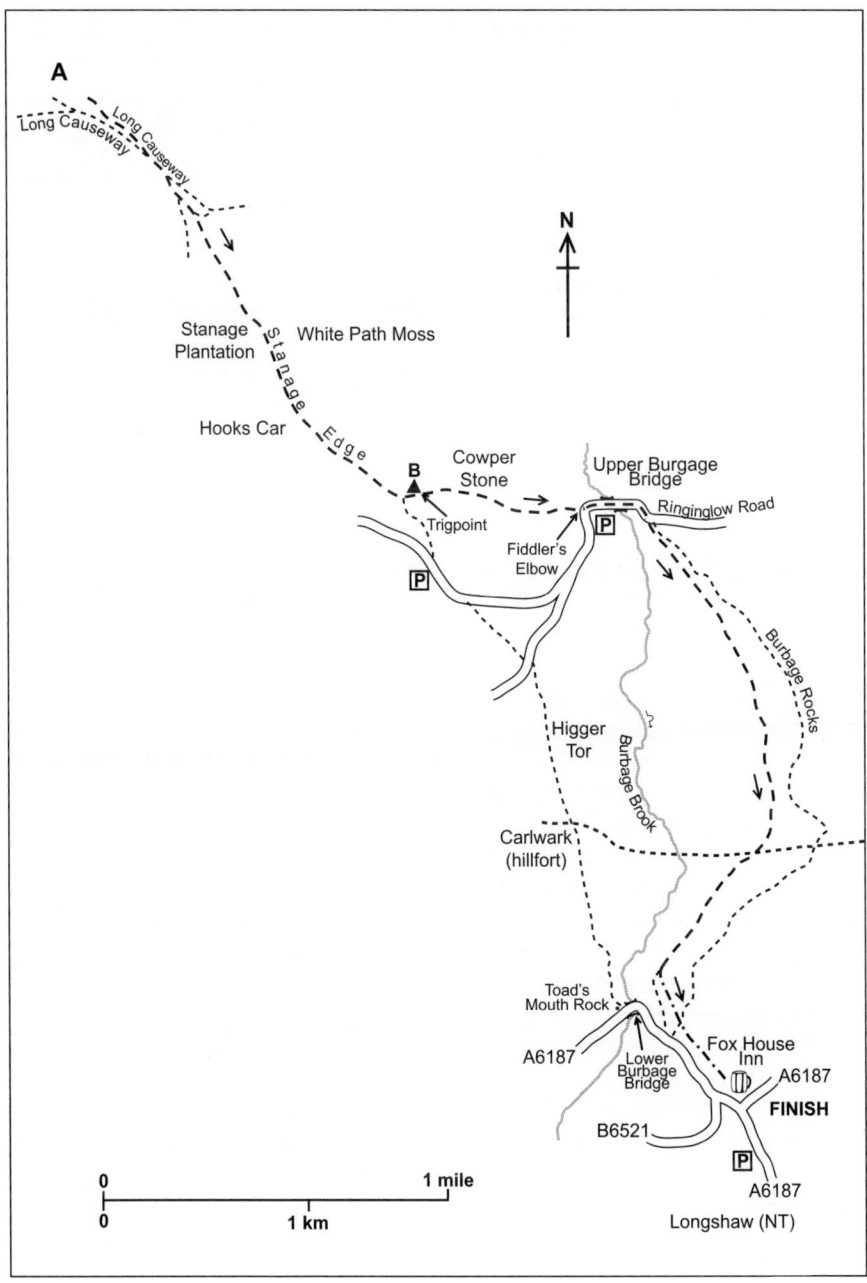

A

Long Causeway

Long Causeway

Stanage
Plantation

White Path Moss

Stanage Edge

Hooks Car

B

Cowper
Stone

Upper Burgage
Bridge

Trigpoint

Ringinglow Road

P

Fiddler's
Elbow

P

Burbage Rocks

Higger
Tor

Burbage Brook

Carlwark
(hillfort)

Toad's
Mouth Rock

A6187

Lower
Burbage
Bridge

Fox House
Inn

A6187

FINISH

B6521

P

A6187

Longshaw (NT)

N

0   1 mile

0   1 km

47

hollow-way, but usually with grand views away to the west. As the path approaches the start of the crags, it passes through a ruined wall in the midst of old gritstone quarry workings. *Note the boundary stones here, marked WM on one side and WW on the other. Whilst you are going along the Stanage path, keep a sharp lookout for the grouse drinking pools, each one numbered. Soon after gaining the top of the crags you pass the first of these, numbered 33. Between this point and the Long Causeway track, see how many of these drinking pools you can spot. I easily found 11 of them before the trig point at High Neb, but only one (number 9) thereafter.*

Grouse watering hole 33, Stannage

The route finding needs no description. Content yourself with strolling along, admiring the views to the west, looking for grouse drinking establishments and watching the antics of climbers. Don't forget to also watch where you are putting your feet, for this is not a nice paved path, but quite rough underfoot and with some awe inspiring drops to the right

After about 2 miles/3¼km you reach the point where Long Causeway crosses. *You'll have spotted this from miles away as a yellowy-orange swathe making its way up the hillside. This is an old road from Hathersage over to Sheffield and in part follows the route of an even older route, the Roman Road from Brough (Navio) to Templeborough (Rotherham).* Cross the Long Causeway and continue along the tops of the crags for a further 1¼ miles/ 2km to the next trig point, which overlooks the Ringinglow-Hathersage road and the popular Higger Tor.

Choices, choices!

You have a choice of routes here. The shortest, but with most ascent, is to drop down from just before the trig point to join the path leading to the road. Cross the road and go up one of the many paths leading onto Higger Tor and from there make your way onto Carlwark, down to Burbage Brook and up to the A6187 road at Burbage Bridge.

The longer route, and the one recommended, has less climbing, and carries on beyond the trig point to Cowper Stone and then descends the obvious path leading to the road at Upper Burbage Bridge. *At weekends you'll find the road and verge parked up solidly with cars, but there are compensations in the form of one or two ice-cream vans.* Assuming you've taken the recommended route, cross Upper Burbage Bridge and its twin companion.

Here again you have a choice of routes. The first stile takes you down the valley of the Burbage Brook on a broad path. The second stile takes you on a path on top of the crags of Burbage Edge. This is a longer route and rougher underfoot, but it ends up at the same place. I chose the lower route, having already walked 10 miles from the Dog and Partridge whilst recce'ing this part of the hike. The path drifts easily down the valley with good views to the right up to Higger Tor and Carlwark and to the left to the climbing crags of Burbage Edge.

When you get within sight of the gate out onto the A6187 road, look out for a narrow path leading away to the left and going slightly uphill. This crosses another path and continues up to reach a cluster of rocks, one of

Carlwark and Higger Tor from Burbage path

which is deeply incised with a large V and the letters IHTT. Precisely what this is all about is a mystery. However, at this point you join a broader track heading right and the Fox House Inn is clearly in view. Go through a small gate, across an equally small field to another gate and so arrive at the back of the pub car park.

The Fox House. 1124 ft/343 metres
Telephone 01433 630374. www.vintageinn.co.uk/thefoxhouselongshaw/
The Fox House Inn is the highest in Sheffield, but is only just within the city boundary. On the opposite side of the A6187 you are in Derbyshire. Indeed, until late on in the 19th century the Derbyshire boundary was drawn around the pub. Another territorial annexation by Yorkshire. Come the revolution... Contrary to popular belief, the Fox House was not named after a small furry animal but after Mr Fox of Callow Farm in Highlow. The original building dates back to 1773, but was extended by The Duke of Rutland, who owned the pub in the 1840s. The Fox House was a favoured resting place for livestock drovers and stagecoach passengers.

Fox House Inn

In a real sense, this hasn't changed because four roads converge at this junction and bus services use all of them, from Buxton, Castleton, Chesterfield, Matlock and Sheffield.

The Fox House specialises in cask-conditioned beers, with regular offerings from Black Sheep, Timothy Taylor's and Marston's breweries. The pub prides itself on its beers and states on its web site that, *'Every pint of our regularly changing real ales is lovingly kept, perfectly poured and Cask Marque accredited for quality, whether accompanying a plate of freshly cooked pub-food in front of the log-fire, or a summer's afternoon spent in our beer garden'.*

Opening times
Monday to Saturday: 1200 to 2300; Sundays: 1200 to 2230.
It is worth noting that the pub may open earlier on certain days depending on local demand so if you would like to visit before midday, give them a ring to ascertain if they're open.

Walk 5: The Fox House to Bretton (The Barrel)

Start	Fox House Inn. GR. SK265802
Finish	Barrel Inn, Bretton. GR. SK200779
The route	Fox House Inn, Longshaw Estate, Padley Gorge, Upper Padley, Leadmill Bridge, Hog Hall, Brook Wood, Stoke Ford, Bretton Clough, Nether Bretton, Barrel Inn
Length	6.82 miles (11 km)
Ascent	1388 feet (423 metres)
Time	3½ to 4 hours (exclusive of stops)
Map	OS OL24 (White Peak)

Getting there

By bus. Daily buses to Fox House from Buxton, Castleton, Bakewell, Sheffield and Matlock. No public transport to Bretton but daily buses to Foolow (1¼ miles from Barrel) from Buxton, Chesterfield and Sheffield.

By train. Nearest stations, Grindleford (bottom of Padley Gorge) or Hathersage (close to Leadmill Bridge). Daily trains to each of these from Manchester and Sheffield.

By car. The Fox House Inn is just in the City of Sheffield on the A6187 road from Sheffield to Castleton. There is pay and display parking at the National Trust car park in Longshaw Estate. The Barrel Inn at Bretton lies on an unclassified road. It is best reached from the A623 (Chesterfield to Manchester) road, leaving this road at Housley and then going through Foolow and up Bradshaw Lane. There is limited roadside parking.

The walk

Fox House to Grindleford

From the Fox House Inn go to the T-junction, cross the road and enter Longshaw Estate. Follow the path down to the house and continue on the drive to Longshaw Lodge. *This used to be a shooting lodge belonging to the Dukes of Rutland, but it is now in National Trust ownership. There's a teashop and visitor centre here, but you surely can't need a cup of tea just yet.* Follow the path round to the right of the Lodge with views across the moor to Higger Tor and Carlwark. At the gate keep right and follow the well-marked path through the estate and Granby Wood, down to the pond, ignoring the sign to Yarncliff. Skirt to the left of the pond and so down to the B6521, passing the discovery barn en route.

Cross the road with care – there's often an ice cream van here and many parked cars – and go over the stile onto a moorland path. Follow the path to the left until you reach a rather fine wooden bridge over the Burbage Brook. Cross

Longshaw Pond

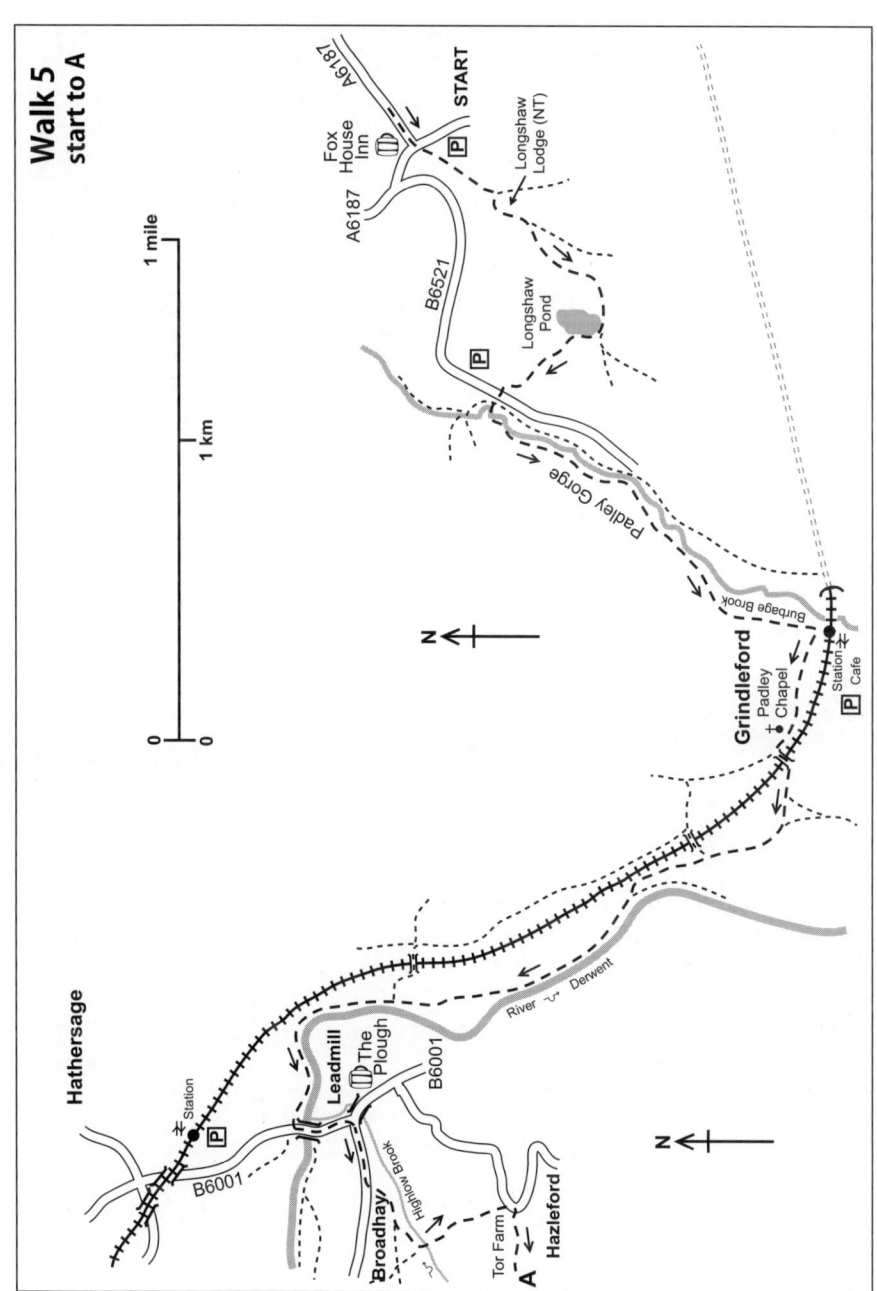

Walk 5
start to A

the brook and go left, soon entering the lovely oak wood, which marks the start of Padley Gorge. *This is a remnant of the ancient woodland which once cloaked much of the Peak District and it very nearly followed the fate of most of the other woodland in the area. Heavy grazing by sheep meant no new growth ever getting going. A series of experimental fences demonstrated that this problem could be tackled; grazing is now excluded and the wood is in fine fettle.*

This is a delightful walk with the stream cascading down a number of waterfalls deep below you. Ignore any paths leading off towards the stream and stay on the main path well above and on the right side of the brook. There is one moment of indecision, where the path begins to go up hill, but a downward trend is soon resumed and you soon pass one of the distinctive valve houses, which sit on the Derwent Aqueduct. *The aqueduct carries water from the Derwent dams near Bamford, to the cities of Derby, Nottingham and Leicester. It was built in the early years of the 20th century and the whole system works by gravity – no pumping being required.*

Once past the valve house you soon enter a steep lane through the Windses estate and then join another rough lane at a T-junction. Grindleford station and its famous café lie a short distance to your left, but your route lies to the right, running parallel with the railway.

Burbage Brook in spate

Millstone in Padley Gorge

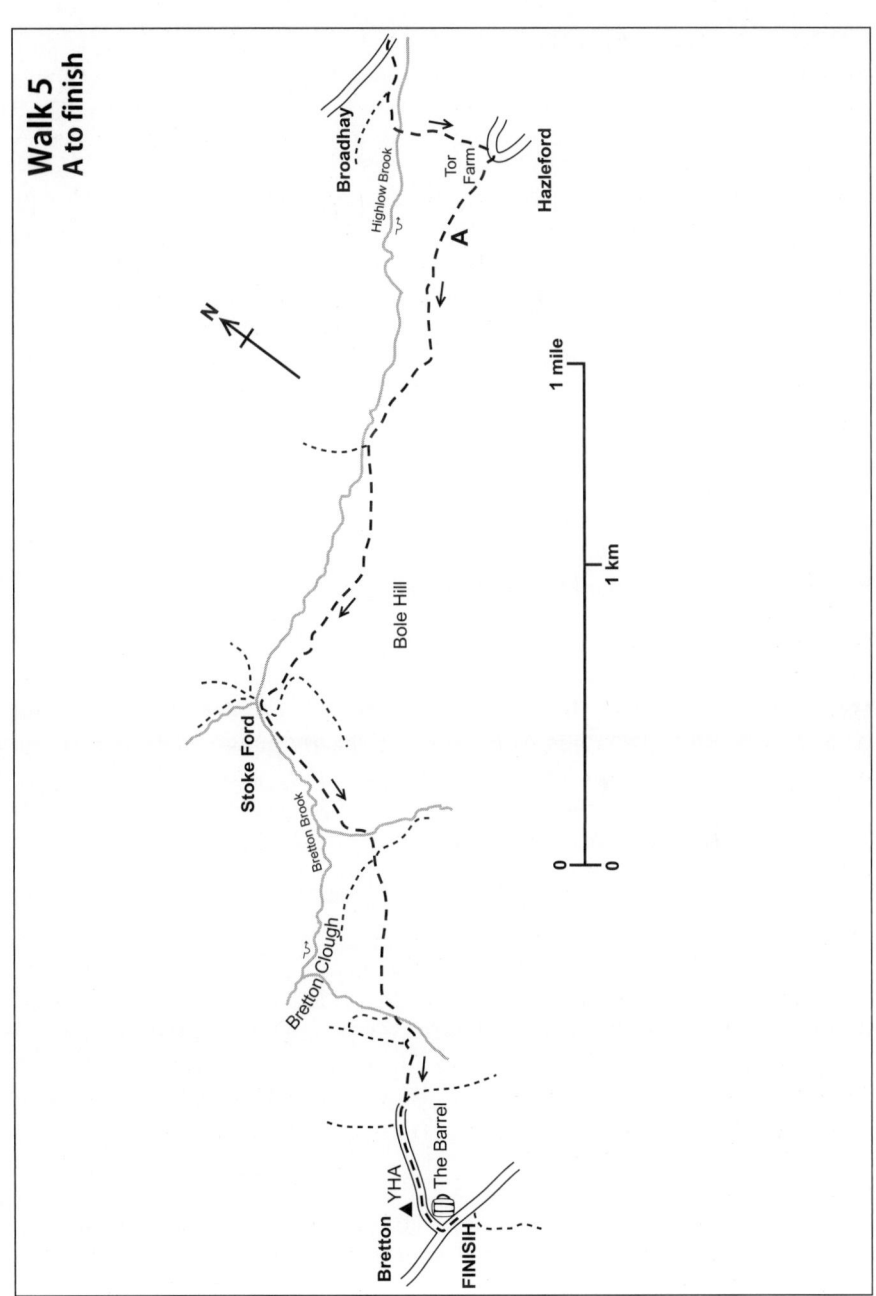

Walk 5
A to finish

Broadhay

Highlow Brook

Tor Farm

Hazleford

A

N

Bole Hill

Stoke Ford

Bretton Brook

Bretton Clough

Bretton

YHA

The Barrel

FINISIH

0   1 km   1 mile   0

Grindleford to Bretton

Follow the lane past Padley Chapel, which is the site of an annual pilgrimage in remembrance of the English Catholic martyrs. Opposite the chapel is Brunt's Barn, now a Peak Park ranger-briefing centre. Just beyond Padley Chapel, the lane passes over a cattle grid and then a bridge, which spans the former railway incline that served the quarries on Millstone Edge. *The incline was built as part of the construction of the Derwent dams. Stone was brought down the incline and taken by rail to Bamford then up the waterworks' private railway to the dam construction site.*

Just past the bridge, turn left and now cross the busy Hope Valley railway line. Follow the path, ignoring the waymark pointing left and the signpost to Leadmill. Continue ahead, soon dropping down to join the riverside path. Follow this path upstream, first through woodland and then open fields until you reach Harpur Lees where you join a lane. Follow the lane, noting the various curious carved stones, and thus reach the main Grindleford-Hathersage road. Here turn left and go over Leadmill Bridge. The Plough Inn lies to your left and is very tempting, but your way is up the little lane on the right, signed to Abney and the Gliding Club.

A short distance up the lane, the road forks and here you keep left, soon crossing a cattle grid and then leaving the lane at a footpath sign on your left. Descend to cross the stream and then climb up beside Hog Hall to reach Hazelford. Turn right and follow the track, which soon enters open fields and passes gently into the delightful valley of the Highlow Brook. *It is worth glancing back every now and then for the view over Highlow towards Burbage Moors and Stanage. Highlow Hall, which can be seen nestling just below Highlow Hill was one of a series of properties owned by local Catholic families at a time when such adherence was severely proscribed. Apparently the various halls are in view of one-another, so their inhabitants could give each other warning of any anti-Catholic activity.*

There is one part of the clough where the planting of conifers some years ago has completely ruined the drainage and this section is always very muddy, but it is soon over. The path dips to cross a stream and then rises onto open moorland (good view back) before descending again to Stoke Ford. There used to be a 'by-pass' here, which obviated the need to drop down to the ford, but recent planting has obscured it. Don't cross the ford (or the bridge) but continue up Bretton Clough. There are one or two muddy patches in this section, but they are mercifully brief and the path is a delight. Another stream is crossed before the path swings into a side clough and then rises in zig-zags to reach the lane at Nether Bretton. *The view across to Abney is very fine, but there is much better to come.*

Follow the lane past the youth hostel and so reach The Barrel. *The pub obscures the view ahead until the last minute, but on reaching the road, the full extent of the panorama is revealed, and it is superb. It must class as one of the best views in the Peak District and certainly one of the most extensive, stretching right down the Derwent valley to beyond Matlock and south-westwards towards the limestone hills of Dovedale and the Manifold. Westwards lie the heights of Axe Edge and Shining Tor, beyond Buxton. Only the occasional quarry mars the view, but this is a working landscape after all.*

The Barrel. 1258 ft/383 metres
Telephone 01433 630856. www.thebarrelinn.co.uk
The Barrel is the highest pub in Derbyshire and lies on an ancient trans-Pennine route that eventually became one of the earliest turnpike roads. The pub dates back to 1597, and retains much of its old fashioned charm, having an oak-beamed bar, flagstone floor, low doorways and studded doors. In every sense it's a traditional country inn. Outside there are seats on the front terrace and at the back of the pub there's a covered courtyard garden. As mentioned above, the view from the front is one of the best in the National Park.

Food is available seven days per week, lunchtime and evening, using only the finest local, fresh produce. The bar normally offers four real ales, which usually include offerings from Greene King and Marston's. There's always a guest beer and this is rotated on a monthly basis.

The Barrel, Bretton

Opening times
Monday to Friday 1100 to 1500 and 1830 to 2300. Saturday and Sunday 1100 to 2300.
Food is served Monday to Saturday 1200 to 1400 and 1830 to 2100. Sunday 1200 to 2000.

Walk 6: Bretton (The Barrel) to Taddington (Queen's Arms)

Start	The Barrel (Bretton) GR. SK200779
Finish	The Queen's Arms (Taddington) GR. SK144711
The route	The Barrel, Foolow, Wardlow Mires, Peter's Stone, Wardlow Hay Cop, Ravensdale, Cressbrook, Litton Mill, High Dale, Taddington (Queen's Arms)
Length	8.1 miles (13 km)
Ascent	1848 feet (563 metres)
Time	4-5 hours (exclusive of stops, but including ascent of Wardlow Hay Cop)
Map	OS OL24 (White Peak)

Getting there

By bus. No public transport to Bretton but daily buses to Foolow (1¼ miles from the Barrel) from Buxton, Chesterfield and Sheffield. There's a daily bus service to Taddington from Manchester, Buxton and Derby.

By train. Nearest station, Buxton.

By car. The Barrel Inn at Bretton lies on an unclassified road. It is best reached from the A623 (Chesterfield to Manchester) road, leaving this road at Housley and then going through Foolow and up Bradshaw Lane. There is roadside parking just east of the pub and you may be able to use the pub's car park if you seek the landlord's permission first. Taddington village lies just off the A6, about half way between Buxton and Bakewell. There's limited on-street parking in the village.

The Walk

Bretton to Cressbrook Dale

On leaving The Barrel, go westwards along the road, keeping left where it forks and descending to Foolow village. There are buses from here to Buxton, Chesterfield and Sheffield. In the village, skirt to the right of the pond and seek out a narrow passageway between stone walls. It is signed, but the sign is frequently obscured by vegetation. Once into open fields, the way ahead is clear enough, with the stiles all in place and some waymarked. The path soon drops into a narrow walled lane and almost at once leaves it again to cut off a corner. Cross a few more fields and thus reach the lane again as you cross Silly Dale. Straight on at the T-junction. Here you join the route of Walk 27, so if you've already done that walk the next section should be familiar.

You soon reach Stanley House Farm, which now has a number of holiday cottages. Just beyond the farm, the track swings right and there's a footpath sign and stile on the left by a gate. A notice warns you to 'Beware of the bull'. Having ascertained that there's no bull in the vicinity, go over the stile and bear right, making for a gate and stile by a trough in the bottom wall of the field. *Wardlow village, Wardlow Mires and the head of Cressbrook Dale can be seen ahead with Peter's Stone prominent.* In the next field keep by the right hand wall to a gate leading into the farm complex. Continue ahead, with the barns on your left and a fence to your right, to another gate, into the farmyard. Go left, through another gate and then right, out onto the A623.

The Three Stags Heads (SK181756 791ft/241 metres), lies just to your right. This pub is legendary, and boasts stone floors and a superb range (the fire) in the bar. The additional time for a visit to the Three Stags is not included in this walk. This pub only opens on Friday nights and at weekends, but if you do find it open, it's well worth a visit. Please do not ask for draught lager as 'a punch in the gob may offend' – as one of the notices says. Also, if there's Abbeydale's 'Last Rites' on offer, resist the temptation for any more than a half, or you'll never reach Taddington unassisted. There are buses from here to Castleton, Chesterfield and Bakewell – and you may need them!

Cross the A623, noting the sign at the entrance to the pub car park, warning you to 'Beware of the guinea pig'. Different! Cross the road leading to Wardlow and then go along the new roadside path to a small gate. Turn left here, round the back of the garage and into a broad green lane, where you turn right. You are now in Cressbrook Dale National Nature Reserve. The walk down the dale is delightful. You pass below Peter's Stone, the top of which can be visited, if you have a mind to. The best ascent is to go round the back and scale it from there. *Don't try the full frontal ascent (or descent) unless you have a death*

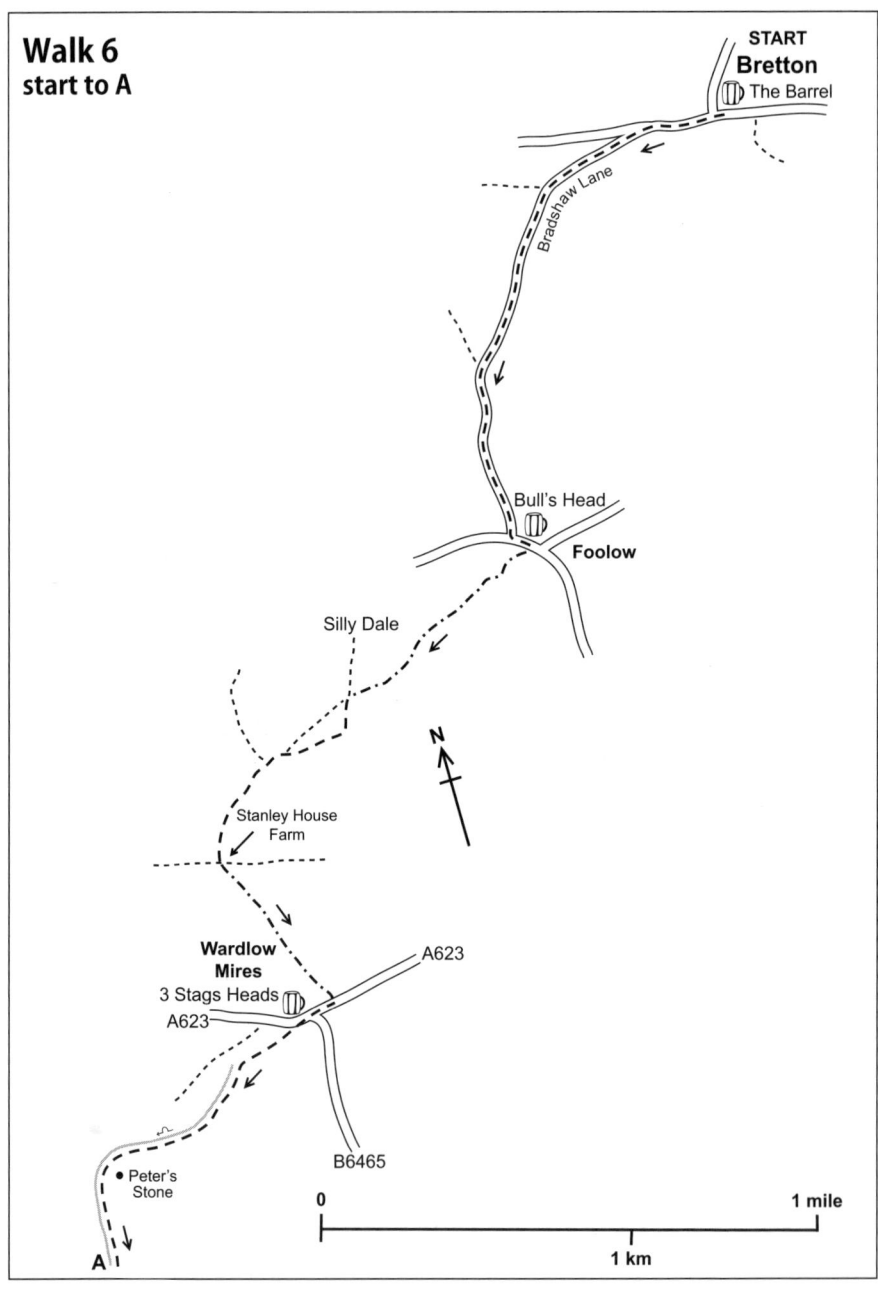

Walk 6
start to A

START
Bretton
The Barrel

Bradshaw Lane

Bull's Head
Foolow

Silly Dale

N

Stanley House
Farm

**Wardlow
Mires**
3 Stags Heads
A623
A623

Peter's
Stone

B6465

0   1 mile

1 km

A

Walk 6
A to finish

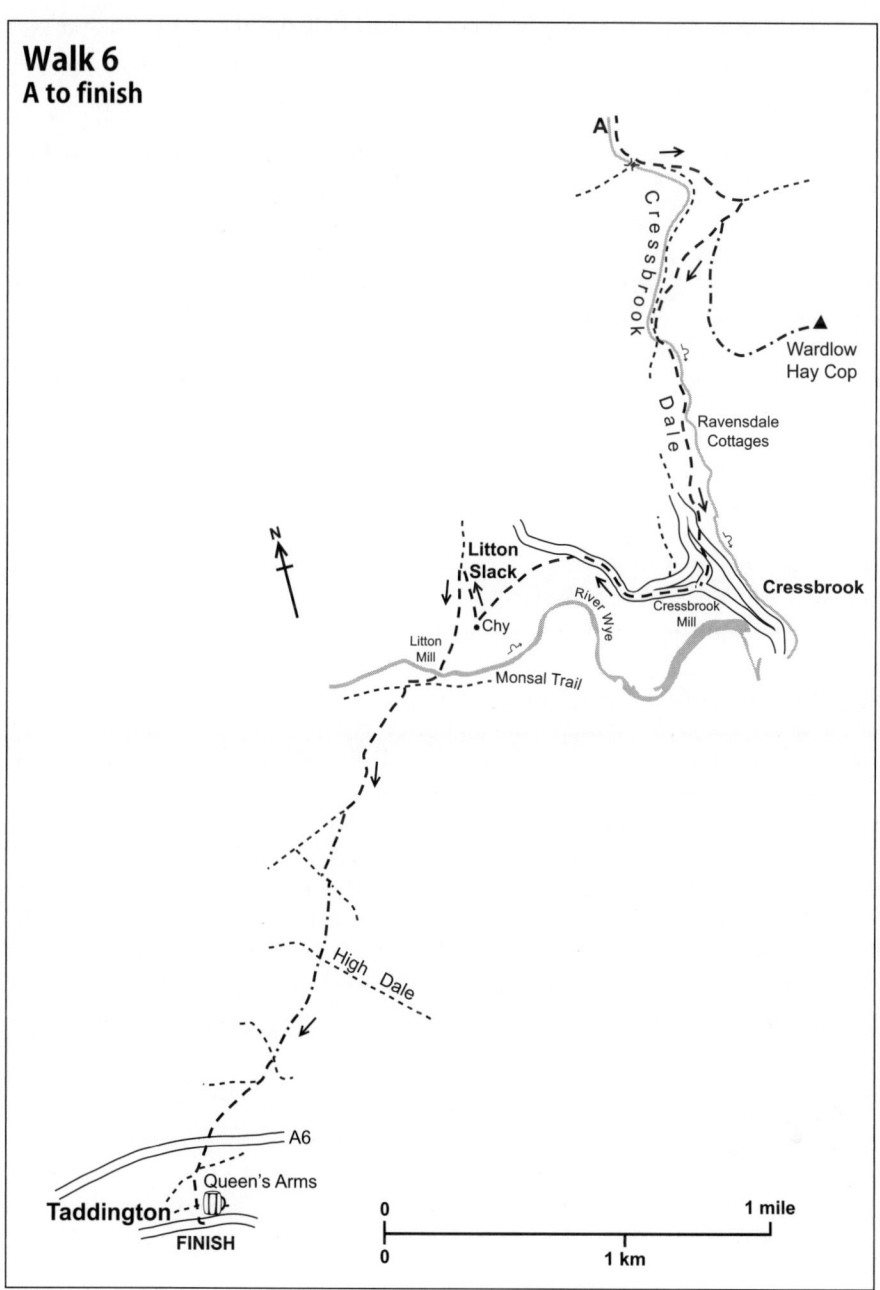

A

Cressbrook Dale

Wardlow Hay Cop

Ravensdale Cottages

Cressbrook

Litton Slack

River Wye

Cressbrook Mill

Litton Mill

•Chy

Monsal Trail

N

High Dale

A6

Queen's Arms

Taddington
FINISH

0   1 mile

0   1 km

wish. Speaking of death wishes, it is worth bearing in mind that the other name for Peter's Stone is Gibbet Rock. In this context it was the scene of the last gibbeting in Derbyshire in 1815. Apparently people came from far and wide to see the grisly spectacle, so much so that a Methodist minister, noting that his congregation was seriously diminished, found them at the site and preached to them in the open air. In this he was following in the footsteps of William Bagshawe, the Apostle of the Peak who is also reputed to have preached to a crowd from the rock in the late 17th century. Interestingly, given the nonconformist religious use of the stone, the name Peter's Stone is said to derive from the similarity of the rock to the dome of St Peter's in Rome!

Having climbed the stone, go back into the dale bottom and continue down the valley, to the new (2012) bridge where a path diverges right to Tansley Dale and Litton. Continue down Cressbrook Dale to a bifurcation of paths at the point where the path skirts round the back of a fenced off lead mine entrance. From here you have the choice of either continuing down the dale or ascending Wardlow Hay Cop. If you don't want to climb Wardlow Hay Cop, skip the next paragraph.

Ascent of Wardlow Hay Cop

If you choose the to climb the Cop, be wary of the additional time, especially if you are banking on catching buses. From here to the summit and back down into the dale again will take about ½ hour, exclusive of any stops for breath or admiring the view. Bear left and go up the gently rising path that makes its way up to the crest of the dale. Here it reaches a stile in the upper boundary wall. Bear right as you near the stile and follow a sketchy path beside the wall until you reach a new gate, complete with the Access Land sign. The summit of the Cop can be seen quite clearly and you can make a beeline for it. The view is tremendous from the top and worth the extra effort. Return the same way and when you reach the point where you turned off the public footpath, turn sharp left to descend into the dale again on a different path from that by which you ascended. This path drops down through woodland to rejoin the dale-bottom path, just before the footbridge. *(Now skip the next paragraph.)*

Cressbrook Dale and Ravensdale

From the fenced off mine working, carry on down the dale, noting that you now have a stream accompanying you. This emerged from the mine workings and runs more or less all the time. You soon enter woodland and the path twists and turns its way through the trees and scrub, sometimes almost in the stream, sometimes well above it. It's a delightful walk but you need to take care because of the tree roots and the polished limestone. Soon you are joined by a path on the left. *This is where your more energetic companions rejoin, having been up Wardlow Hay Cop.*

Descend to the footbridge and bear left, still following the stream. Ignore the path going off to the right. The dale bottom path continues to twist and turn through woodland until you reach a gate and stile by a water trough and the hamlet of Ravensdale. *As you pass the cottages look up at the towering limestone crags, a playground for rock climbers.*

Ravensdale

Cressbrook to Litton Mill

From Ravensdale, follow the tarmacked lane, which rises gently to join the Monsal Head to Litton road. Go straight across the road onto a footpath and continue upwards to join another, narrower road in Cressbrook village. Bear left here, following the road down a short way to a crossroads. (*The route straight ahead leads only to Cressbrook Hall.*) Your way is to the right, up the hill. This is quite steep, but it is soon over. At the top of the hill the road levels out and you have a view down Monsal Dale to Monsal Head. Continuing along the road, with a nature reserve on your left, you soon pass the small church of St. John the Evangelist on the right. Just beyond this, bear left along a rough track, signposted to Litton Mill and Millers Dale.

This track begins as a narrow walled lane, but soon emerges onto open hillside with a superb view down into Water cum Jolly Dale, and a fine vantage point from which to appreciate the precipitous limestone cliffs. You'll also notice a fine stone chimney. The track continues to descend, soon reaching a gate and stile, beyond which is access land. Here you join another track coming down from the right.

This is Litton Slack, 'slack' being an old word for steep hill. Go left here, soon getting very close to the chimney you saw earlier. This chimney was once part of the Litton Mill complex. These mills gained considerable notoriety in the 19th century because of their harsh employment practices, especially in their use of female and child labour. The exposure of this appalling treatment was instrumental in bringing about the first factory acts, which regulated the employment of children and introduced the idea of an independent factory inspectorate. From the chimney, the track swings sharp right and into a side dale, with a very steep grassy slope on the left. *This was the scene of an escapade by the author of this book when he and a colleague decided to take a short cut from Cressbrook to Millers Dale in the author's car. We got as far as this hairpin bend and viewed the remaining descent with alarm. Turning round was not an option (as you'll see), nor was reversing, so down we went. At one point, my colleague decided that he would be better off getting out and making sure that the car didn't go over the edge. A wise move and it is a pity the author couldn't do the same. Incredibly we got down in one piece, but I've never attempted it again, and nor should you.*

Stroll down the track, which drops into the side dale and then turns sharp left to reach the cottages of Litton Mill. It would be possible to descend the grassy slope more or less direct, but the track is easier and more comfortable. A gate and stile takes you into Litton Mill hamlet. The mill complex, which is now private housing, is to the left. Your route lies to the right along the road, to the cottages. Look out for a path to the left. This leads to a bridge over the mill-race and the River Wye.

Litton Mill to Taddington

Go over the bridge and climb the bank on the south side to reach the Monsal Trail. Don't go onto the trail but follow the path up and over the bridge, which spans the former railway. From the bridge, the path wriggles steeply upwards, through a patch of scrub to reach a stile by a gate. The cottages of Litton Mill now seem far below. A sign proclaims that this is a nature reserve, but it is also open access land. The multiplicity of lead workings should be sufficient to deter all but the most ardent access enthusiast from wandering too far and the advice is to stay on the well-marked path. Go over the stile into the area of lead mine remains and continue your ascent with a wall close by on your right and with former lead workings everywhere around. Where the path levels out, you cross the main lead rake. It is worth pausing here for the view (and to catch your breath). *The lead mine remains stretch away to your left and to your right. The view from here is extensive. From here you are looking across Millers Dale to Ravenstor youth hostel and up Tideswell Dale, to Tideswell and Win Hill, to the Barrel Inn at Bretton and to Wardlow Hay Cop at the top of Scratter.*

Follow the lead rake across the hillside on a well-defined path to a stile by a gate on your left. This takes you out of the lead mining area and into a field.

Follow an ill-defined path beside the left-hand wall to a stile that exits onto Bulltor Lane – merely a rough green lane. At Bulltor Lane, turn left and then, almost at once, go right, through a bridle gate and descend into High Dale. *This delightful quiet dale would have been very different had the proposals for the Lancashire Derbyshire and East Coast Railway come about in the 1890s.* The continuation of your route can be seen on the opposite side of the dale running in a pronounced zig-zag to a sign-posted stile in the top wall. Cross the dale-bottom path and climb up the south bank along an obvious beaten path. Part-way up, a less obvious path goes right, still climbing and then bears left, straight up the hillside to the stile you saw earlier. Go through the stile and into fields, following the narrow but

Litton Mill from the platelayers' path

obvious path until you reach a narrow walled lane. The left hand arm of the lane is gated. The right hand arm only takes you back towards High Dale and Priestcliffe, so it's the straight ahead route that you need. *This lane is one of a number around Taddington, now mainly the preserve of walkers, but still the main means of access for farm traffic, despite their narrow width.*

Follow this green lane, which soon descends to the A6. The A6 is a dual carriageway at this point and has some very fast traffic, so take care when crossing. The green lane continues on the far side of the main road and soon reaches the outskirts of Taddington. There are a number of options for getting to the main street, and there's nothing to choose between them. At the main street go right, unless you are calling at the Queen's Arms, in which case, go left for a short distance.

The Queen's Arms 1052ft/321 metres
Telephone 01298 85245. No website

The Queen's Arms features in *Best Pub Walks in the White Peak* by Sigma Press. For many years the pub has been a popular calling point for ramblers. The

Queens has been a pub since 1736, at which time it sat on the main road to Buxton. Now the village is (mercifully) by-passed and the pub is a very pleasant quiet place in which to enjoy a jar. The pub apparently boasts two resident ghosts: a little black dog and a young girl. On entering the pub there's a small bar to the left, which now doubles as a pool-room and village shop. Most people head for the larger L-shaped bar on the right. In this room there's a large attractive fireplace with a lovely warm fire in the winter and it is very spacious with plenty of traditional seating away from the bar.

The Queens sells a range of cask beers, usually including several local brews e.g. from the Buxton and Barnsley breweries.

This is a great community pub, which welcomes walkers. Families and dogs (on a lead) are also welcome. There's limited seating outside.

Opening times
1200 to 2300 every day (2230 on Sundays).
Food is usually available at all opening times and on Sundays lunch/dinner is available from 1200 until 2100. Buses to Buxton, Bakewell, Matlock and Derby stop outside the pub.

Queen's Arms, Taddington

Walk 7: Taddington (Queen's Arms) to Pomeroy (Duke of York)

Start	Taddington (Queen's Arms) GR. SK144711
Finish	Pomeroy (Duke of York) GR. SK119675
The route	Taddington, Sough Top, Chelmorton, Church Lane, Highstone Lane, Pippenwell Lane, Pomeroy
Length	3.94 miles (6.34 km)
Ascent	551 feet (168 metres)
Time	Around 2 hours (exclusive of stops)
Map	OS OL24 (White Peak)

Getting there

By bus. There's a daily bus service to Taddington from Derby, Buxton and Manchester. There's a daily bus service to Pomeroy from Ashbourne and Buxton.

By train. Nearest station, Buxton

By car. Taddington lies just off the A6, midway between Bakewell and Buxton. There's limited on-street parking in the village. Pomeroy is on the A515 between Buxton and Ashbourne. There's no on-street parking. If you park at the Duke of York, ask permission first and make sure you patronise the pub!.

The Walk

Over Sough Top to Chelmorton

Walk up Main Street, passing the church on your right, noting the unusual dedication to St Michael and All Angels. At the junction of Main Street, School

Walk 7

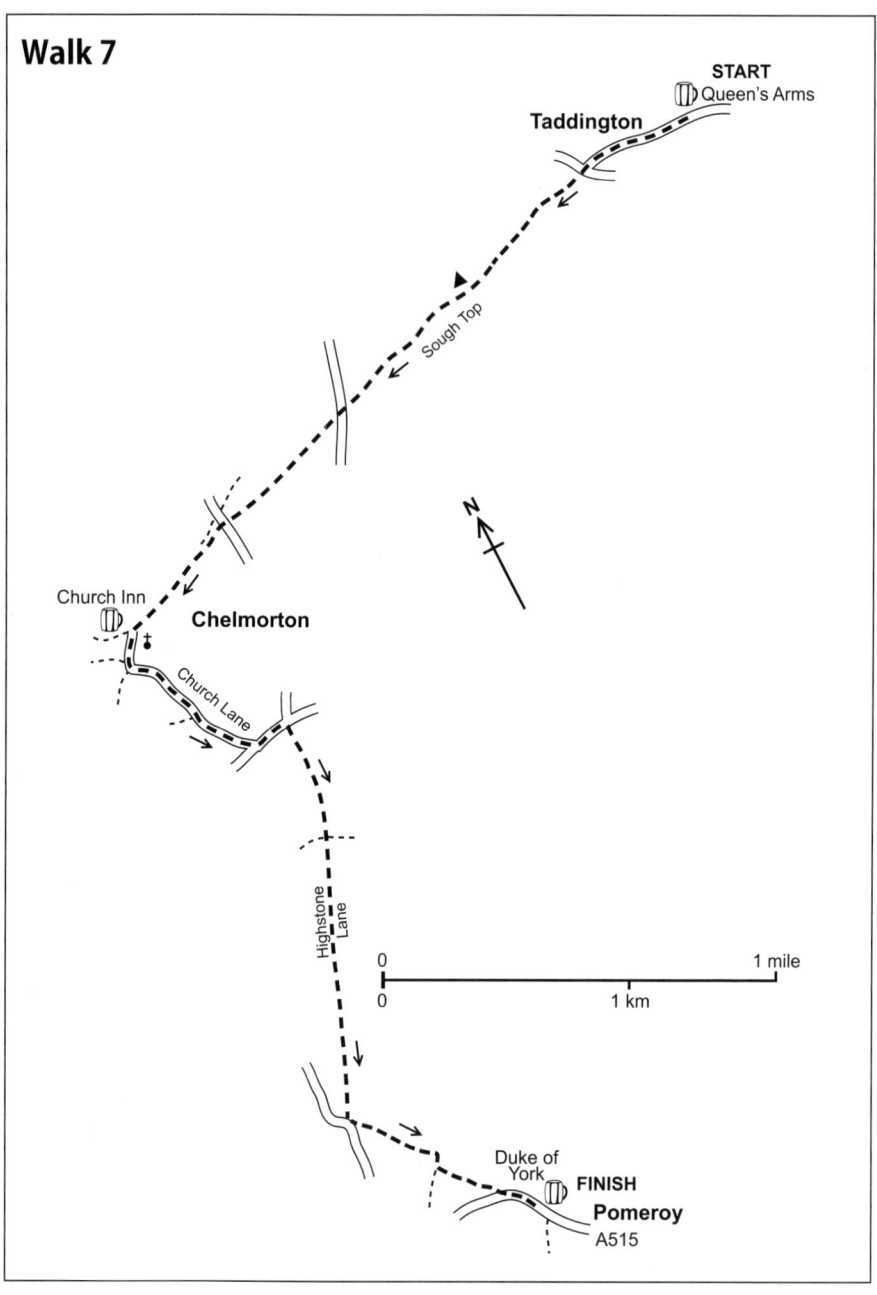

START
Queen's Arms

Taddington

Sough Top

N

Church Inn
Chelmorton

Church Lane

Highstone Lane

0   1 mile
0   1 km

Duke of York

FINISH
Pomeroy

A515

Lane and Humphrey Gate turn sharp left and almost at once, seek out a narrow path on the right, between two houses. Easily missed, especially if the hedge hasn't been trimmed.

The narrow section is soon over and the path gains open fields. It rises steadily to another stile onto Slipperlow Lane. Cross the lane, go over another stile and continue upwards, with increasingly good views back over Taddington towards Longstone Edge and beyond to The Barrel. *The deeply incised dales are almost entirely hidden from this viewpoint.* As the path tops the hill, you'll see in front of you the communication masts and a flat-topped mound. *This is not a well-preserved tumulus, but a modern reservoir.* The path keeps to the left of the mound to a stile and then bears right to follow a wall line across the broad expanse of Sough Top.

A steady stroll alongside the wall and over a series of stiles, soon brings you to another green lane, Sough Lane. Cross over and continue alongside the wall, with Five Wells farm now in view to your right. Another easy stroll brings you to a junction with Pillwell Lane (or Pillwell Gate) and here you have a number of choices.

Leaving Taddington behind

You may have noticed from the map that there is a 'chambered cairn' marked to the north of Fivewells Farm and it is from this ancient burial mound that the farm gets its name. The cairn is accessible by turning right, along Pillwell Gate and then using the signed concession path to the cairn. You'll have to return to this same point if you chose this option and you should allow yourself at least ½ hour.

The second option is to turn left at Pillwell Gate and follow the Pennine Bridleway down to the junction with the Chelmorton-Flagg road and then across onto Highstone Lane. If you take this option, ignore the next paragraph.

The third option (and the 'official' route of this walk) is to cross Pillwell Gate and carry on along the bridleway, which here runs either side of an old lead rake. *In spring, the flowers on the spoil heaps are a picture, but don't venture too close to some of the deep hollows. Who knows what delights could await you there? Best not to find out. To your right and ahead, rises Chelmorton Low and further away, the view stretches to the high moors behind Buxton. In fact you can probably see a couple of the other high pubs from here, though it's difficult to be certain.* The path now begins to descend quite sharply and the village of Chelmorton comes into view.

Chelmorton

Just before you reach the first houses, you pass the Illy Willy water, which rises alongside the lane just above the church. *Chelmorton owes its existence to this spring. In former times it ran in channels through the village before disappearing down a swallow hole, but it has now been culverted.* The path swings left and becomes a metalled road. *To your right is The Church and to your left is the church. One church dispenses spiritual refreshment; the other more basic food and drink. Before you deviate into The Church take a look at the church (not the pub). Look at the weathervane and whilst you are in the pub or on the walk try to work out what type of insect it represents. Then, when you've found that out,*

Chelmorton church

use that knowledge to work out to which saint the church is dedicated. Here endeth the RE exam.

The Church Inn (SK114702, 1224 ft/373 metres), *is a fine village hostelry with an enviable reputation for both its food and drink. Well worth deviating for. It features in the companion book to this one, 'Best Pub Walks in the White Peak' also published by Sigma Press.*

Chelmorton to Pomeroy

From the pub, go down the main street and then turn left up Church Lane. As you climb away from the village you get an almost bird's eye view of its layout. *The one main road runs between a line of limestone houses and farms, each one of which has strips of land leading up the hillside towards you, or stretching away to the west. These are ancient strip fields, now fossilised by drystone walls. They are amongst the finest examples in the country. At the time of the recce' it was clear that one resident was clearly expecting global warming and sea level rise on a massive scale as he'd got a narrow boat in the back garden.*

Continue up Church Lane to its junction with the road to Flagg and there turn left. Follow the Flagg road for a little less than 200 yards/metres to the cross roads with Flat Lane and Highstone Lane and here go right, joining the Pennine Bridleway.

Expecting the worst at Chelmorton

Highstone Lane is no more than a rough track. *As well as being the Pennine Bridleway it is also part of the Midshires Way, which as you might gather, runs through middle England.* The track imperceptibly changes its name to Nether Blindlow Lane and then gives out onto a metalled road, the delightfully named Pippenwell Lane. Don't go along the road, but turn left, to go over a stone step stile into a field. Follow the drystone wall on the right, cross a stile and continue ahead to go over another boundary wall, before crossing a stile near to the electricity pylon. Walk over to the opposite field boundary and then turn left, ignoring the stile in this wall. *At this point you are following the alignment of the Roman road from Buxton (Aquae Arnemetiae) to Derby (Derventio).*

Go through the gateway and walk to the corner of the field where a stile exits onto the main road, the A515. *From here, the A515 is also on the alignment of the Roman road at this point and this is indicated by the Street Farm place name given to the farm on your right. A 'Street' name usually indicates the presence of a Roman Road, and that is the case here.* Turn left to walk the short distance on the road verge to the Duke of York pub at Pomeroy. Thankfully it is a short stretch. Along the main road to the right is a boundary stone marking the different quarters of the Hartington townships or parishes. Be careful hereabouts because the traffic travels at speed – the Romans knew what they were doing when they laid out this road!

The Duke of York, 1237ft/377 metres
Telephone 01298 83345. www.thedukeofyorkpomeroy.co.uk
The Duke of York at Pomeroy is a Robinson's pub with extensive gardens and a camping/caravan site behind. The building was originally a farm in the 15th century. In the early 17th century it was converted to a coaching inn to serve the growing trade on the road from Buxton to London. This continued as Buxton became more popular as a place to take the waters in the next century. The coaching trade declined with the arrival of the railways in the 19th century, but the inn has continued to welcome passers-by since those heady days. The pub welcomes walkers, but please clean your boots on the scraper provided.

There's a main lounge bar that has a roaring fire on a winter's day. An unusual feature on the wall was a list of all the landlords and landladies that have served here since 1618. (It is understood that this has now 'vanished', though it may hopefully be reinstated). The inn prides itself on its locally sourced home-made food and of course stocks the usual range of Robinson's excellent beers, plus guest ales.

The Duke of York

Opening times
The Duke is open every day, Monday to Sunday: 1200 'til midnight.
Food is available from 1200 to 2030 every day. The Buxton-Ashbourne bus stops at the pub and runs daily.

Walk 8: Pomeroy (Duke of York) to Earl Sterndale (Quiet Woman)

Start	Pomeroy (Duke of York) GR. SK119675
Finish	Earl Sterndale (Quiet Woman) GR. SK089670
The route	Duke of York, High Peak Trail, Dowlow, Earl Sterndale
Length	2.45 miles (3.94 km)
Ascent	192 feet (59 metres)
Time	Allow 1-1¼ hours (exclusive of stops)
Map	OS OL24 (White Peak)

Getting there
By bus. Both Pomeroy and Earl Sterndale have daily bus services from Buxton and Ashbourne.
By train. Nearest station, Buxton
By car. Pomeroy lies on the A515 between Buxton and Ashbourne. The only car parking is at the Duke of York so please ask the landlord's permission first. There's on-street parking in Earl Sterndale, but please park considerately.

The Walk
This is the shortest walk in the book and also has the least ascent. It could easily be combined with Walk 7 or Walk 9. Alternatively you could just regard it as a pleasant afternoon stroll. You could park at Pomeroy, stroll to Earl Sterndale, have a jar and stroll back to the Duke of York for a meal.

Pomeroy to Earl Sterndale
From the Duke of York, cross the A515 with great care and go over the stile to the left of Street House Farm. Skirt to the left of the farm buildings, through a gateway and then follow the wall on the right, until you spot a bridge ahead

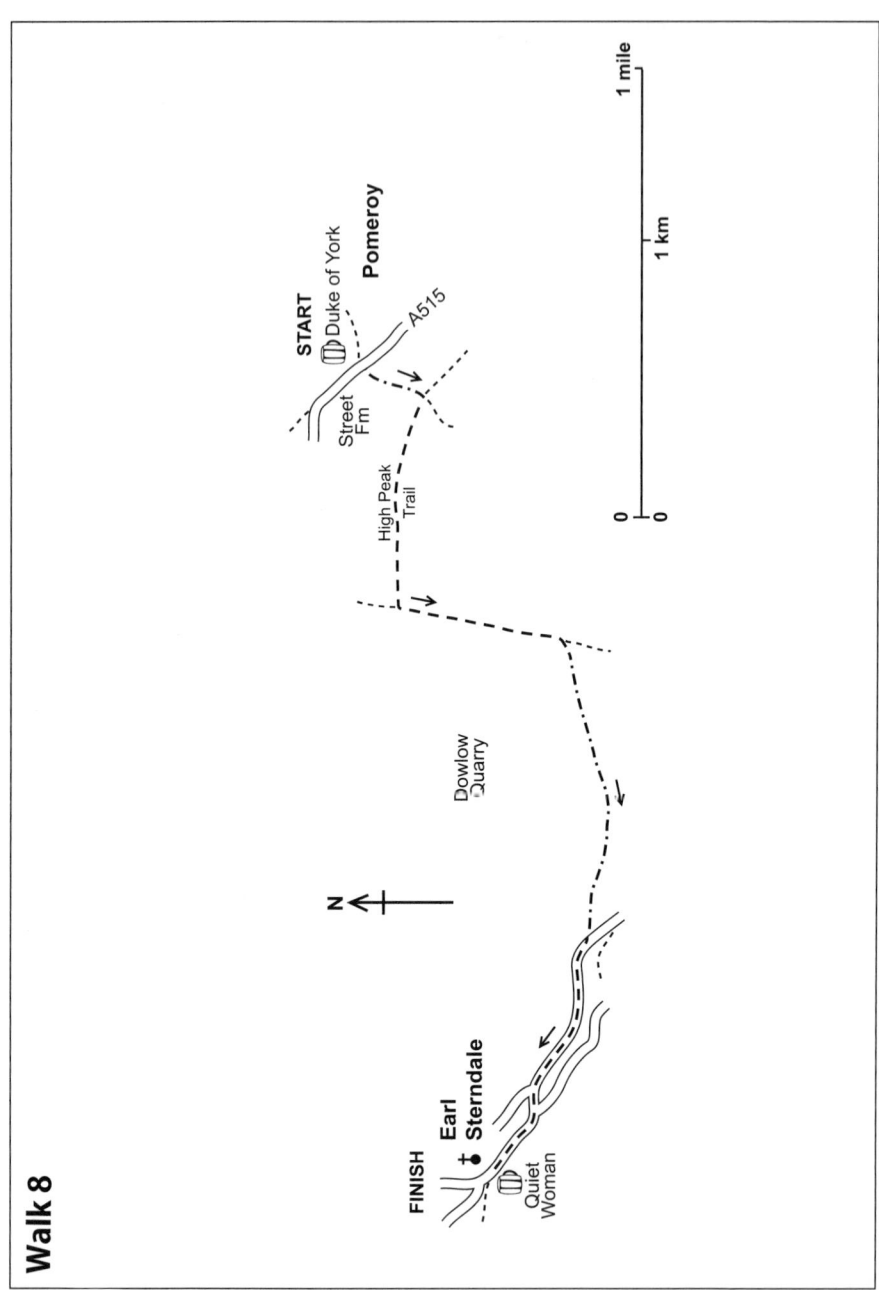

Walk 8

START — Duke of York — Pomeroy
Street Fm
A515
High Peak Trail
Dowlow Quarry
N
Earl Sterndale
FINISH
Quiet Woman

0 — 1 km — 1 mile

of you and slightly to your left. Make a bee-line for this, but don't cross it. Instead, drop down the left hand side of the embankment to a stile, which takes you onto the High Peak Trail. Turn right and pass under the bridge. *The High Peak Trail runs from Cromford to Dowlow. For the most part it follows the alignment of the Cromford and High Peak Railway, one of the pioneer railways and the first trans-Pennine rail route,*

Bridge on High Peak Trail

opening in the early 1830s. It finally closed in 1967 and was subsequently converted into a cycling and walking route. The section you are on now was not part of the original route, but was opened on 2ⁿᵈ January1869 to avoid a rope worked incline with a 1:16 gradient.

An easy stroll along the former railway soon brings you to the current end of the Trail at Dowlow, where there is an information board. There used to be a bridge here too, but it was demolished when the Trail was opened. *Beyond this point there is a short section of disused trackbed and then the railway is operational, serving Dowlow and Hindlow quarries.* Pass through the gate and turn left, following the signs to Earl Sterndale. *To your right lies Dowlow quarry, securely fenced and apart from the fencing, more or less invisible, surrounded as it is by an earth bank. It is only when you realise that the green rolling hills just to your right are actually revegetated quarry overburden that you begin to understand the size of this undertaking.*

A short distance further on, you cross the original route of the Cromford and High Peak Railway. *To your left, a line of trees on an embankment marks the old line. To your right, the continuation of the route is immediately lost in Dowlow quarry.* You have been climbing gently to this point, but now you top the rise.

A sudden view opens out ahead, over Dove Dale and towards the Staffordshire moorlands.

Go over the signposted stile on your right, into a field, making to the right of the prominent conical hill (High Wheeldon) seen ahead. Continue ahead through another field. *Note the improving view to your left, which now takes in Sheen Hill and the hills around Wetton and Alstonefield. Looking south you can make out the distinctive tree-topped outline of Minninglow.* Head now for the centre of a line of trees to locate a small gate. This takes you into the tree belt, and another small gate takes you out the other side. *At this point the reef knolls of the Upper Dove suddenly come into view. The course of walk 9 can be seen stretching ahead to the horizon, where a cluster of buildings could well be those at Flash Bar. They look a long way off!*

Bear left in this field to another small gate and here bear right to yet another little gate. Here the path bears left and downwards to join a cart track, which then swings right. Follow this down to a field gate on the left, but don't go through it. Instead carry on alongside the wall to a sign-posted (small) gate in the field corner. In the next field head slightly left to yet another gate (there's a plethora of the things on

High Wheeldon

this walk) and across the next field to reach the road. Go right here and follow the road into Earl Sterndale, soon passing Sterndale Hall and the chapel on your left, and reaching The Quiet Woman pub in the centre of the village.

The Quiet Woman, 1084ft/330 metres
Telephone 01298 83211. No website

The Quiet Woman at Earl Sterndale is not one of the 'High Pubs' featured in this walk. It features in *Best Pub Walks in the White Peak* also published by Sigma Press. It nevertheless ranks high in the table of grand National Park hostelries. It is an unpretentious Peak District pub, not given over to food but focusing on good hospitality for both locals and visitors. The name is unusual and the inn sign includes the words 'Soft Words Turneth Away Wrath', referring to the tale of an earlier landlord who chopped off his wife's head to stop her ranting at him all night and day. The gory pub sign illustrates a headless woman. Evidently, the villagers at the time happened to be 100% behind his rather desperate action.

The main room is the bar and, whilst there has been ongoing upkeep, this has been undertaken in a sympathetic manner including the restoration of natural beams. The open fire in winter is a real plus for the walker – and the settles and wooden tables make this a place to get comfortable. This is especially the case on Sundays when folk music is sometimes played. There are Marston's and Jennings beers on hand pull and often a guest beer on tap too. Food is available in the form of marvellous pork pies produced in the Buxton area. On the bar local produce is often for sale, including free-range eggs and cheese. There's also camping in the field behind the pub. A very good watering hole during or after any walk.

Opening times

The Quiet Woman is usually open daily at lunchtimes from 12 noon until 1500 and in the evening from 1900.

The Quiet Woman

Across the road and village green is the church, the only rural church to be the (unintended) target of a bomb in the Second World War. In true British spirit, a wedding, due to take place the following day, did so in the ruined chancel.

Walk 9: Earl Sterndale (Quiet Woman) to Flash Bar (Travellers' Rest/Knights' Table)

Start	Earl Sterndale (Quiet Woman) GR.SK089670
Finish	Flash Bar (Travellers' Rest/Knights' Table) GR. SK032678
The route	Earl Sterndale, Glutton, optional ascent of Parkhouse Hill, Hollinsclough, Washgate, Gamballs Green, Flash Bar
Length	4.53 miles (7.29 km)
Ascent	1040 feet (317 metres)
Time	2½ to 2¾ hours (exclusive of stops and ascent of Parkhouse Hill)
Map	OS OL24 (White Peak)

Getting there
By bus. Earl Sterndale has a daily bus service from Buxton and Ashbourne. Flash Bar has a daily service from Buxton and Leek.
By train. Nearest station, Buxton
By car. Earl Sterndale lies just off the B5053 midway between Longnor and Brierlow Bar (A515 Buxton-Ashbourne road). There's limited on-street parking in the village so please park considerately. Flash Bar is on the A53 Buxton-Leek road. There's parking at the pub (with permission of course) and some limited roadside parking.

The Walk

Earl Sterndale to Hollinsclough
From the front door of the pub, turn left and follow the footpath sign alongside the main building and then round to the left. Here the path forks. Take the

right hand path, passing through four gates in quick succession to emerge into a field. The serrated top of Chrome Hill is a good marker, as is the perfect mountain shape of Parkhouse Hill. Head across the field towards these, ignoring the obvious stile and gate in the right hand corner of the field, and soon reaching a gate (what else?) in the left hand corner, into another field. Go straight on across the field to a rather awkward stile. Once over this obstacle, bear right down the hollow-way, with a good view over to the reef knolls of Parkhouse and Chrome hills. Don't let your attention wander

*Parkhouse and Chrome Hills
from Glutton*

too much, as the path includes some steep and well polished limestone, which can be treacherous in wet conditions. The path descends through a sweeping left curve to reach a stile. This drops you into a field, which when this walk was recce'd, was very wet underfoot. *I watched a raven being mobbed by jackdaws here.* The path bears left to a stile and thus you reach the road.

Cross the road with care and go over the stile opposite. Head across the field to a waymarked gate. Here you have a choice. There is a possibility of climbing Parkhouse Hill from this point, but you need to be aware that this will take you an extra 15 minutes and involve a further 250 feet/77 metres of ascent. It is also not a suitable route for anyone with acute vertigo. If you are not going up Parkhouse, skip the next paragraph.

Ascent of Parkhouse

A path heads off diagonally right, making for a gate at the base of the ridge. From there a steep and narrow path scrambles up to the top. *The traverse of the crest is exhilarating and this miniature mountain and its nearby companion (Chrome) are by far the best ridge walks in the Peak District. It's only a pity they are not a couple of thousand feet higher, because they would then rank with some of the best in the country.* As it is, the traverse of the crest is over all too soon and you descend the far end equally steeply – avoiding the limestone pinnacle en route, to reach the Dowell Dale road. Turn left here and go down the road for about 250 yards/230 metres, to rejoin the main route of the walk. Skip the next paragraph.

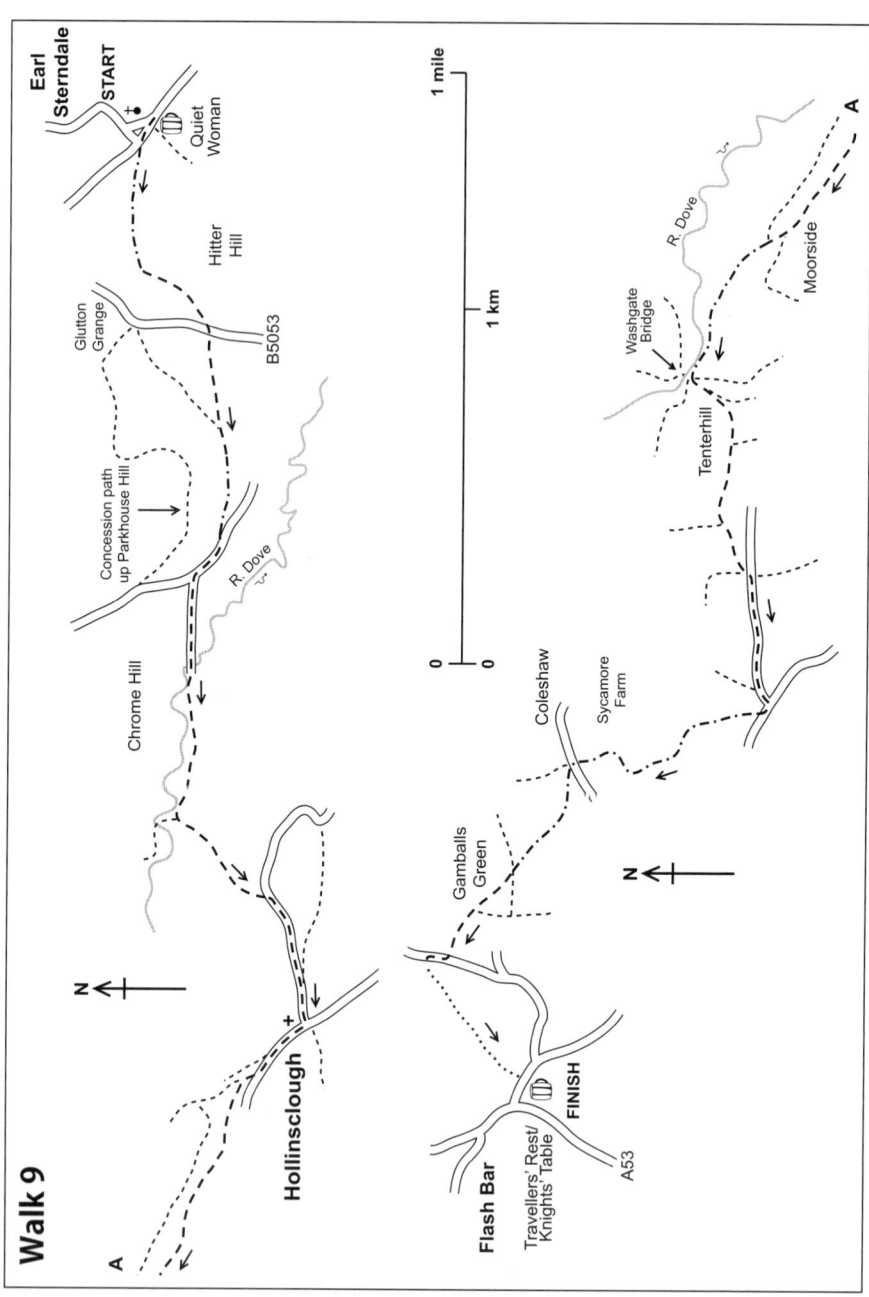

Walk 9

Earl Sterndale

START

Quiet Woman

Hitter Hill

Glutton Grange

B5053

Concession path up Parkhouse Hill

R. Dove

Chrome Hill

Hollinsclough

Gamballs Green

Coleshaw

Sycamore Farm

Tenterhill

Washgate Bridge

R. Dove

Moorside

Flash Bar

Travellers' Rest/ Knights' Table

FINISH

A53

0   1 km

0   1 mile

On to Hollinsclough

From the gate bear left, up the field, which can be very wet, making for the corner of the fence/hedge. Follow the fence/hedge to a gate and from this point you can see Hollinsclough ahead. Make your way across the field to the road and continue along the lane until it forks. *The intrepid mountaineers who have ascended Parkhouse will rejoin you at this point.*

Go down the track towards Hollinsclough, passing over the cattle grid and through the ornate gateway for Stannery Farm. Where the track forks, keep right and carry on to the ford and footbridge over the River Dove. Here you leave Derbyshire and enter Staffordshire. *Looking down from the footbridge you can see the former stepping stones.* The track continues through fields to a T-junction where you turn left, following the signs for Hollinsclough. *The route to the right is signed, 'No public right of way', which is a pity as it keeps close to the river.* The track soon joins a narrow road at another cattle grid. Bear right, soon passing the school and in about 325 yards/300 metres arrive in the great metropolis of Hollinsclough.

Hollinsclough is a classic example of the loss of amenity in rural settlements. There's no longer a post office, shop or pub here and the only bus is a pre-booked dial a ride service. At the T-junction turn right, passing the Bethel chapel dating from 1801, built by local jaggerman, John Lomas. *A jaggerman was responsible for leading teams of packhorses through the Peak District and the trough, which used to be situated here, would have been to refresh the packhorses.*

The wilds of Upper Dovedale

Go up the narrow road for a short way, passing a small barn, before locating a rather battered and decrepit signpost on the right, advertising the presence of a bridleway. Go through the gate and begin to descend towards the Dove again. In about 50 yards/metres (if that), there is a waymarked path on the left. Go left here and follow the well-blazed path along a terrace on the hillside, with a view down into the Dove valley and a grand view back down the dale to Chrome, Parkhouse and High Wheeldon. *The path has what appear to be sleeper marks across it, but this is purely the action of cattle, not, unfortunately, the remains of the Leek and Manifold Railway's Buxton extension.*

You pass a small ruined building on your right and from here on the path begins to deteriorate. Once over a stile you will find that the path forks. In practice it doesn't matter which way you go, for the two routes rejoin a little further on. Of the two, the upper path is marginally less muddy. After the paths have rejoined, you follow a ruined wall. However, there is a suspicion that this is not actually the definitive line of the path, though it is the trodden route. A glance at the 1:25000 map confirms this. The true path is a little way down the hillside on a faint terrace (and a very wet one too). Eventually the route alongside the ruined wall is blocked by a combination of fallen trees and bog and walkers have obviously descended to the lower route at this point. From here on it is relatively distinct, though still very wet underfoot.

Continuing along the path, you soon see a more obvious cart track coming down the hillside. When you reach this, bear right, following the cart track down to a well preserved barn. The path skirts to the right of the barn and then forks. A waymark post indicates the line of the 'true' path, but the other, left hand path, is the more used. Both are wet and muddy, the true path being the more so – hence the existence of the other route. At the bottom of the slope, the two paths rejoin and what follows is a real quagmire, through which it is difficult to find a dry route. You extricate yourself from this morass by bearing right to cross a small stream by a single stone clapper bridge. Just the other side of this, to your left is a wall, a stile and a waymark post with a myriad of different arrows on it. This is Washgate. Once over the stile, you'll see on your right a delightful little packhorse bridge spanning the Dove. *The bridge is accompanied by a large highway sign warning intending users of a*

Washgate bridge

severe width restriction. Seems a bit superfluous, as one would have considerable difficulty getting a large vehicle down to this point in the first place. On the opposite side of the bridge, you are in Derbyshire.

The map shows a path leading up the hillside from the Staffordshire side of the bridge to New Colshaw Farm. Take it from me, it doesn't exist and an attempt to find it involves a desperate scramble up the bank side only to find there are no stiles where they should be, so the only course of action is to retrace one's steps. Go up the stony track on the Staffordshire side of the bridge. This track climbs away from the river and soon becomes a very narrow, muddy lane, obviously frequented by motor-cyclists. There are some deep ruts and puddles that look too deep for comfort. Having avoided these, you soon come to Tenterhill Farm. Here you join a tarmacked road. What a delight that is, after the muddy struggle from Hollinsclough. The map shows a variety of paths between here and Gamballs Green, which is your next objective, but you may well feel that you've had enough of jungle warfare and opt instead for the easier life of using the road. Console yourself with the knowledge that the road sees very little use and at least it has the merit of (usually) being dry underfoot.

Go up the lane for a couple of hundred yards/metres to a T-junction with Hollinsclough Rake Lane. *It will come as no consolation to realise that this is the road on which you left Hollinsclough!* Turn right and continue up the hill for about 400 yards/370 metres to a crossroads, where you join the Longnor to Flash bar road. *Wimps may decide to walk along the road from here, but although the views from this ridge-top route are good, the walking is not pleasant as the road is quite narrow and without a verge in places. The traffic also tends to come on here at quite a pace.*

Just up the road to the right, there's a stile. Go over this and then down the rough field, making for Sycamore Farm, which you'll see on the opposite side of the valley. You'll soon spot a stile in the fence at the bottom of the field. Once over this, bear left, through a boggy stretch to a small stream (no bridge). Cross the stream and make your way up towards the farm, keeping the fence/hedge to your right. When you are almost at the farm, there's a stile on the right and the path skirts round the buildings to a track. Go right here and through a gate, which isn't waymarked, and follow the track up towards another farm. A stile on your left gives access into fields again. Go up the field to a stile, marked by a prominent signpost and thus emerge onto a lane. There are two footpaths signposted from here. The one you want is the left hand one. The stile is easy enough. It's getting up from the road to stile level that's the tricky bit. The path is not distinct but heads across the field towards the left hand end of Top Colshaw Farm. *Half way across the field you cross, imperceptibly, the alignment of a Roman Road.* The path passes through a stile onto the farm access and here you go left for a short way. Go through a small gate on the right, just beyond the farm and skirt round the farm complex, following the waymarks. Gamballs Green can be seen away across the fields and thankfully, you can also see the main A53 Leek-Buxton road, Flash Bar and the Travellers' Rest. Salvation is in sight.

Go down the field to a stile and then across another field to a double stile. The map shows four paths converging here, but you'd never know. Bear right, across the field, making for a gate in the far right hand corner, adjacent to Lower Gamballs. The path wriggles its way through the back garden of Lower Gamballs, your passage only disturbed by the occasional duck. Once on the access lane continue ahead, through the gate and so down to the lane. There's a stile and footpath signs almost immediately opposite the driveway, but no-one has ventured that way for many a long year and the route looks decidedly boggy. A short distance to the right there's a gateway on the left and another signpost, minus arm. Go through the gateway onto a track.

The map shows a path heading off left, straight up the hillside, with a shallow valley just to your right. There's nothing obvious on the ground to say that this is ever used and in any case, at the top, you come into a quagmire (now there's a surprise). Locals apparently carry on along the track for a short way then turn left up the right hand side of the shallow valley. There's a semblance of a path here – and it's dry. At the top of the valley there's a stile into a small field, another stile and then you are out onto the road. The Travellers' Rest, or The Knights' Table lies just to your right.

The Travellers' Rest or The Knights' Table, 1516 ft/462 metres
Telephone 01298 23695. www.theknightstable.co.uk

The Travellers Rest is an 18th century coaching inn on the A53 Leek Buxton road. At 1516 feet/462 metres above sea level it is reputedly the 3rd highest pub in England, beaten only by its near neighbour the Cat and Fiddle (2nd highest at 1690 feet/515 metres) and the Tan Hill Inn (in North Yorkshire 1732 feet/528 metres). It is only fair to say that there is some doubt about this, especially given the close proximity of The New Inn at Flash, which claims to be the highest village pub in the UK and in a village which, according to *The History of the County of Staffordshire* is 1526 feet/465 metres above sea level. The Travellers Rest is situated almost exactly on the main English watershed. To the west the rivers flow to the Irish Sea. To the east they flow to the North Sea. The Knights' Table at the Travellers Rest, has been extensively refurbished with a medieval Knights' theme (reflecting the local legend of Sir Gawain and the Green Knight). The pub serves meals daily, both lunchtimes and evenings and has a range of real ales on hand-pump. Walkers are welcome, even in muddy boots, but please stay in areas without carpets. There's an outdoor seating area behind the pub, with terrific views over the Peak District, especially down the Manifold and Dove valleys. For anyone doing this high pubs circuit in one long walk it's worth knowing that the Travellers also does accommodation. A very welcoming pub and a worthy inclusion in this high pubs circuit.

Opening times
Monday to Thursday and Sunday: 1200 to 2230; Friday and Saturday: 1200 to midnight.
Food is served: Monday to Thursday and Saturday 1200 to 2000; Friday 1200 to 2100; Sunday 1200 to 1800.

Travellers Rest

There's also the Flash Bar Stores. At 1518 feet/463 metres this is supposedly the highest shop in England. It serves sandwiches, snacks and (non alcoholic) drinks daily.

Walk 10: Flash Bar (Travellers' Rest) to the Cat and Fiddle

Start	Travellers' Rest (The Knights' Table) Flash Bar. GR. SK032678
Finish	Cat and Fiddle Inn. GR. SK001719
The route	Flash Bar, Knotbury, Blackclough, Three Shires Head, Danebower Quarry, Danebower Hollow, Cat and Fiddle
Length	4.32 miles (7 km)
Ascent	817 feet (249 metres)
Time	2¼ to 2½ hours (exclusive of stops)
Map	OS OL24 (White Peak)

Getting there

By bus. There's a daily bus service to Flash Bar from Buxton and the Potteries and a daily service to the Cat and Fiddle from Buxton and Macclesfield.

By train. No train service. They never built the High Peak and District Light Railway, which was supposed to have a stop at the Cat and Fiddle! Nearest station is Buxton.

By car. The Travellers Rest at Flash Bar is on the main A53 Leek-Buxton road. With permission from the landlord, there's car parking at the pub or on the roadside just to the north of the pub. The Cat and Fiddle is on the main Buxton-Macclesfield road (A537). With permission from the landlord, there's car parking at the pub and in a large lay-by on the opposite side of the road.

The Walk

Flash Bar to Three Shires

From the front door of the Travellers' Rest, go up the A53 for a short way and cross to the bus shelter. Carry on a little further and then go left, along the minor road signed to Knotbury. In about 100 yards/metres you cross the English watershed. *You are now in the catchment of the River Dane, which eventually flows into the Mersey. As you top the slight rise that marks the watershed, Shuttlingsloe comes into view ahead, along with the communications mast on Croker Hill. Shuttlingsloe looks decidedly mountainous from this angle. Miniature cars can be seen moving across the moor on the A54, Buxton-Congleton road. To your left you can see down to Ramshaw Rocks and The Roaches.* The lane begins its descent into the Dane valley, passing Oxensitch Farm on the left and the lane leading to Hilltop Farm on your right. Descending further, you soon reach a T-junction. Turn right here and climb through increasingly wild moorland scenery to the farm at Readyleach Green. Keep on along the lane, ignoring the road to the right, leading to Drystone Edge. You go past a small derelict barn. *This was up for sale when the walk was recce'd and would definitely require a large dose of tender loving care to make it fit for anything. As you reach the top of the hill, pause and look back at the view, which takes in not just The Roaches, but hills far beyond the Peak District towards Shropshire. The isolated conical hill is almost certainly The Wrekin.*

The lane now passes through a narrow cutting and begins to descend into Black Clough. Almost at once, there's an unsigned path veering off to the left. This descends steeply to rejoin the road a little further on and cuts off a corner. Just before rejoining the road you cross Blackclough Brook and you have crossed back into Derbyshire from Staffordshire without realising it. Turn left at the road and follow it downstream. There's a footpath sign

In Black Clough

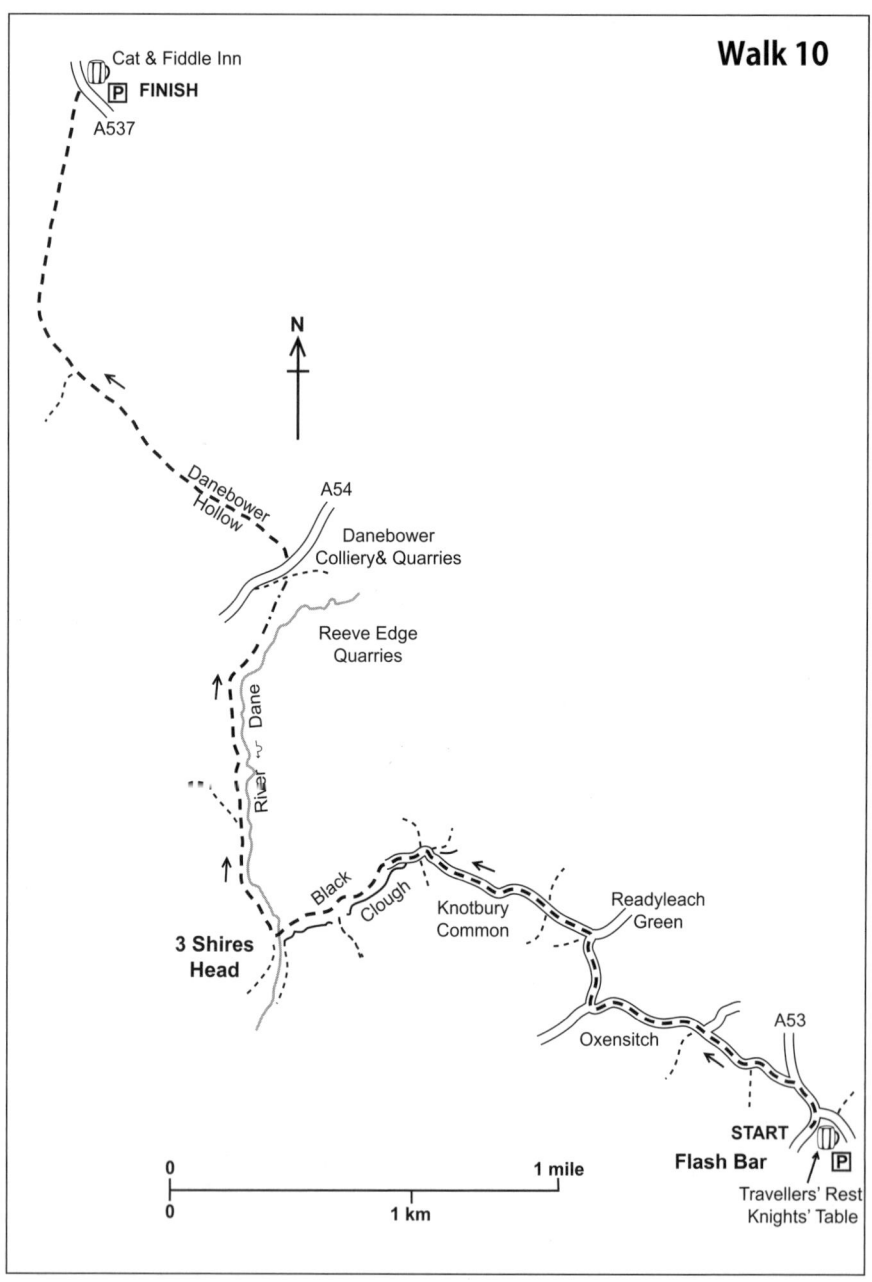

Walk 10

Cat & Fiddle Inn
FINISH
A537

N

Danebower
Hollow

A54
Danebower
Colliery& Quarries

Reeve Edge
Quarries

River Dane

Black
Clough
Knotbury
Common

Readyleach
Green

3 Shires
Head

Oxensitch

A53

START
Flash Bar

Travellers' Rest
Knights' Table

0   1 mile
0   1 km

on the right. This path leads to Danebower Quarry, avoiding the descent to Three Shires Head. You can use this if you have a mind to, but a visit to Three Shires is really not to be missed, so carry on down the lane. In about 200 yards/metres, just beyond the track leading up to Blackclough Farm, the tarmacked road ends and the continuation down to Three Shires is a rough stony track, with the stream churning away on your left. Keep company with the stream, ignoring paths and tracks leading off to the right and thus you come to a T-junction where a track from Knotbury trails in from the left. *There's a delightful little packhorse bridge here, that's worth a picture.*

Three Shires Head

Carry on down Black Clough and in about 325 yards/300 metres you reach Three Shires Head. *What's in a name? Some call this place Three Shires Head, others call it Three Shire Heads, others just Three Shires. There's also the place name of Pannier's Pool shown on the OS map. Whatever name you give it, it is an idyllic spot, where Cheshire, Derbyshire and Staffordshire meet. All the tracks leading to it are actually public roads, but in practice they are rough tracks on which most motor vehicles are banned. The bridge to your left spans the Blackclough Brook and would take you into Staffordshire. The bridge in front of you spans the River Dane and takes you across into Cheshire. The two bridges and the various waterfalls make for a charming picture, especially when bathed in sunshine. However, this used to be a notorious spot, an easy place for the coin counterfeiters of Flash to escape across into another county if the 'law' came too close for comfort.*

Up the Dane Valley Way
Cross the bigger of the two bridges, noting the former stepping-stones below on the left, and so enter Cheshire. Go right and begin your ascent of the Dane Valley, along the Dane Valley Way. This is waymarked by DVW signs. What follows is a lovely walk alongside the river on a broad, but rough track. *You'll*

not have it all to yourself, for this is prime mountain biking country. However, there's room and to spare on this route. After about 540 yards/½km you pass a small ruined building on your right and almost immediately afterwards you go over a side stream and are faced with a gate. The obvious track goes on through the gate and climbs away from the river, but the DVW is signed over a stile to the right. This is your route. The path keeps close to the Dane and crosses some very wet ground. *Fortunately for all concerned, large stretches of the route have been flagged with stone slabs. This avoids the worst of the mud and puddles, but there are some curious gaps in the flagstones, so you'll be lucky to avoid muddy boots.* The DVW waymarks are not numerous, but they do crop up if there's the slightest hint of uncertainty in the route. Not that there's much to worry about, with the flagstones under foot and the river to your right. You'd have a job losing your way here.

The valley makes a gentle curve to the east and, as it does so, you'll see a ruined building ahead and a prominent chimney. *To the right of the chimney are the unmistakeable outlines of spoil tips. You are approaching the sites of Danebower colliery and Danebower and Reeve Edge quarries.* Soon more buildings come into view and as you get nearer the sheer scale of the quarry spoil tips becomes apparent. *Despite the ruins and tips, this is still an attractive area and all the more fascinating for its industrial past.* To your right as you near the chimney, there is a fenced off area surrounding a collapsed shaft. *The chimney is a fine dry-stone structure and used to be connected by a flue down the hillside to a stationary steam engine that seems to have been used for shaft haulage. The colliery was last worked as late as the mid 1940s, but then only on a part-time basis. Full time working had*

Danebower chimney

ceased in the 1920s. The quarries on the other hand, appear to have been abandoned earlier. They produced stone roofing slabs and this material fell out of fashion once cheaper and more easily worked Welsh slate became readily available with the coming of the railways in the 19th century. More recently

90

(1996), with the increased interest in building conservation, Reeve Edge quarry was investigated as a source of roofing stone, but no work has yet taken place. At a gate by the ruins the path is waymarked up the hillside towards the chimney. Go up to the chimney, from which vantage point there is a view back down the valley to The Roaches. *Looking down towards the river you can make out the site of the steam winding engine. The mine was thoroughly explored in 1987. It extends beyond the A54 road towards the Cat and Fiddle for about 510 yards/467metres and at its maximum depth was 340 feet/105 metres below ground level.*

Continue up the hillside from the chimney, soon reaching a track that slices down the slope from the main road. This was the access track for the mine and quarry. A quick left and right here and then you continue your upward tramp, alongside a derelict fence. A final pull lands you at a stile, out onto the verge of the main road. Here you are confronted by a crash barrier, the height of which is just that bit too much for anyone with normal length legs. Find a lower bit and go over the barrier and then over the road to a signposted gate on the far side.

A broad stony track leads up onto the moor. This is Danebower Hollow and the views either side are constrained by slightly higher ground for about 500 yards/460 metres. Eventually the track levels out and a wide view opens up to the left. *When the walk was recce'd you could see not only nearby Shuttlingsloe, Croker Hill and Bosley Minn, but clear across the Cheshire Plain to the hills at the back of Helsby and beyond that to Moel Famau in the Clwydian Hills. There is also a surprising view back the way you've come with the Travellers' Rest being visible on the skyline and the traffic on the main A53 Leek-Buxton road.* The rest of the walk needs little description. The broad track continues over the moor, soon being joined from the left by a path coming up from Cumberland Cottage. *This is marked by one of the famous green signs of the Peak and Northern Footpaths Society.* 300 yards/metres further on you breast the rise and the Cat and Fiddle comes into view with its attendant communications mast and array of parked cars and motor-cycles. Shining Tor, the highest part of Cheshire and included in the next stage of this walk, lies just to the left of the Cat. The remainder of the walk to the pub is no more than a gentle stroll for the final ⅔ mile/1km. *There are buses to Macclesfield and Buxton from the Cat every hour.*

The Cat and Fiddle. 1690 ft/515 metres
Telephone 01298 78366 (0900-2100 only). www.catandfiddleinn.com
At 1690 feet/515 metres, the Cat and Fiddle is reputedly the 2nd highest pub in England, beaten only by the Tan Hill Inn. This is all the more amazing given

the fact that the Cat is in Cheshire – not a county noted for is high places. The pub is adjacent to the A537, the main road between Buxton and Macclesfield. Although this is a relatively modern road, only being built in the early 19th century the pub was there long before, serving the earlier packhorse routes and the original turnpike. The pub is at the hub of several ancient tracks over the hills, and has long been a popular refreshment stop for walkers and others. It goes without saying that the Cat specialises in catering for people in outdoor gear, whether they come on foot, on bikes or motorcycles and you'll find most such people in the Moorland Bar, which offers an open fire in winter. There's a separate lounge bar and restaurant for families and groups. The website states that 'dogs and boots are welcome'.

The Cat & Fiddle sign

Opening times

Daily 1100 to 2300.
Food is served from 1200 to 2000. (Tea and coffee served with hot snacks from 1100).

The Cat & Fiddle

Walk 11: Cat and Fiddle to Whaley Bridge

Start	Cat and Fiddle Inn. GR. SK001719
Finish	Whaley Bridge station. GR. SK011814
The route	Cat and Fiddle, Shining Tor, Oldgate Nick, Pym Chair, Windgather Rocks, Taxal Farm, Taxal Moor, Toddbrook Reservoir, Whaley Bridge station
Length	7.33 miles (11.8 km)
Ascent	630 feet (194 metres)
Time	Allow 3 to 4 hours (exclusive of stops)
Map	OS OL1 (Dark Peak) and OS OL24 (White Peak)

Getting there:

By bus. Daily buses to the Cat and Fiddle from Buxton and Macclesfield. Daily buses to Whaley Bridge from Buxton, Glossop, Macclesfield, New Mills and Stockport.

By train. Daily trains to Whaley Bridge from Buxton, Manchester and Stockport.

By car. The Cat and Fiddle is at the summit of the A537 road from Buxton the Macclesfield. There is car parking in the layby opposite the pub. Whaley Bridge is on the A5004, just off the Manchester end of the A6 Chapel by-pass. There is free (but very limited) parking at the station, and free parking on-street close to the railway station on the A5004.

The walk

The views on this walk can be spectacular, especially across the Cheshire Plain, where, on a good day it is possible to see right to the Clwydian range in north

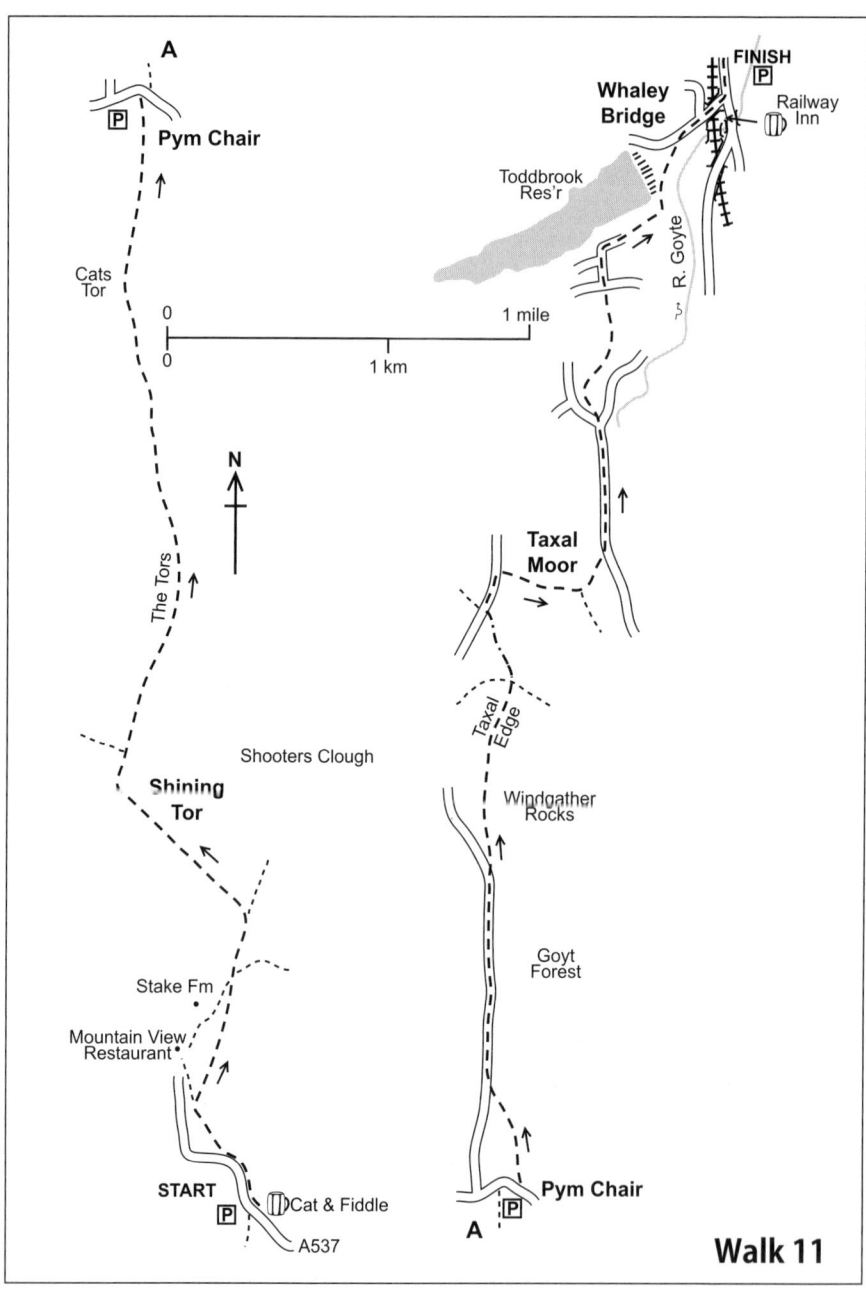

A

P
Pym Chair

Cats
Tor

Toddbrook
Res'r

**Whaley
Bridge**

FINISH
P
Railway
Inn

R. Goyte

0

0

1 mile

1 km

N

The Tors

**Taxal
Moor**

Taxal
Edge

Shooters Clough

**Shining
Tor**

Windgather
Rocks

Goyt
Forest

Stake Fm

Mountain View
Restaurant

START
P
Cat & Fiddle
A537

Pym Chair

A
P

Walk 11

Wales and the Llangollen hills. On a bad day (and they are numerous on this part of the Peak District), you will be fortunate to see your hand in front of your face. However, the route finding is never difficult, in part at least because for a long way it follows the Derbyshire/Cheshire county boundary and this is marked by a wall or fence.

Cheshire's high point

From the Cat and Fiddle, turn right, heading along the A537 towards Macclesfield. There is an adequate verge, but the proximity of the road is not the most pleasant start to a walk. At the first left hand bend bear right, following the old Macclesfield road and leaving the A537 behind. In a short distance the track forks. The old road continues straight ahead, but bear right here along a more prominent track, which soon brings you onto the top of the moor. Continue along the track until you come to a signpost directing you left to Shining Tor. In clear weather you wouldn't need the sign as Shining Tor is clearly in view from the very start, but in low cloud you could easily carry straight on and end up in the Goyt Valley.

The path to Shining Tor has been repaired at some time, but it could do with some tender loving care now, as there are bits of matting and plastic mesh showing through in a lot of places. The ascent to the summit is easy and the view (possibly) excellent. *The trig point lies on the Cheshire side of the boundary wall. Purists and railway enthusiasts should visit it, if only because it's the highest hill in Cheshire and has a railway engine named after it.*

Down to Whaley Bridge

Leave Shining Tor heading north, signed to Pym Chair. The path is on the Derbyshire side of the wall and for most of its length it is paved with large stone slabs, so there's no chance of losing your way. *There has been a lot of attention paid to trying to prevent erosion here and you'll see numerous examples of attempts to try to re-establish vegetation and slow down water run-off. You are on top of a ridge for the whole of this stretch so the views are very good, with some grand rock scenery near Oldgate Nick as you approach Pym Chair, though sadly there seems to be no way of getting to the rocks, certainly from the Derbyshire side – Cheshire guarding their assets presumably.* As you near Pym Chair the path forks and you bear right, signed to Windgather.

Cross the Errwood to Jenkin Chapel road and join the path, again signed to Windgather. This path is not paved and can be quite muddy. *At this point, when recce'ing the walk there was a curious incident. There is a substantial drystone wall to the left and I was suddenly conscious that there was a bike speeding along the top of the wall. What was even more curious was that there was no-one riding it. No great mystery, because of course the bike was perched on top of a car, which couldn't be seen. I have to admit to doing a double take and thinking I had finally gone mad.* The path reaches the road and according to the map you should join the road here, but you are on access land and there is a well-blazed path alongside the wall and off the road. In very wet weather it may be advisable to use the road, but otherwise use the path. Follow the path (or road) for about ⅔ of a mile (about 1km), to the fine rock outcrop of Windgather, normally festooned with climbers, even in inclement weather. It's a fine place to sit and admire the view.

Continue along the ridge, descending now to Taxal Farm. Turn right there, heading up the hill, with a wall to your right until you regain access land. Now go left alongside another wall for a traverse of Taxal Moor. *This is a delightful section with grand views to each side and towards Whaley Bridge and Toddbrook Reservoir. The wind-blasted oaks give a good indication of the direction and strength of the prevailing wind at this point.* The ridge keeps high and you begin to wonder what the descent to Whaley Bridge will be like. Soon you reach a rough track, which services a water company installation and here turn right. Almost at once, bear left, leaving the track to your right and beginning to descend on a path, passing the remains of a seat and a nice stone trough. At the bottom of the path, just before it joins a narrow road, go left, over a stile and follow this path down to the main road.

Cross the main road with care and in about 300 yards go left along Reddish Lane. This is the Midshires Way. Follow the Midshires way-markers, soon passing the dam wall of Toddbrook Reservoir on the left. *The reservoir was built in 1831 to provide extra water for the Peak Forest Canal, which starts from Whaley Bridge.* The path descends quite sharply, with the reservoir overflow to your left and the river a good way below. Soon you join a path alongside the River Goyt and here go left, crossing the bridge over the reservoir stream and thus reaching Whaley Bridge Memorial Park. Keep the river to your right and either go up the tarmacked drive to the road, or continue on the muddy path alongside the river. Either way, on reaching the road, go right, soon sighting the railway bridge. *If you want trains for Manchester turn left just before the bridge. If you want trains for Buxton go under the bridge and turn left up the main station approach. The main bus stops are on the A5004 just by the Jodrell Arms. Either way, if you've got time to kill, Whaley Bridge has a number of hostelries. The Railway Inn is nearest, just to the right beyond the railway bridge and, as its name suggests, it's right next to the railway station.*

Walk 12: Whaley Bridge to Broadbottom

Start	Whaley Bridge railway station GR. SK011814
Finish	Broadbottom railway station GR. SJ992938
The route	Whaley Bridge station, Peak Forest Canal, Bugsworth basin, Overhill Road, Piece Farm, Birch Vale, Lantern Pike, Matley Moor, Cown Edge Rocks, Coombes Edge, Charlesworth, Warhurst Bridge, Broadbottom station
Length	11.94 miles (19.2 km)
Ascent	2084 feet (641 metres)
Time	Allow 6 hours, exclusive of stops
Map	OS OL1 (Dark Peak)

Getting there

By bus. Daily buses to Whaley Bridge from Buxton, Glossop, Macclesfield, New Mills and Stockport. Daily buses to Broadbottom from Glossop, Hyde and Manchester.

By train. Daily trains to Broadbottom from Manchester, Hyde and Glossop. Daily trains to Whaley Bridge from Buxton, Stockport and Manchester.

By car. Whaley Bridge is on the A5004, just off the northern end of the A6 Chapel by-pass. There is free (but very limited) parking at the station, and free parking on-street close to the railway station on the A5004. Broadbottom can be reached off the A57 from the junction at Mottram, or from Charlesworth by a very narrow bridge over the River Etherow. There is a large free car park at the railway station

Walk 12
start to A

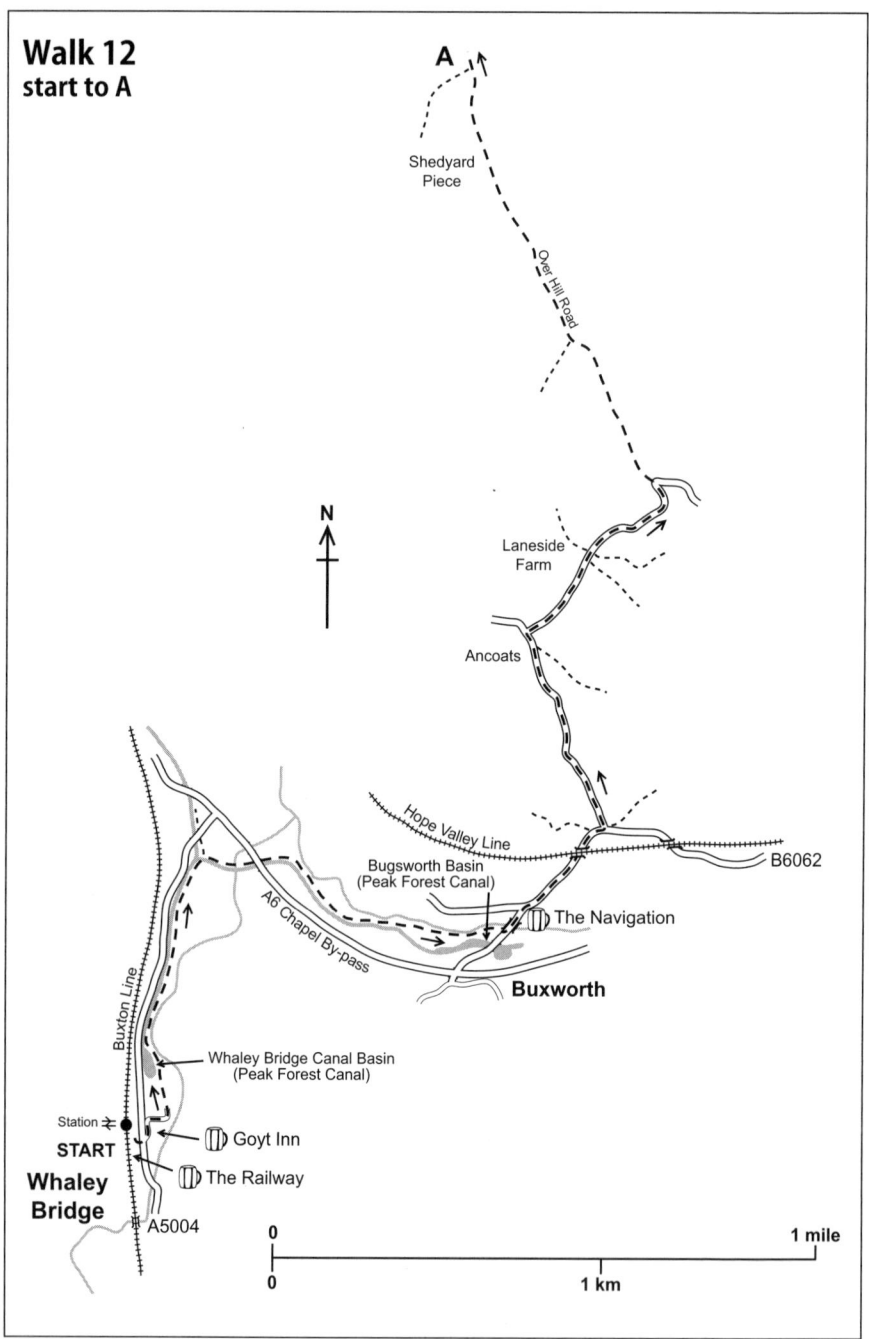

A

Shedyard Piece

Over Hill Road

N

Laneside Farm

Ancoats

Hope Valley Line

Bugsworth Basin
(Peak Forest Canal)

B6062

The Navigation

A6 Chapel By-pass

Buxworth

Buxton Line

Whaley Bridge Canal Basin
(Peak Forest Canal)

Station

START

Whaley Bridge

Goyt Inn

The Railway

A5004

0

0

1 mile

1 km

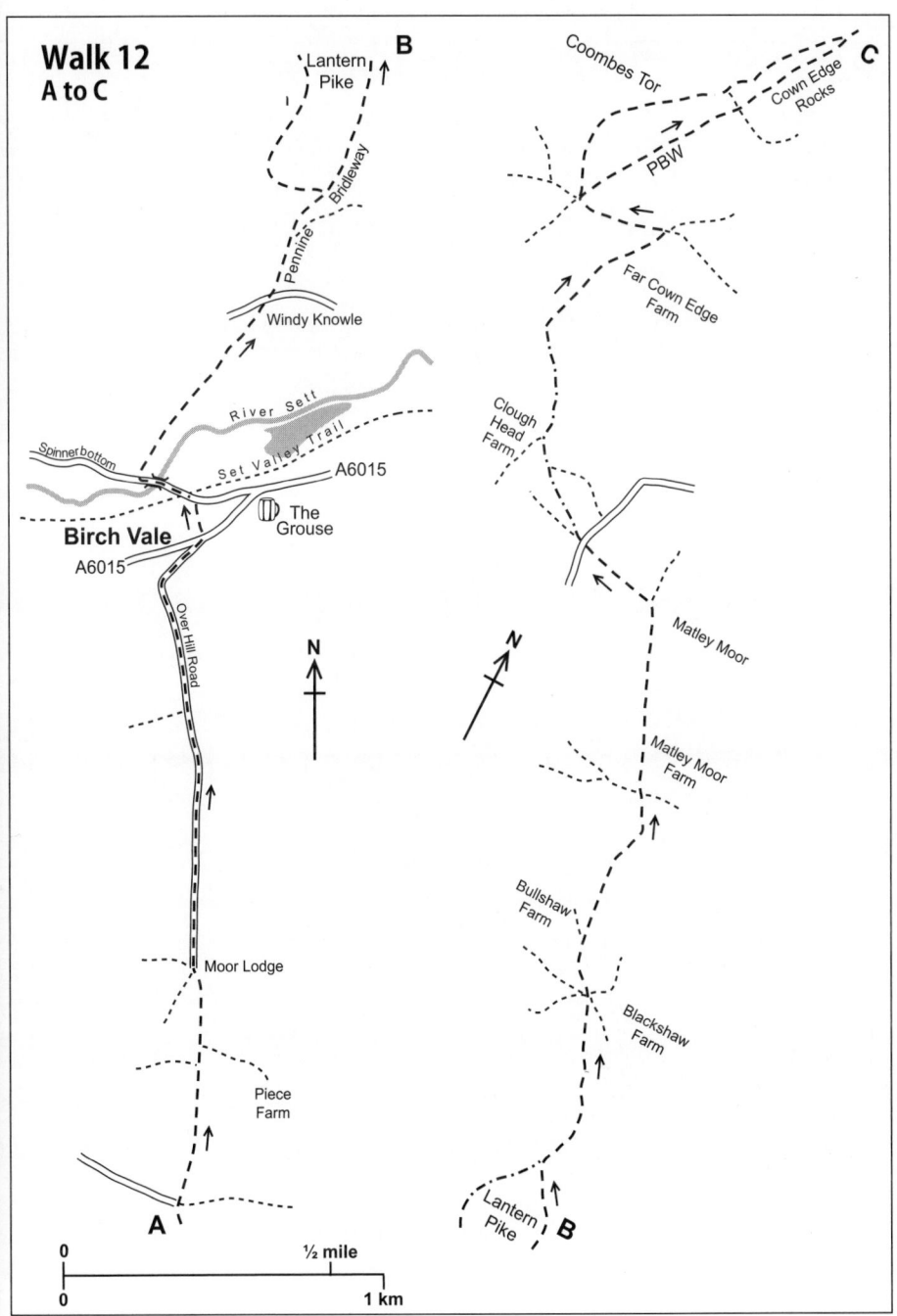

Walk 12
A to C

Lantern Pike **B**

Coombes Tor

Cown Edge Rocks

C

Pennine Bridleway

PBW

Windy Knowle

Far Cown Edge Farm

River Sett

Sett Valley Trail

Spinner bottom

A6015

Clough Head Farm

Birch Vale

The Grouse

A6015

Matley Moor

Over Hill Road

N

N

Matley Moor Farm

Moor Lodge

Bullshaw Farm

Piece Farm

Blackshaw Farm

A

Lantern Pike **B**

0

½ mile

0

1 km

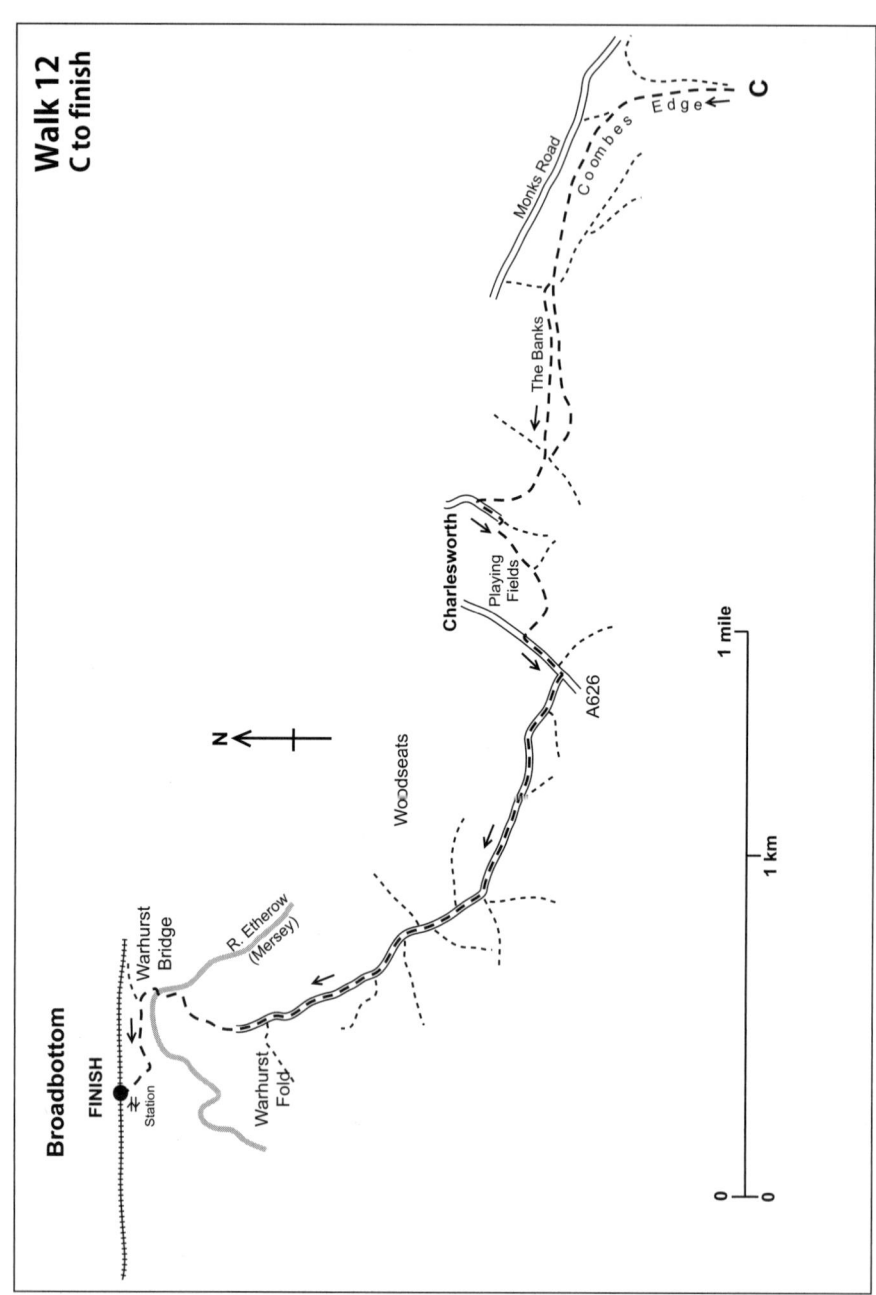

Walk 12
C to finish

C

Coombes Edge

Monks Road

The Banks

Charlesworth

Playing Fields

A626

Woodseats

N

R. Etherow (Mersey)

Warhurst Bridge

Warhurst Fold

Broadbottom

FINISH

Station

0   1 km

0   1 mile

The walk

Whaley Bridge to Birch Vale

From Whaley Bridge station cross the main road and then go down the signed route to the canal basin, down Canal Street, passing the post office on your right. At the canal basin, take a few moments to look round this historic site. *The canal warehouse lies to your left. It was opened in 1801 as the terminus of the Whaley Bridge arm of the Peak Forest Canal. In 1831 it became a transhipment warehouse between the canal and the newly opened Cromford and High Peak Railway, the first trans-Pennine railway line. Canal/rail traffic continued until the closure of this section of the CHP in the 1950s. Quite a complex of railway sidings developed over the years, some taking traffic to the canal but latterly most freight went up the Whaley Bridge incline to join the main line railway just east of Whaley Bridge station. The Whaley Bridge incline is walkable and lies to the east of the canal basin. Worth a look if you've time. Locomotives were never used either on the canal-side tracks or to take the waggons from the top of the incline to the mainline, as there was a very low bridge that precluded their use. The incline itself was also worked by a horse 'gin.*

From the canal basin, follow the towpath, soon crossing the overflow weir and then passing numerous moored boats of various shapes and sizes. You pass under the access road to the Tesco supermarket and soon reach the junction with the Bugsworth arm of the canal. A footbridge spans the Bugsworth arm. Don't attempt to continue on the east side of the canal at this point as the path only serves the moorings. A horse tunnel dives down to the right and passes under the Bugsworth arm, though this must have made for a tricky manoeuvre for horse drawn boats coming to or from Whaley Bridge. Follow the towpath to Bugsworth basin for one of the great waterways sites in England.

In its day, Bugsworth Basin was much more important than the Whaley Bridge. It was a massive complex of wharves, each served both by a canal arm and by sidings from the Peak Forest tramway. Forget any notion of an electric tramway like that in Manchester, Sheffield or Nottingham. The Peak Forest Tramway dates back to the 18th century and was always horse worked, using L shaped rails rather than the modern 'edge' rail used on today's mainline railways or the grooved rail used on-street tramways. None of the tramway is now extant, but there are numerous interpretation boards, which explain how the tramway operated, and the various industries that were dependant on the canal and its associated tramway. The last tramway traffic ceased in the mid 1920s after which the tramway was removed and the Bugsworth basin became more and more derelict. Heroic efforts and no little injection of cash have

Peak Forest Canal, Bugsworth Basin

managed to bring the basin back to life. On the occasion of the recce' for this walk there was a rally of canal boats going on, which gave an impression of what the place must have been like in its heyday. The assembled boats were a myriad of shapes, sizes and colours. The names too seemed to indicate some amazing flights of fancy. Each boat has to be registered with British Waterways and has a unique number. Quite how the numbering system is structured is not obvious, but it surely cannot be the case that there really are in excess of 550,000 boats registered on Britain's waterways, which is what the numbering would imply. Any offers of an explanation?

Still musing on the boat-numbering problem, continue alongside the basin and up to the road. Opposite you is the excellent Navigation Inn (SK023821, 548 feet (169metres)), which is well worth a visit. **www.navigationinn.co.uk** It is the only pub on this section of the route until you get to Broadbottom, so you may well be tempted. Turn left at the road and go up to join the B6062. Turn right here and go up the hill, passing the school and the former Primitive Methodist chapel. As you approach the railway bridge, which carries the Manchester to Sheffield (Hope Valley) line, look up to your left to see the former Bugsworth station house. *The station closed to passengers in 1958, but the house is still occupied.* Pass under the railway bridge, noting the width of the bridge, which used to carry four tracks though there are only two now. Still following the road, you swing to the right and soon reach the junction with Dolly Lane. Turn left here, leaving the main road and the railway and beginning your first serious climb of the day. About ½ mile of steady uphill plodding brings you to a T-junction by Brookdale cattery. Here you turn right and resume the uphill plod. The lane is narrow and has neither verge nor footway, but this doesn't really matter as it also sees very little traffic.

As you climb, take the opportunity to pause every now and then to admire the increasingly wide view (a good excuse). You can see over Whaley Bridge to Toddbrook Reservoir, the communication mast on Eccles Pike and beyond that to Castle Naze and Combs Edge. After a further bout of climbing you reach another T-junction, where you join Over Hill Road. The tarmacked road turns sharp right, but your route lies straight ahead on a broad stony track. Now you can bowl along with ease as the first lot of climbing is done.

The track marks the boundary of the Peak District National Park. The views to the west are very extensive, looking down the Goyt valley, over New Mills towards Stockport and Manchester. The highest tower block that you can see is the Hilton Hotel, Manchester's answer to London's Shard. The hills in the far distance are those at the back of Horwich. As you progress along the lane the view becomes even more extensive westwards, taking in the whole of the Cheshire Plain, Fiddlers Ferry power station and the sandstone escarpment near Helsby. On a clear day you should be able to see the Clwydian range of hills in North Wales.

Continuing along the track you pass Shedyard Piece Plantation on your left and then the lane dips briefly to cross the upper reaches of Shedyard Clough Brook. About 100 yards/metres from here you come to a cross-roads. Go straight ahead, soon passing Piece Farm and so reaching Moor Lodge. Here the National Park boundary swings away to the right. You go straight on, along what is now a tarred road, hemmed in by high and well-built dry-stone walls, which restrict the view to either side. However, you can clearly see your onward route as it climbs the flanks of Lantern Pike. *You quickly realise to your annoyance that you are about to lose most of the height you have gained, only to have to regain it all again.*

Descend the steepening road, soon passing Arden Quarry landfill site on the right, with the usual plethora of 'Keep Out' notices and fences – though why anyone would want to go in at all defeats me. The road widens considerably at this point, presumably to take lorries destined for the landfill site. There's no footway and not much verge either, so take care. As you approach Birch Vale, the road swings sharp right at a blind bend. You are advised to keep on the left hand side of the road round the bend. Just past the bend you reach the first houses of Birch Vale. *Beware dogs! When the walk was recce'd the author was given a nasty nip by a dog which charged out of one of the houses and took a hearty dislike to my left leg.*

Go down the footway to the main A6015 road and cross with care. Turn right and in less than 100 yards/metres, just before Zion House (a former chapel), go left down a steep track, signed 'No horse riding', but without any footpath sign. This path leads down beside the former chapel to emerge on Station Road, just at the point where the Sett Valley Trail crosses. Cross the road, go through the gate and turn left, emerging onto the road again just above the river bridge.

Birch Vale to Matleymoor Farm

Go down Station Road, passing the Birch Vale Industrial Estate on your right and so reaching Spinnerbottom. Cross the River Sett and go past The Crescent, a lengthy terrace of attractive stone-built houses. Just past The Crescent, at the Pennine Bridleway sign, turn right and go up the cobbled path away from the road. As you climb, you look down onto the backs of The Crescent, from which vantage point you can more readily see how it got its name. After a steady climb of a little less than ½ mile you come to another road, opposite a short terrace of houses. If nothing else, they've got a grand view across the valley, back towards Chinley Churn and up towards Kinder Scout. Go right at this point and then immediately left just past the last house in the terrace. This narrow lane is still part of the Pennine Bridleway. Indeed you will be on this long distance route for some considerable time, but you are more likely to meet mountain bikes than horses. Still climbing, you soon reach Sunnyside – an apt name and here the road degenerates into a rough track. The track forks and the Pennine Bridleway keeps to the left hand path. Still climbing, you'll now see a National Trust sign ahead, just beyond a gate. This proclaims that you are now on Lantern Pike, and of course, this is access land. Here you have a choice.

The Pennine Bridleway contours around the flank of Lantern Pike and is easily followed. However, to your left a rough path rises steeply alongside the NT boundary wall leading towards the summit of the Pike. Unless you are feeling really worn out, this is the recommended route.

Climb up beside the wall until you reach the ridge and then follow the narrow, but obvious path to the right, which leads unerringly to the viewfinder on top of Lantern Pike (1224 feet/373 metres). *It is worth the climb as the view is very extensive. Eastwards you have a clear view to Kinder Scout, the highest part of the Peak District. Hayfield can be seen down in the valley bottom and looking south there's Chinley Churn, South Head and Mount Famine. To the north lie Matley Moor and Coombs Tor, whilst to the west the view stretches out over the Cheshire Plain. On a good day it would be a fine place to stop and linger, but on a windy and cold day, as on the day I did the recce', it was decidedly not a place on which to hang around.* A well-blazed path carries on along the ridge northwards and soon descends to a gate where you rejoin the Pennine Bridleway. Continue northwards to yet another gate, which brings you out onto open moorland.

It would be easy to go wrong here. An obvious track bears right, across the moor, but a less obvious – and unsigned, path diverges left, making for a gate, stile and signpost about ¼ mile away, where no fewer than six routes converge. This is your route. The path across the moor is not well marked underfoot, despite it being the Pennine Bridleway. *Perhaps this is because the moor is open access and thus you can make your way across to the gate however you choose, but a way-mark at the point of divergence would be useful.* At the six-way junction, go through the gate onto a narrow, rough lane

Hayfield from the Pennine Bridleway

and bear left. In about 150 yards/metres you pass the access to Bullshaw Farm on your left, firmly marked with 'Private Road' signs. The rough lane continues for a further ¹/₃ mile or so to Matleymoor Farm and a T-junction.

Matleymoor Farm to Cown Edge Rocks

At the T-junction, go left and follow the track round to the right, still on the Pennine Bridleway, tightly constrained between dry-stone walls. Your route ahead can be seen away to the left, climbing (again) towards the top of Coombes Tor. After almost ½ mile you reach a gate and the track turns sharp left. Ignore the tempting path through a gate on the right, leading further onto the moor, and instead follow the broad track down to the road. Here you leave the Pennine Bridleway. Go over the road and climb over the stile into the field. The signpost clearly indicates two routes through this field, neither of which is obvious on the ground. Bear right, making your way diagonally across the field, heading towards a large tree and a stile in the bottom right hand corner. Climb this stile to emerge onto a farm track and go left, still descending, until you almost reach Cloughead Farm. Do not go down to the farm, but keep your eyes peeled for a waymarked path on the right. This skirts the farm buildings, passing between a metal tank and the house wall. You go through a bit of the garden (waymarked) to reach a bridge over a stream. Go over another stile and into fields again. The first bit of this path is marked with widely spaced concrete blocks, presumably to help you across what in normal circumstances would be a muddy mess.

Beyond the concrete blocks the path is indistinct, but you go up the field, roughly following the telephone poles until you can see Far Cown Edge Farm above and to your right. You'll also discern a stile in the wall at the far side of the field, marked by one of the ubiquitous Peak and Northern Footpaths Society signs. Make for this stile and go over it. An equally indistinct path follows a wall on the right towards the farm. Here another P&NFPS sign shows you are on the right route and a small gate on the right leads into the farmyard and thus onto the farm access. Go along the lane, still climbing slightly, until you reach a T-junction where you rejoin the Pennine Bridleway. Go left here and climb the short stretch into a deep cut V between the two parts of Cown Edge Rocks. A stile on the right gives access onto the open moor and here you leave the Pennine Bridleway again.

Choices, choices!

Once over the stile, you have a choice. A well-blazed path heads straight across the moor, making for the right hand side of the plantation, which can be seen ahead. The views from this path are extensive but not spectacular.

The alternative is to bear left, following the fence to the edge of Coombes Tor, where you pick up a path to the right, along the lip of the pronounced valley from which Coombes gets its name. This is spectacular and well worth a visit, but not for anyone with a fear of heights.

If you've chosen the path across the moor, you'll soon come to a stile close to the edge of the wood. To your right here there is a sudden drop (Cown Edge Rocks) down to Rocks Farm and Plainsteads, plus a view across to Kinder. The path then continues, with the trees to your left until you reach the end of the wood and there join up with anyone who has ventured along Coombes Edge. Even here there are alternatives. There's a path right alongside the edge, with great views down into the valley. Alternatively there's another path, separated from the first by a fence and a little further away from the edge. Both go to the same place eventually. The left hand path keeps on the left side of the fence and soon drops into a pronounced hollow-way, shown on the map as being part of the Pennine Bridleway, though it's hard to see how this can be the case. The right hand path keeps to the right of the fence to a small gate then drops into the hollow-way. You can either follow the hollow-way down or, preferably climb out onto the bank on the other side and then carry on along the path with extensive views either side.

To your left, the view is down into the hidden valley of Coombes, backed by the spectacular Coombes Rocks and beyond to the hills at the back of Macclesfield and Congleton. Ahead the view stretches over most of the Manchester conurbation, whilst to your right you can discern the hills at the back of Horwich, Alphin Pike and the high rise blocks in Oldham. The path is a delightful trot over closed cropped grass, tending steadily downhill, accompanied some times by a derelict wall and at other times by an equally derelict fence. *To your right you'll spot the roof of Charlesworth chapel.* At the sheep pens keep to the right. There are no fewer than four stiles here, in quick succession, though two of them are totally redundant. The third and fourth stiles land you on the access track to Coombes Farm.

Here again you have a choice of routes. Immediately ahead is a deep cut hollow-way. To the left, through a gate clearly marked 'Private', you'll spot a stile in the fence. The hollow-way has the merit of being very obvious, but the view from it is constrained, so the advice is to use the paralleling footpath instead. In this manner, continue downhill, with Charlesworth now being visible ahead and below, and your ultimate objective, Broadbottom station, also in view. The path comes close to the hollow-way at a junction of paths. Go straight on, over a couple of stiles into fields and continue down the hill, soon reaching the outskirts of Charlesworth. Carry on down the hill, with the houses to your right. The path turns sharp right to a stile at the bottom of the gardens. A steep bank leads you down onto a rough lane. Here you go left, only to leave the lane almost at once via a stile on your right by an electricity pole. (You will have spotted this in any case as you came down the previous field.) The map shows that the path goes down the right hand side of the field and then goes left along the bottom boundary. In practice, it seems that users cut across the field diagonally left and so reach a stile in the corner by the playing field.

To the left is the cricket pitch, home to Charlesworth and Chisworth Cricket Club. To the right is an assortment of play activities including football pitches, a zip-wire and slide. Keep to the left hand side of the playing field to reach the access track to the cricket ground, and there go right.

Charlesworth to Broadbottom

On reaching the road, go left. Follow the road over the brow of the hill, passing Dyson's shop on your right and then turning right, down Woodseats Lane. *Woodlands Tea Room is just on your right. Unfortunately it was closed when this walk was recce'd, because I could have done with a cup of tea at this stage.* Woodseats Lane gets narrower as you progress along it. It only serves a few properties and traffic is minimal. The lane bears right at Woodseats Farm. *Just beyond this point, the map shows that there has been the possibility of a footpath alternative from Charlesworth. However, when this walk was recce'd the stile from Woodseats Lane merely dropped you onto a plank bridge which only spanned half of a large pool of water, so the lane was clearly a wiser choice. Just past this point, there is a small cluster of buildings and most incongruously a speed limit de-restriction sign. Why this is thought necessary here is incomprehensible and it is surely a candidate for removal of signing clutter. You'd have difficulty doing more than 20mph anyway. Away from these buildings you now get a good view of Broadbottom viaduct and you realise how extensive the structure really is. It is not just the high steel viaduct over the Etherow, but a lengthy stone arched structure almost back to the station.*

The lane comes to an end at three farms, Rivendell, Silvandale and Warhurst Fold. Surely only the last name can be of any antiquity. The three farms are on your left and a wide, signed path continues ahead. It has obviously been surfaced at some time in the distant past, because there are traces of tarmac here and there is a good stone surface elsewhere. As the path descends and swings round to the left, the River Etherow comes into view below. The path drops steeply to reach a bridge over the river with gritstone crags on either side – an unexpected sight. Once over the bridge, you are now in Tameside and there is an information board to your right. *This refers to the Broad Mills Heritage Site and gives details about the various buildings that were on site and what can still be seen today. In their heyday, the mills must have been very impressive and closely akin to those seen even now at New Mills. Spend some time looking round the site and reading the various information boards. With any luck the information centre at Lymefield will be open and can supply even more material.*

Having looked round the Broad Mills site, return to Warhurst Bridge and follow the signposted route to Housefold. This climbs steeply with a good view down the Etherow to your left. At a T-junction, go left, still following signs to Housefold and with the railway viaduct rising to your right. The path squeezes between the railway and the steep drop into the river. In winter you will catch a glimpse of the weir far below. The path levels out at a terrace of houses. Pass to the left of these on a track and at the far end of the houses go right, up a waymarked path. Where this reaches the back of the terrace the path forks and here you go left. (The right hand route only goes to the back doors of the houses.) Still climbing, you go up through the trees and thus reach another junction of paths, with unmistakeable signs of railway influence in the form of signs and lights. The path to the right leads up to a gate onto the Manchester bound platform. That to the left goes up steps onto the road. On the assumption you've come by train for this walk, the right hand path is for you. If you want a train to Hadfield or Glossop then merely go over the footbridge

If you are in need of liquid refreshment, go up the station approach road from the Glossop bound platform, pass the former goods shed and seek out the Harewood Arms.

Broadbottom station

Harewood Arms

Walk 13: Broadbottom to Uppermill (Cross Keys or The Church)

Start	Broadbottom railway station GR. SJ992938
Finish	Uppermill (Cross Keys) GR.SE008062
The route	Broadbottom station, Gorsey Brow, The Hague, Melandra Roman fort, Trans Pennine Trail, Wooley Bridge Rd, Waterside, Goddard Lane, Bottoms Reservoir, Tintwistle, Arnfield Lane, Pennine Bridleway, Ogden Clough, Chew Reservoir, Dovestones Reservoir, Oldham Way, Pots and Pans, Pob Green, Cross Keys or The Church Inn
Length	12.01 miles (19.3 km)
Ascent	2737 feet (834 metres)
Time	6¼-7½ hours (exclusive of stops)
Map	OS OL1 (Dark Peak)

Getting there:

By bus. Daily buses to Broadbottom from Glossop, Hyde and Manchester. There are no buses up to Pob Green, but frequent services on the A670 in Uppermill, to Ashton, Stalybridge, Oldham, Manchester and Huddersfield.

By train. Daily trains to Broadbottom from Manchester, Hyde and Glossop. Daily trains to Greenfield (nearest station for Uppermill), from Ashton, Huddersfield, Manchester and Stalybridge.

By car. Broadbottom can be reached off the A57 from the junction at Mottram, or from Charlesworth by a very narrow bridge over the River Etherow. There is a large free car park at the railway station. Devious is the only way to describe the road approach to Pob Green and 'limited' is an exaggerated description for parking, except at the pubs.

The walk

Broadbottom to Melandra

From Broadbottom station, go up the station approach, passing the Etherow centre on your right. *This was originally the goods shed.* At the road, turn right, following the Trans Pennine Trail sign. *Go down through the village, passing the Harewood Arms and noting, on your right the reuse of the goods yard as a riding area for disabled children and then, a little further on, the remains of the coal drops.* Just before the viaduct, turn left up Gorsey Brow and then almost immediately, bear right onto Hague Road. Despite its name, this is little more than a rough lane and is clearly signed as a footpath only, though the OS map shows it as a bridleway. The lane swings left, away from the railway and through a substantial rock cutting, high above the Etherow. *The noise of the weir far below can be heard clearly and you can also catch a glimpse of the Etherow viaduct through the trees.*

A short distance along the lane brings you to a substantial house known as The Hague. This does not correspond with the place name 'The Hague' on the OS map. *From here you can look back and see the Etherow viaduct spanning the gorge. Also from this point there is a view across the valley to the site of Melandra Castle and the hills of the Peak District, with the houses of Gamesley estate intervening.* Carry on along Hague Road until you reach the collection of buildings, which the OS map refers to as The Hague. Here the track forks, but the way ahead is clearly to the left as the others are all obviously private. At another junction, although the map seems to indicate a route straight ahead, the footpath is firmly signed to the left, through a gate and then the farmyard. The exit gate was fastened with rope when the walk was recce'd and, being a very wide gate it was not the easiest to open and close. Once through this gate, turn right, along a rough road, Pingot Lane, which appears to be heading straight for a set of high ornamental gates. Just before the gates there is a signpost directing you to the right for Melandra castle and sure enough, the lane does swing right and begins to descend towards the river.

Note the stone-lined well on your right. Don't lean too far over, especially if you have anything about your person that is likely to fall off, as recovery could be problematic!

The lane ends abruptly in the courtyard in front of a house, but ahead there is an archway cut into the hedge and your route lies through this. Here you rejoin a rough lane, which looks suspiciously like the one you were following before you were diverted through the farmyard. Go left and follow the lane, from which there is a view across the valley to Melandra Castle, the earthworks of which are very obvious. A quick descent soon brings you to a junction of paths adjacent to the water treatment works. Go straight on, across the bridge and thus enter Derbyshire. You are now on a tarred road and will remain on this for some time. Its one merit is that it's flat and sees little traffic. The lane runs alongside the former sewage works, which are now derelict and rapidly developing into woodland. The hillside on your right rises steeply and you can begin to see why the Romans chose this site for their fortress.

As you pass the recycling site on your left and approach a bridge, look out for a stile on your right. From here a path goes steeply (and muddily) up to the fortress. (If you miss the stile and reach the bridge, turn sharp right here (not along the Trans Pennine Trail route) and follow the made path to the first hairpin bend then strike up the hillside on the path already mentioned.)

Melandra/Ardotalia fort

The fort is rather a disappointment. There is no obvious interpretive material and the concrete blocks at each 'gateway' are either devoid of information or merely tell you that the place is in the care of the Ministry of Public Buildings and Works. As this government department no longer exists (and hasn't done so for many years), this is scarcely useful information. The walls of the fortress appear as raised earth mounds and form a complete rectangle in the classic 'playing card' shape, enclosing an area of about 3½ acres (1.42ha). Whatever the fort's function was in Roman times, nowadays its major usage seems to be as 'doggie' walking territory for the residents of the Gamesley estate, which borders the southern edge of the site. In the centre of the fortress further structures can be discerned, including the foundations of the fort's main buildings, but there is no descriptive material on site.

The name Melandra does not appear in any Roman records so far discovered and its origin is a mystery, though it is thought likely to have been coined by John Watson, the then Rector of Stockport. He visited the site in the early 1770s. At this time substantial stone remains existed and it seems likely he witnessed the demolition of the ruins of the fort's bath house. It would seem that the Romans called the fort Ardotalia. The derivation of this name is obscure but it is thought to come from an ancient Celtic word 'talia' meaning 'steep hill' so the full meaning would be the 'place of the high, dark hill'. However, other scholars have suggested that the fort and the river Etherow both derive their names from the winding, heather covered valley of Longdendale.

The Archaeology Department of Manchester University has done excavations at the fort and it is from this work that much of the information about the fort has been derived. The fort was built around 78 AD, initially of turf and wood. This was the period when Agricola was Governor of Britain and was in the

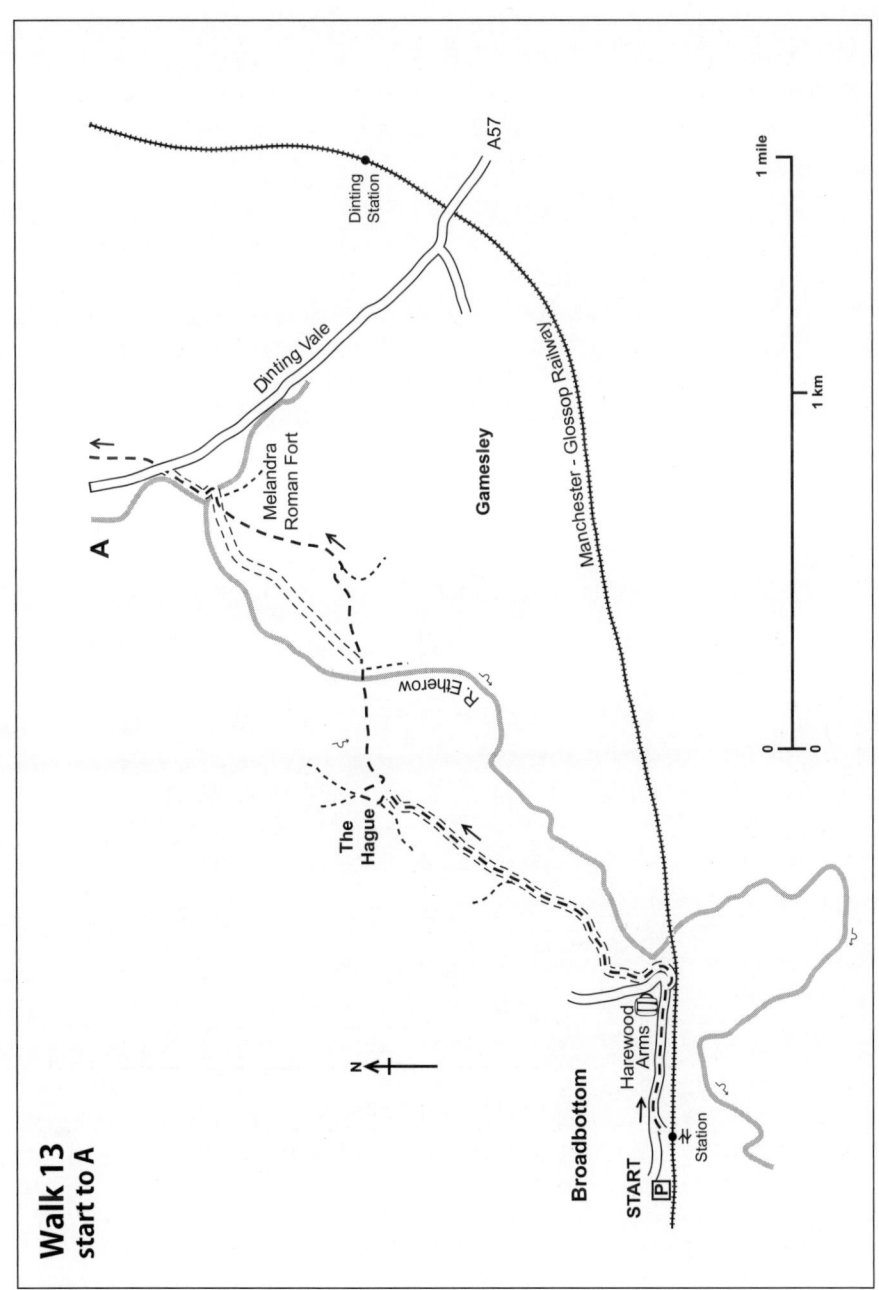

Walk 13
start to A

A

Dinting Vale

Melandra
Roman Fort

Dinting
Station

A57

Manchester - Glossop Railway

Gamesley

R. Etherow

The
Hague

N

Broadbottom

Harewood
Arms

START

P

Station

0   1 km   1 mile

0

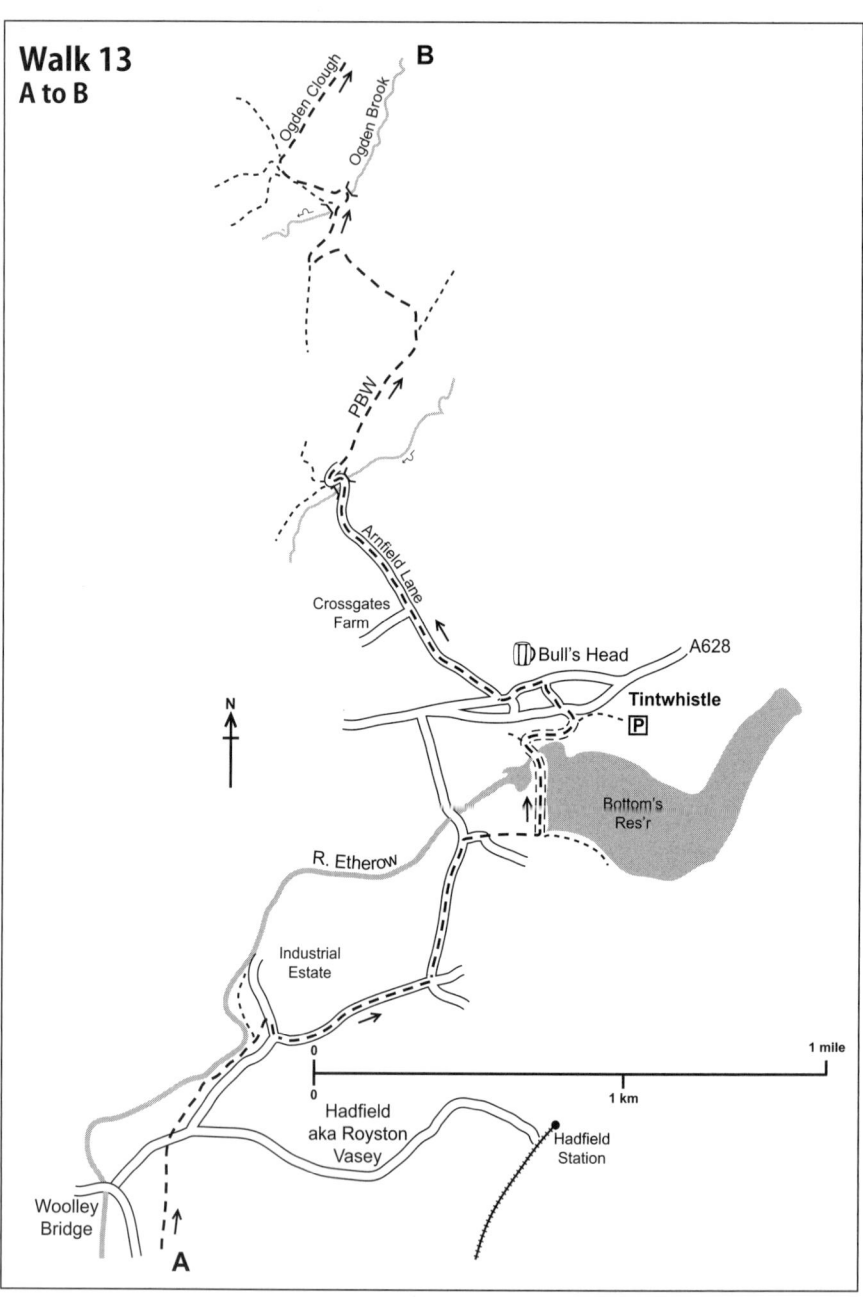

Walk 13
A to B

B

Ogden Clough

Ogden Brook

PBW

Arnfield Lane

Crossgates
Farm

Bull's Head

A628

Tintwhistle

P

N

Bottom's
Res'r

R. Etherow

Industrial
Estate

1 mile

0

0   1 km

Hadfield
aka Royston
Vasey

Hadfield
Station

Woolley
Bridge

A

Walk 13
B to C

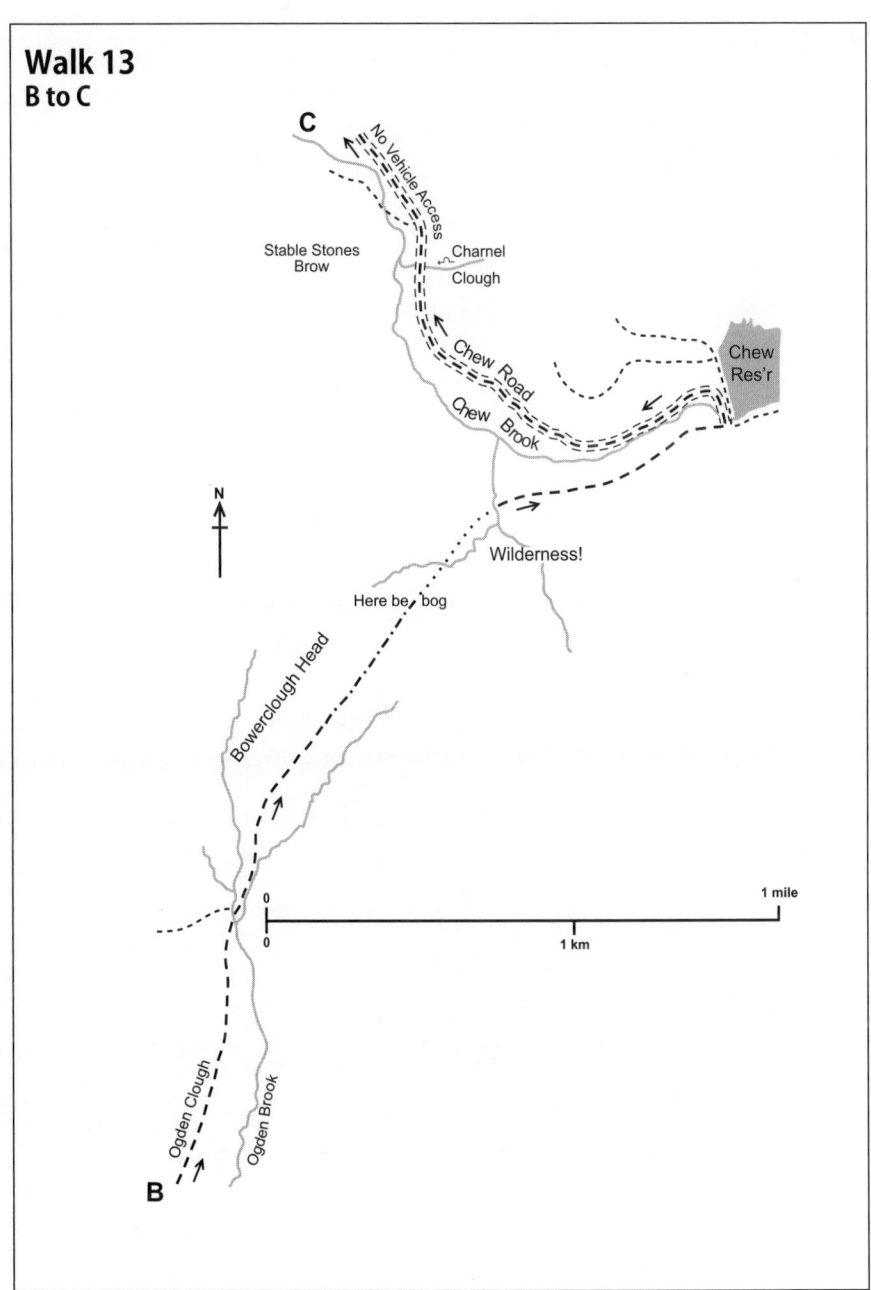

C

No Vehicle Access

Stable Stones Brow

Charnel Clough

Chew Road

Chew Brook

Chew Res'r

N

Wilderness!

Here be bog

Bowerclough Head

0

0

1 mile

1 km

Ogden Clough

Ogden Brook

B

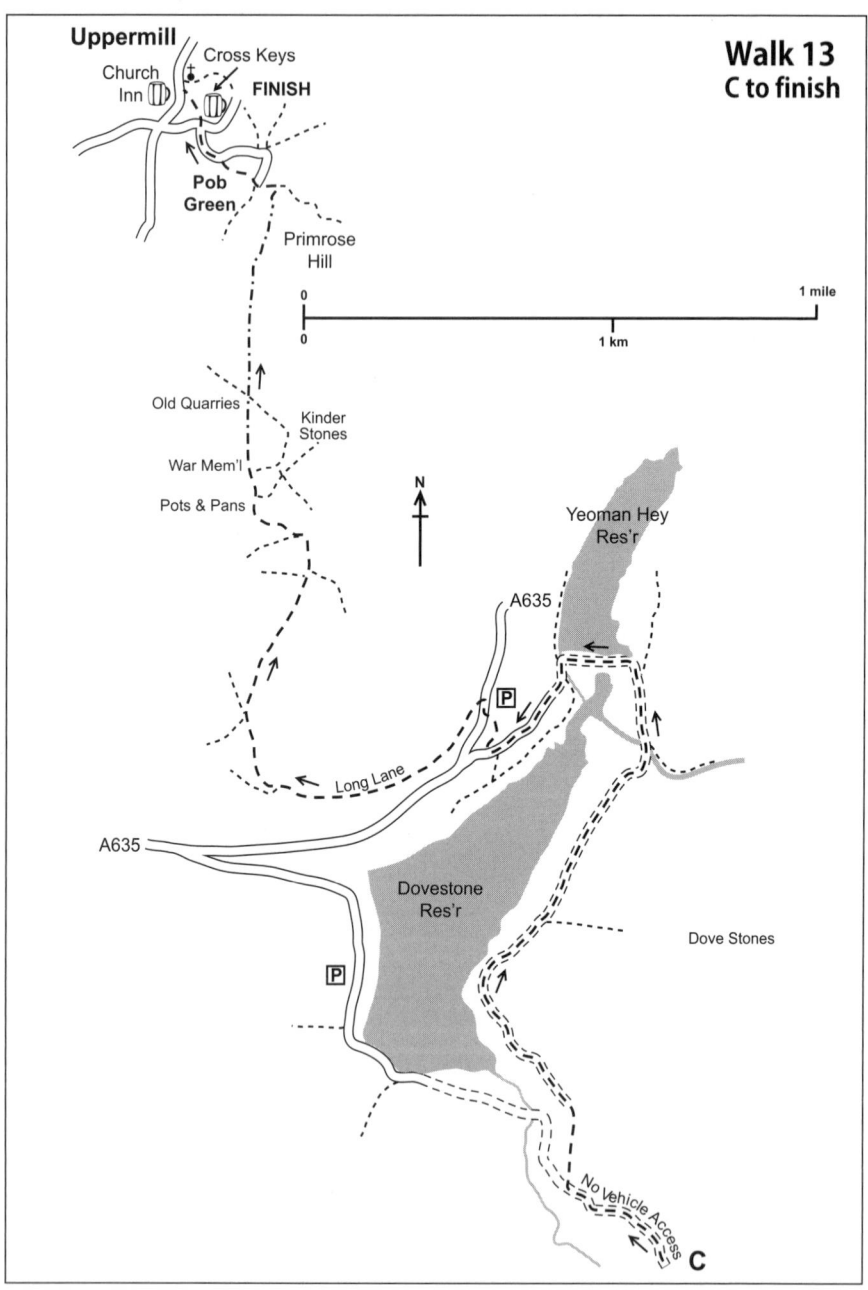

Walk 13
C to finish

Uppermill
Cross Keys
Church
Inn
FINISH
Pob
Green
Primrose
Hill

Old Quarries
Kinder
Stones
War Mem'l
Pots & Pans

N

0   1 mile
0   1 km

Yeoman Hey
Res'r

A635

P

Long Lane

A635

Dovestone
Res'r

Dove Stones

P

No Vehicle Access

C

process of expanding Roman influence northwards. (He eventually reached as far north as Inverness and in AD 83 fought and won the Battle of Mons Graupius near Aberdeen, against the Caledonian tribes. This marked the high water mark of Roman expansion in Britain.)

Around 500 auxiliary soldiers would have manned Melandra/Ardotalia. As with all Roman forts there would have been a headquarters building, barracks, granaries and a bathhouse. Archaeological evidence suggests that there was also a civilian settlement nearby. In around 110 AD, the fort was rebuilt in stone, but evidence suggests that it was abandoned only 30 years later. The stone version of Melandra/Ardotalia was built by the 1st Cohort of Frisiavones and the 3rd Cohort of Bracara Augustani. Evidence of this exists not only from the building stone found at the site but also from various Roman records. These two units were auxiliaries and were apparently attached to the Legion XX Valeria Victrix based in Chester. Which of these two auxiliary units manned the fort is uncertain.

Following its abandonment in about 140 AD, the fort saw one last military use when the remains of the south-west tower became a Home Guard machine gun post during WWII. By this time, the stone fort had long been regarded as a convenient source of stone, rubble and gravel for local builders and examples of re-used Roman stone work have been found at Woolley Bridge, Melandra Farm and Mottram church.

Despite appearances and what the 'information' panels say, the fort is a scheduled monument in the care of English Heritage. For further information on the fort, key in Melandra Castle Roman fort on the Internet.

A forced march to Tintwistle

Leave the fort by your approach route and descend to the bridge over the Glossop Brook. Follow the Trans Pennine Trail signs towards Longdendale, soon passing the confluence of the Glossop Brook and the River Etherow. Continue along the trail, mainly beside the river, until you reach the A57. Cross at the pelican crossing and go up the path on the far side of the road. *You are now on the former Waterside branch railway. This line left the Glossop branch just west of Dinting viaduct and descended quite steeply before crossing the Glossop Brook on a substantial steel viaduct and then the A57 on a bridge. The single-track branch was 2 miles 16 chains long (3.54 km). It opened in 1879 and the last portion of it closed in 1964, though a date in 1965 has been mentioned. Other than the occasional special, it never carried a passenger service, its sole raison d'etre being to serve a series of mills and factories. Unlike the Woodhead and Glossop lines it was never electrified. In retrospect, it is a shame that passenger services were not introduced, as an electrified railway* serving the lower part of Hadfield, Hollingworth and Tintwistle would have been a great asset now.

Follow the course of the former railway, soon reaching and crossing Woolley Bridge Road. There used to be a level crossing here. The Trans Pennine Trail continues ahead, passing one of the formerly rail-served mills on the left and then coming close to the Etherow again. Where the river swings to the left, leave the tempting riverside path (which goes nowhere) and go up the track to the roundabout at the end of Graphite Way and thus back onto Woolley Bridge Road. *The Roman Catholic church dedicated to St Charles Borromeo is to your right.* Go up Woolley Bridge Road to the mini roundabout at the bottom of Station Road.

If you are a fan of the League of Gentlemen television series, you will recognise Station Road, for it was here that many of the scenes were filmed. If you walk up Station Road towards the station, see how many of the locations you can distinguish. Unlike the fictional town in the series, Hadfield is easy to leave, with a half hourly train service and plenty of bus routes too. However, it can be a bit disconcerting when you see a bus coming towards you with the destination blind displaying 'Royston Vasey'.

The route of the walk turns left at the mini roundabout and goes down Waterside, following the Pennine Bridleway signs. At the bottom of the hill, turn right, into Goddard Lane, just before the river bridge. Pass through the gate and where the path forks, bear right on the pedestrian route of the Trans-Pennine Trail. At the dam wall turn left.

Bottoms Reservoir

When this part of the walk was recce'd, there'd been very heavy rain. The overflow weir at Bottoms Reservoir was in full spate and 'Bateman's Fountain' was spectacular. Bottoms Reservoir was one of a series of reservoirs constructed for Manchester Corporation in the mid 19th century. The engineer was John Frederick Bateman, who is widely regarded as one of the greatest

Bottoms Reservoir overflow and Bateman's fountain

reservoir builders of all time. When the various reservoirs in Longdendale were completed in 1877 they were the largest chain of reservoirs in the world. As you reach the north side of the dam, there's an information board on the left describing the construction of the dams and the overflow arrangements. The building down below, by the side of the overflow weir, used to house turbines, which provided electricity for the other reservoir buildings and for the waterworks railway. It is also worth looking at the building at the end of the dam, on the right. There's an impressive stone plaque in the north wall, setting out the chairmen and vice chairmen of the water committee, plus the engineers and clerk. This was in the days when local authorities meant something and had a hand in most utilities, water, roads, trams, gas and electricity. They built to last and were proud of their achievements and rightly so. Take the opportunity to look at the twin overflow weirs, just past the building.

Over't'moor to Chew

Return to the dam and go right, following the Pennine Bridleway signs up to the A628. Cross the main road with great care. This is a very busy road, with a lot of lorry traffic. Go up Chapel Brow, a steep ascent, with the unusual terraced cemetery on your right. The centre of the road is cobbled with gritstone blocks. At the top of the road, turn left. Go past The Bull's Head pub and the war memorial. It is worth bearing in mind that the Bull's Head is one of the few pubs you pass between Broadbottom and Pob Green and it's the last one for miles. If you feel tempted (and you may), just bear in mind that the bulk of the climbing and mileage has yet to come.

Turn right along Arnfield Lane, which is signed as the Pennine Bridleway. This lane is a delightful stroll. The first section is cobbled with gritstone blocks and passes the allotments on the left, with views down the valley to Arnfield Reservoir and Mottram church. There's even a seat, should you be in need of a rest. Like Bottoms Reservoir, Arnfield was also a Manchester Corporation development, being finished in 1854. The lane forms the National Park boundary at this point. At the T-junction by Crossgates Farm, keep straight on along the tarmacked road. Look out for a stone on the left, inscribed with the initials HWW. This refers to Mottram and Hollingworth Water Works and there's a small covered reservoir in the field, just over the wall. The lane soon descends past the gamekeeper's cottage and crosses Arnfield Brook, by a fine, stone bridge that clearly bears the marks of water company construction. Beyond the bridge the road rises towards Arnfield Farm.

Just before the farm there's a signpost. The Pennine Bridleway goes sharp right at this point, signed to Brushes (Stalybridge Country Park). It is possible to carry straight on, round the farm and along a field path, but the route of the walk is along the bridleway. Go up the bridleway, which is now a rough track, between walls. *Beware mountain bikers, who seem to believe that they have a god-given right to charge down the bridleway irrespective of anyone else. I was nearly mown down by half a dozen who came careering down the track at great speed, without any warning.* The track eventually emerges onto Arnfield Low Moor and forks. Keep left here, still following the PBW waymarks. *The view to the left is extensive, but to the right it is constrained by a belt of conifers.* As you top the rise you can see Ogden Clough ahead and the continuation of the bridleway, making its way up the far side. The track now bends sharply to the left and begins to descend into Ogden Clough. You can make out the path you need to take, running up the clough at a high level. *The scene here will be very different in a year or two as there's been extensive planting of trees.*

Follow the bridleway down. There's a footpath alternative dropping steeply down the bank side to the footbridge below, but the bridleway is preferable. At the sharp right hand bend there's a ladder stile in the wall ahead. This is where you would come out if you take the footpath route at Arnfield Farm. When you reach the footbridge you can either cross it (with care, because some of the planks are missing or rotten), or continue ahead and go over the culvert carrying the bridleway across Ogden Brook. The latter is to be preferred, not only because it's safer, but also the gradient on the far side is easier.

Follow the bridleway up the hillside. Where it levels out, there's a PBW waymark. The bridleway continues straight on, but a track heads off to the right, unsigned. This is shown on the OS 1:25000 map as a concession path, but you are in access land here in any case. After only a few paces, leave the track and bear right along a narrow but distinct path, marked by a small cairn and a rotten post. This is the path you saw earlier. It continues at this high level, above the clough, steadily climbing and always distinct. The path is marked by occasional small cairns, but these are not really necessary as you'd have a job losing the route. There are no difficulties or nasty bogs to cross (at this stage). *A glance at the map will show that you are no longer in the National Park, having left it when you crossed Ogden Brook. As there's no obvious landscape reason for this, both sides of the clough being very similar, one has to look for a political justification, and so it proves. At the time the National Park boundary was being drawn in the late 1940s the moorland you are on now was in Cheshire, but under the jurisdiction of Stalybridge Borough. Including this moor would have meant another authority having a seat on the National Park Board, so the moor was excluded. The same reasoning applied with half of Alphin Pike and the some of the moors around Buxton. The boundary has never been re-visited, though logic would suggest it ought to be, in order to remove such anomalies.*

The path follows the clough upwards and swings in a more northerly direction. Ahead you'll see a fence, running across the moor. At a bridge you cross from Tameside into Derbyshire and in so doing re-enter the National Park. Take care as the planks on the bridge are slippery when wet. Carry on up the path, still marked by cairns in places, until you reach a stile in the fence. *Look back from here. There's an extensive view, right across the Cheshire Plain, with Jodrell Bank telescope very prominent. The two small reservoirs you can see are Higher and Lower Swineshaw. For a change, these were not built for Manchester, but for the Ashton, Stalybridge and Dukinfield Water Works at around the same time as the Longdendale dams.*

Once over the stile, the gradient steepens somewhat, and the path becomes rougher underfoot. There's one short stretch where the heather moorland gives way to rushes and this always means wet conditions. It's soon over and after a final pull the path reaches the top of the moor. *Somewhere here is the boundary between Derbyshire and Oldham, though no right thinking Yorkshireman would ever accept that fact. To such a person, this is still part of the West Riding of Yorkshire, irrespective of the 1974 reorganisation of local government!*

Just when you thought how easy this bit of the walk had been, there's a sting in the tail. The route of the path is marked by a series of posts, but these are of little use in wet conditions. The moor is a squelchy bog and to cross it involves many a twist and turn. In fact there are two sets of posts and it is better to go for the right hand set, which give a marginally drier passage. Path there is not! You'll spot Chew Reservoir away to your right and the crags of Stable Stones Brow to your left. The best advice at this point is to find a northward flowing grough and make your way alongside it until you reach the clear path from Alphin Pike to Chew. When you spot this, you'll be gazing down the impressive gorge carrying Chew Brook and the reservoir access road. Bear right, along the path until you get to the dam wall.

Chew to Pob Green (Uppermill)

Drop down the path to the base of Chew Dam and then go left along the reservoir road. (You can also walk across the dam and descend to the road at the far end). The road goes down the valley of the Chew Brook with some impressive crags on the left. The road soon swings north, opening up a view down to Dovestone Reservoir and Greenfield. Continue down the road until you reach a junction where a narrow path goes off to the right, signed as the Oldham Way. *If time presses or your legs are about to give out, it is possible to carry on along the reservoir road at this point, descending to Dovestone Dam, where there is a car park, toilets and usually an ice cream van and/or a tea van. The nearest bus stop is at The Clarence. Follow the reservoir access road to the A635 and there turn left. The pub is about ½ mile/805 metres, down the main road.*

The Oldham Way bears right, leaving the reservoir access road. A narrow path traverses the hillside and is soon joined by a much wider and well-used path coming up from Dovestone Dam. Carry on along this path, with excellent views over the reservoir and back towards Alphin Pike. You pass through a belt of trees, the inevitable conifers beloved of all water undertakings. This section is soon over and you are in open country again with the rugged head of the valley becoming more apparent with every step. *Across the valley is Alderman's Brow, looking quite formidable.* The path soon reaches the head of Dovestone reservoir and passes across the dam wall of Yeoman Hey reservoir. Once over the dam, go left and follow the access road up towards the A635. Just before you reach the main road there is a small gate on the right, signed as the Oldham Way. Go through the gate and ascend the flight of steps through the wood to reach the small car park. At the car park entrance, go over the A635 and through a gate opposite – again signed as the Oldham Way. A lovely green track climbs away from the main road, soon

Dovestone Reservoir from Binn Green path

becoming walled. (*The stile on the right is for the path to the summit of Alderman's Brow. This is not part of the walk route, but if you feel fit enough the ascent is worth the effort as the view from the top over the reservoirs is magnificent and the route thence to Pots and Pans is easy going.*) Carry on along the green lane with grand views over Dovestone reservoir and its attendant gritstone edges. *The view also opens out westwards towards Oldham and Manchester and, as the track swings around the flanks of Alderman's Brow, the hills north of Saddleworth come into the picture.*

Where the track begins to descend, and with the war memorial on Pots and Pans clearly in view on your right, there is a junction of tracks. The Oldham Way goes right, through a gate. A steady plod up a fine grassy path soon takes you to a gate and stile, beyond which the path becomes much rougher and steeper. *Pauses for breath can be justified by admiring the extensive view to the left and by the thought that the view from the top must be even better.* The path soon reaches old quarry workings, long abandoned and overgrown. Skirt to the left of these to reach the rocks that give Pots and Pans its name and also to reach what must be one of the finest sited war memorials in the country. *The view is magnificent, north, west and south. Eastwards the view is blocked by Kinder Stones, which, at 1388 feet/427 metres are marginally higher than Pots and Pans.* Leave the war memorial and pass through the gap in the metal fence, and skirt round the left hand side of Kinder Stones to pick up a track, which then runs above the quarry edge, descending all the while in a roughly north easterly direction.

This is the route used by people attending the annual Remembrance Day service if they have parked near the Cross Keys. On 11th November 2012 there must have been hundreds of people making their way across the moor on this route. The only point of note is a prominent gateway of two large stones in an otherwise semi derelict wall. Pass through this on what is by then a more obvious track and then continue to descend, making for the tower of the St Chad's church at Pob Green, until you come up against a rather more substantial wall. Follow this down to the right, quite steeply in places,

War Memorial on Pots and Pans

until you join another path running in from your right. Go left here, down to the stile and past the house. *After the Remembrance Day service, we had to queue at the stiles at Pob Green.*

(From Pots and Pans it's also possible to reach Pob Green by going through the gap in the metal fence and then following the broad track down into the dip and then up to Dick Hill. Continuing along this track you'll reach a gate and stile, where a path branches off to the left. Go down this and join the main route of the walk at the Pob Green stile. This route is not shown on the sketch map in this book, but is clearly marked on the OS 1:25000 map and on the ground).

At Pob Green, don't go across the front of the house, but go straight ahead, down a narrow walled track, which descends steeply and roughly to reach a lane. *(If it is particularly muddy or icy, the route across the front of the house is a right of way, so go down the drive to the lane and turn left, soon passing the exit from the path mentioned above.)* Follow the lane down, soon passing Peter's Farm and so reaching a T-junction. The Cross Keys pub is immediately ahead and just below the road. You should need no instructions from here on. To get to The Church Inn, there's a footpath starting in the car park of the Cross Keys! This leads unerringly down to the other pub. If you visit both pubs you'll need someone to give you a lift because there are no buses or trains up here.

Cross Keys. 862 ft/263 metres
Telephone 01457 874626. www.crosskeysinn.co.uk

The Cross Keys was built in 1745 and opened as a pub in 1753. Although it may seem an odd place for a pub nowadays, in the 18th century it was situated on the main packhorse route across the Pennines to Marsden. The inn hosts what claims to be the longest running Folk Clubs in the North West of England. The club meets on Wednesday evenings.

The pub specializes in freshly prepared, home cooked food. The pub is a J.W. Lees house and has a selection of their cask ales, plus guest beers. Both the beer and the food are heartily recommended, but you'll need to book a table, especially at weekends. Even on a miserable Sunday afternoon in January, the place was packed.

Just in case you need it, the Cross Keys is also the base for the Oldham Mountain Rescue Team.

The Cross Keys

Opening times

Monday to Thursday: 1200 to 2330; Friday to Sunday: 1200 to midnight.
Food serving times are: Monday to Friday: 1200 to 1430 and 1730 to 2030;
Saturday: 1200 to 2030; Sunday: 1200 to 1930.

The Church Inn, 789 ft/240 metres
Telephone 01457 820902. www.churchinnsaddleworth.co.uk

Like its near neighbour the Cross Keys, the Church Inn served the old
packhorse routes across the Pennines, plus of course attending to the
congregation of the adjacent St. Chad's church in their 'thirst after
righteousness'. The Church Inn is sited at the head of Capper Clough, a steep
wooded steep valley that overlooks Uppermill. This is a pub full of
character(s), with gurning championships, handbell ringing, morris dancing
and a number of resident peacocks.

Not only does the pub serve good food, it also brews its own beer and you
could find up to 11 different varieties available, plus guest beers at times. The
Saddleworth brewery opened here in
1997, thereby restoring an old
tradition by reusing what had been
the original brew-house. The
strapline for the brewery is
'Purveyors of mental distortion'.
You'll enjoy sampling their beers!
Like the Cross Keys, this is a very
popular pub and you'll need to book
a table if you wish to eat, especially
at weekends. We couldn't get into
the pub at all one Sunday afternoon
in January, and when we visited
again in February the place was

The Church Inn

packed again – but we'd booked that time. Both the food and drink come
highly recommended.

Opening times

Monday to Friday: 1200 to midnight (0100 on Saturday); Sunday: 1200 to
2230.
Food serving times are: Monday to Friday: 1200 to 1430 and 1730 to 2100;
Saturday, Sunday and Bank Holidays: 1200 to 2100.

Part 2: The Circular Walks

Introduction

The 17 circular walks vary in length from just over 5 miles (8 km) to 12.4 miles (19.96 km) and the ascent ranges from 602 feet (185 metres) to 2747 feet (845 metres). It'll come as no surprise that the longest walk also has the most climbing. (It's also the only walk in the book that gets above 2000 feet (610 metres.) However, the shortest walk doesn't enjoy the least climbing. That would be too easy. One walk in this section (Walk 20, Owler Bar) is actually a linear walk and requires either two cars or preferably use of the bus service.

Walk 14: Flash (New Inn)

Start and finish	Flash Bar GR. SK024671
Alternative sttart and finish	Gradbach car park GR. SJ998662
The route	Flash, Flash Bottom, Adders Green, Little Hillend, Sniddles, Bradley Howe, Gradbach, Wicken Walls, Flash
Length	5.19 miles (8.35 km)
Ascent	1086 feet (334 metres)
Time	2½-3 hours (exclusive of stops)
Map	OS OL24 (White Peak)

Getting there:
By bus. Daily bus service between Leek and Buxton stops at the Travellers Rest at Flash Bar.
By train. Nearest station is Buxton.
By car. A53 from Leek or Buxton to just south of Flash Bar, then through Flash village (no parking) and follow the lane and signs down to Gradbach car park. From A54 from Congleton to Allgreave, then very sharp right onto the minor road to Gradbach. The car park at Gradbach is just in Staffordshire, signed to the right (a very sharp turn) down an even more minor lane.

The Walk

Flash to Adders Green
From the back door of the New Inn, go down onto the road and turn right. Go down the road past the Council depot, complete with its salt pile in readiness for the inevitable snow. Continue along the road for about ⅔ mile/1km until you reach the driveway for Lower House Farm. Just beyond this, there's a

signpost and a small gate on the left leading into the fields. Go through the gate, down the steps and bear right, noting that even the relatively minor road you have just left is supported on a considerable stone retaining wall. Pass through a gap in the wall ahead and continue across the next field to a gate out onto the driveway to Flash Bottom Farm. Go left here and follow the waymarked path that diverges from the driveway and skirts round the right hand side of the farm. In this manner you'll reach a footbridge over the stream.

Cross the bridge and go up the path through the trees. The path seems to double up as a stream-bed at times and there are various methods of avoiding the water. On

Old chapel, Flash

emerging from the trees, continue up beside the stream, eventually crossing it. The path pursues an unerring course up the hill, soon breasting the rise and giving a clear view ahead to Adders Green Farm. You are in access land at this point, though there have been no signs to indicate this. As you begin to descend towards Adders Green it is worth noting that the route from that farm over to Gradbach is notoriously wet underfoot, so it may be worth exploring the option of going up the hillside on your right, skirting round the back of Ann Roach Farm (which is now an acupuncture clinic!) and then dropping down to the path again at GR. SK017652. This has not been recce'd, but it may be worth a try. You won't avoid all the bog but you should avoid some.

If you choose to continue to Adders Green you pass through a waymarked gate/stile and with the wall to your right you encounter the first muddy stretch. At the farm there's a crossing of paths. (It is possible to combine this walk with Walk 24 from this point. This makes for a lengthy hike, but it does take you to The Roaches and Lud's Church and it also avoids the Adders Green to Little Hillend bogs.)

Adders Green to Gradbach

At the crossing of paths turn right along a broad green track to a gate. Here bear left alongside a ditch, fence and ruined wall, making your way across a quagmire. *(In fairness it has to be said that there had been torrential rain the day before the recce' and one farmer I spoke to mentioned the fact that a couple of the rivers in the vicinity had burst their banks that day.)* A signposted stile gives out onto the access track to Ann Roach Farm. Unfortunately this is no help, because the path continues straight ahead, over a plank bridge across a ditch and then into another morass. Make your way alongside the ruined wall to a junction of paths with a footpath sign. Beyond this point the wall is intact and here there is a small gate onto the access land on your right. *(This is not the gate referred to in the previous section.)* Continue muddily beside the wall to a stile and gateway. Here is another gate onto the access land. *This is the one previously mentioned as a possible way of avoiding some of the bog.* Unfortunately, once you get over the stile and begin the descent to Little Hillend you are into an area of rushes and reeds, which can only mean 'damp' conditions underfoot – and so it proves. The saving grace is the view ahead to Croker Hill and Shuttlingsloe. Thankfully you soon reach the garden gate that gives you access to the driveway of Little Hillend. Go down the drive to the road and then straight ahead down a good, firm and dry track.

Head along the track to the semi-derelict buildings. The path skirts round the right hand side of the buildings and onto a walled track. Go along this and it soon emerges into open fields. An indistinct path heads across the field making for a stile and gate well to the right of the little barn. Once through this stile, bear left, down the field to another stile leading out onto the road, close to the delightfully named Sniddles – now there's a place name for you. Go right and follow the road down until you are almost at Bradley Howe Farm. Look out for a waymarked stile on your left and go over this into fields again.

There's no obvious path in this field, so bear right, keeping to the right of the electricity pole and thus locating a stile in the wall. The stile is defended by a sea of rushes and the usual accompanying quagmire. This can be circumvented with relative ease. The next task is to cross the stream on your left. The map indicates an immediate crossing, but the sheep know better. Keep on the right hand bank for a short distance and cross where they do! Then bear right, up the bank through more rushes and reeds, keeping well to the right of the barn. There's no obvious path here, but sheep have obviously wandered through the jungle so there's some evidence that there's a way through. Eventually, you'll spot a footpath sign and a path materialises. Cross a small stream and go through the gate/stile on the other side. Bear right, up the bank, making for the wall corner and then follow the wall on your left to another stile, which is not only waymarked, but has its own television aerial. Straight on now, making for Greensitch Farm, which can be seen ahead. You can see Gradbach car park below you, to the right. Pass through a couple of

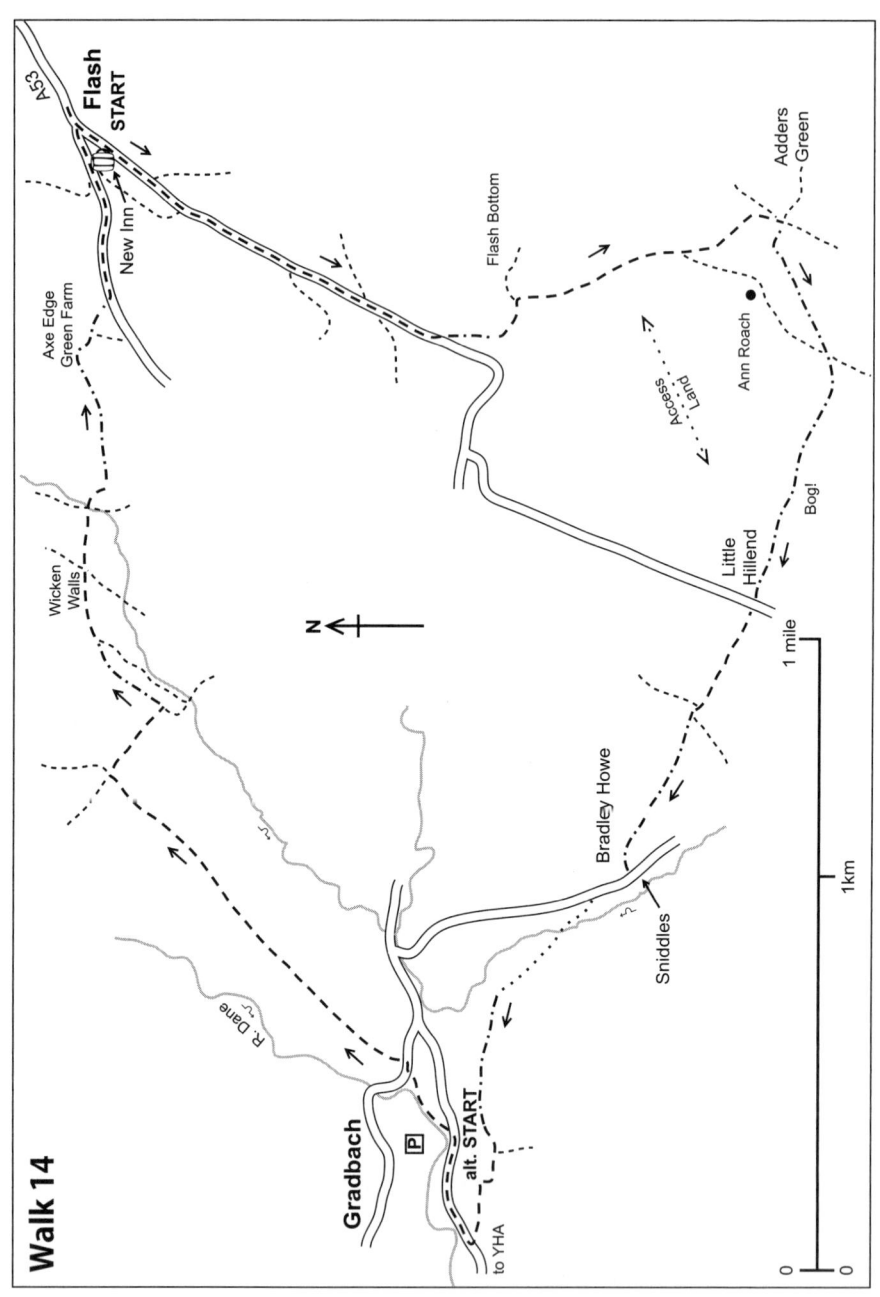

Walk 14

Flash
START
A53
New Inn
Axe Edge
Green Farm
Wicken
Walls
R. Dane
Gradbach
P
alt. START
to YHA
Bradley Howe
Sniddles
Little
Hillend
Bog!
Ann Roach
Access
Land
Flash Bottom
Adders
Green

N

0   1km   1 mile
0

gates and then follow the waymarked path round the left-hand side of the farm. Cross the bridge and then go right, down to the farm access. *(If you are heading for Gradbach youth hostel you go left here, along the farm access to the road and then follow the road to the hostel.)* Cross the farm access and go down the hillside a short way then right, across another bridge. The path now descends steeply to the road, almost opposite the entrance to Gradbach car park.

Gradbach to Flash

From the car park, follow the riverside path to the footbridge over the stream. Cross the bridge and bear right, alongside the River Dane. The path veers away from the river to a gate and stile leading out onto the road. Go right here for a very short distance and then go left, up the access to Dane View House, immediately going right, through a waymarked gate, into fields.

Keeping the wall to your left, follow this track/path up the hillside, with a view up the Dane Valley towards Three Shires Head. After about ⅔ mile/1km of steady uphill plodding through a series of fields, you come to a gate and stile into an area of rushes and reeds. In the midst of this, there's a Peak and Northern signpost and here you turn right. Follow the broad green path down towards the stream until you get to another P&N sign. Here you go left, along the path signed to 'Flash via Wicken Walls'. A faint path leads away through the rushes, paralleling the stream, but keeping to higher ground. As you approach a wall across your line of march, you'll spot a stile below you, in a pronounced hollow-way. You can drop down to this stile, or continue ahead and so locate another stile in the same wall, but at a higher level. Either stile will do, and, as this is access land it doesn't matter if you stray off the right of way. The two paths join about 100 yards/metres beyond the wall, with the lower path climbing to meet the upper. Both then carry on alongside a fence, making for Wicken Walls Farm, which can be seen ahead.

The path keeps to the right of the farm and carries straight on, alongside a wall to a stile. Cross an open area and then descend the steep and rough zig-zags to the stream, where there is a crossing of paths and a footbridge. Go over the footbridge and steeply up, on a narrow slippery path to an awkward stile. Here bear right, still climbing until the path runs alongside a wall. Go through another stile, with Axe Edge Green Farm to your left, then straight on across the middle of a couple of fields to a stile leading out onto the driveway to the farm. Go right here.

Go along the lane for less than 100 yards/metres and then go left, over a stile and up a steep grassy slope. *At the top of the slope turn and look back*

Axe Edge Green

to admire the view which stretches down the Dane valley to Bosley Minn. Pass through a number of stiles in quick succession and so emerge onto the road.

Go left and up the hill to Back of the Cross, where the view suddenly widens appreciably. *You can see over Flash to the Dovedale and Manifold hills, with High Wheeldon being particularly prominent. The Roaches can be seen and of course there's the view back down the Dane valley to Bosley Minn and beyond.* The lane now drops down to Flash and the front door of the New Inn. Flash Bar and the bus stops lie about $^1/_3$ mile/½ km further on.

The New Inn (Flash) 1516 ft/462 metres
Telephone 01298 22941. No website

The New Inn at Flash lays claim to being the highest village pub in the UK. Apparently there was some dispute about this, with Wanlockhead in southern Scotland also laying claim to the same title. Flash won. However, there is some dispute whether the New Inn is higher than the Travellers' Rest at Flash Bar, as Volume 7 of *A History of the County of Stafford* states that Flash is 1526 ft/465 metres. There can't be much in it, but the landlady of the New Inn is prepared to concede the point, having secured the other title.

The New Inn, Flash

During the week, the pub normally opens in the evenings only, but by arrangement can open for a party of walkers. Make arrangements in advance by phoning. We were lucky on the day of the recce' because this is just what had happened. The group had been and gone, but a couple of other walkers had spotted the opportunity and stopped to buy drinks, so we did likewise. The pub has an excellent friendly atmosphere and serves a good drop of Storm Brewery ale. No food served – they leave that to the Travellers'. Well worth a visit, but don't ask the landlady whether she likes Carling by the barrel!

Just to the north of the village is Oliver Hill, 1684 ft/513 metres. This is the highest point in Staffordshire. Save it until you've finished the walk and had a jar.

Walk 15: Hollingworth Head (The Grouse)

Start and finish	Hayfield car park and bus station) GR. SK035869
The route	Hayfield car park/bus station, Sett Valley Trail, Birch Vale, Lantern Pike, Matley Moor Farm, Hollingworth Head, The Grouse, Burnt Hill, Mill Hill, Ashop Head, Kinder Downfall, Red Brook, Kinder Low, Bowden Bridge, Hayfield
Length	12.4 miles (19.94 km)
Ascent	2747 feet (845 metres)
Time	Allow 6½ to 7½ hours (exclusive of stops)
Map	OS OL1 (Dark Peak)

By bus. There's a daily bus service from Buxton, Hayfield and Glossop to The Grouse. There are frequent buses to Hayfield from Stockport and New Mills, plus those from Glossop and Buxton

By train. Nearest station, New Mills Central, but the Glossop and Buxton buses serve their respective stations

By car. Hayfield car park is on the north side of the A6015, just a few yards west of its junction with the A624 (Glossop-Buxton road). The Grouse is on the A624 at Hollingworth Head, mid way between Glossop and Hayfield. There's parking at the pub with permission from the landlord or there's a large lay-by just the Glossop side of the Grouse.

The Walk

If you do this as a complete circuit it is almost the longest walk in the book and it has the most climbing. It certainly gets higher than any other walk in the

book and comes within 11 feet/3.35 metres of the highest point in the Peak District. However, you potentially get three walks for the price of one here, because not only could you do the whole circuit, but you could do the Hayfield to The Grouse bit as one walk (and catch the bus back), or do The Grouse to Hayfield section on its own, by catching the bus up the hill from Hayfield. I have to confess that this is the way it was recce'd.

Hayfield to Birch Vale

Hayfield car park and bus station is on the site of the former railway station and is the start of the Sett Valley Trail. The Trail follows the route of the erstwhile Hayfield branch railway, which opened in 1868 and closed in 1970. Its closure was a tragic loss as it was one of the main access routes to the Peak District from Manchester and played its part in the well-known 'Mass Trespass' in 1932. The closure seems to have had more to do with local politics than the infamous Dr Beeching. The route was purchased by Derbyshire County Council in 1973 and was converted into a multi-user trail over the next few years.

From the car park/bus station, stroll easily along the Trail for about a mile/1½ km, until you reach the Birch Vale-Thornsett road. Here you turn right and join the route of Walk 12. **Use the instructions in Walk 12 covering the section 'Birch Vale to Matleymoor Farm'.**

Matleymoor Farm to The Grouse

At the T-junction at Matleymoor Farm go right, along a track for about 150 yards/metres to a signpost indicating a path to the left. Initially this runs in a walled and fenced green lane, but soon reaches a stile out onto open hillside. A myriad of paths run up and over the moor, always keeping the wall to the right. As you climb, the view to the right becomes increasingly good, taking in Kinder and its satellites, plus South Head and Mt. Famine. At the next gate and stile you re-enter a walled, fenced lane, alongside a plantation. The path bears right and joins the rough track coming down from Knarrs Farm. Continue down this track, with a view to the right showing the route of the rest of the walk up Burnt Hill and Kinder, but with no pub in view at all. The track now drops down towards Monks Road, with an extensive view over Glossop towards Black Hill and Alphin Pike. At Monks Road, turn right and follow the road to its junction with the A624 at Hollingworth Head. Here you turn left for The Grouse or go straight on if you are not calling at the pub. The pub lies 300 yards/276 metres down the road. There's no footway and precious little verge so take great care and remember that, if you are doing the full circuit, you've got to retrace your steps to the junction.

Walk 15

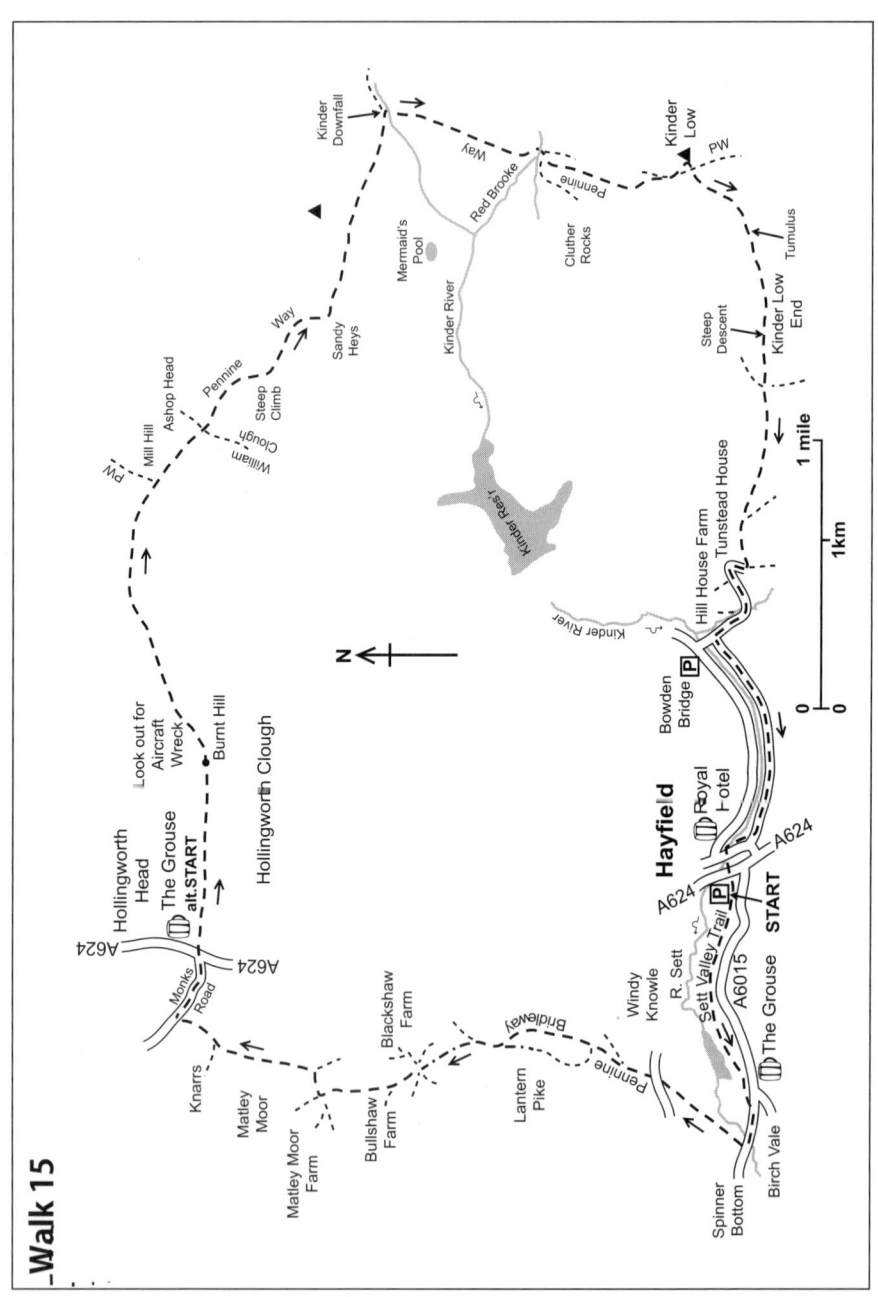

The Grouse 1058 ft/322 metres.
Telephone 01457 852603. www.grouseinnglossop.co.uk

The Grouse Inn stands almost at the top of the road from Hayfield to Glossop. This is an ancient route, turnpiked in the late 18th century, so there may well have been a pub here even then. The present building is certainly recorded in 1820 when it was a farm. However, it may well also have served as a pub and certainly after it was granted a licence in 1861, it functioned as both farm and pub for a long time.

Opening times
Monday to Thursday: 1200 to 1800; Friday to Sunday: 1200 to 2300. Food is served daily and the pub boasts real ales from Thwaites, plus guest beers.

The Grouse, Hollingworth Head

The Grouse to Ashop Head

From The Grouse, turn left and go up the A624 to the road junction at Hollingworth Head, taking great care as you do so. At the T-junction with Monks Road, there's a stile on the left leading onto access land. Go over the stile, which is signed as a concessionary path and follow a good stony path up beside the wall. *There's a grand view to the north over Glossop and beyond to Alphin Pike.* As you climb Burnt Hill the view gets better and better, especially to the south and looking back to Lantern Pike. *To your right, the big, whale-backed lump in the near distance is The Knott, which looks higher than anything else, but there's just a glimpse of Kinder beyond it.* Ahead, the land rises gently and the climb is easy.

At a gate you reach National Trust land and the character of the path changes. There's no accompanying wall now, just a narrow path through the heather. This soon widens out to become a broad path through the peat. No chance of going wrong here, as it is a well-blazed route. *To your left you'll spot the trig point on Harry Hut, but there's no obvious way to get to it other than tramping across pathless heather, so carry on, upwards.* The path runs in a stony slot then reaches the top of Burnt Hill where the gradient eases. *Again you've got an extensive view to Bleaklow and Holme Moss in the north, to Kinder and the hills around Chinley on your right. It's also worth looking back to see the route of this circular walk over Lantern Pike and Matley Moor.* From here on the path is paved with large stone slabs. These have the merit of reducing the erosion on the peat moorland, but in icy conditions they can be very slippery. This is particularly the case on any descent and there's just a short section of this after the top of Burnt Hill. Other than that, the slabs make an excellent firm path and one that's easily followed.

In a short distance, you'll spot some silver grey wreckage on your left. *Closer inspection reveals it to be bits and pieces of an aircraft, including an engine. The aircraft was a B24J Liberator en route from Burtonwood to Hardwick, which crashed on 11ᵗʰ October 1944. Miraculously, the two-man crew escaped, though not uninjured (one had a broken jaw). The remains of the aircraft were subsequently burned and most of it buried. There are two obvious bits of wreckage close together and as you climb further you will probably spot more.*

Where the paved path bears right, a narrow trod trails in from the left. *Looking back along this other path, you can see what appears to be more aircraft wreckage.* Still climbing, you soon reach the junction with the Pennine Way on the summit of Mill Hill. This is marked by a large cairn and a small waymark. *The frowning north edge of Kinder looms to the right; Ashop Clough*

Kinder from Mill Hill summit

and the distant Derwent hills lie ahead; Bleaklow and Featherbed Moss to the left. Bear right, along the Pennine Way, making for Kinder. Initially the path is merely a stony track, but it is soon paved again as you descend to Ashop Head, which is marked by a large Peak and Northern guide stoop. If you've had enough, or if you've run out of time, or the weather has turned really nasty, you can turn right here and follow the signed route to Hayfield via William Clough. Initially it's quite rough underfoot and steep, but it is a quick way down and it cuts off a considerable mileage and ascent.

Ashop Head to The Downfall

Gird up your loins. The ascent route looks and is, steep, but it's mercifully short. Follow the Pennine Way up the steep and rocky flank of Kinder. *Part way up, I was surprised to hear the sound of a train horn not once, but twice. Presumably from trains on the Glossop line, but it's amazing how the sound carries, albeit there was a north-westerly wind.* Once on the plateau the path is a broad stony track with stunning views to the right over Kinder Reservoir towards Hayfield. *Looking back you can see Bleaklow and Black Hill and even the hills beyond Saddleworth. Each twist and turn in the path reveals new views and contorted rock formations.* The path closely follows the crags on the right – but not too closely – we don't want to call out the Mountain Rescue.

The path makes a significant swing to the left as you approach the great cleft that contains Kinder Downfall. *Mermaid's Pool can be seen below, but the legends of its depth have been greatly exaggerated.* The path passes through a fence at a kissing gate. *You may have spotted a fence away to your left. The installation of fencing on Kinder Scout has not been without controversy, but it is part of a major effort to control grazing and restore the heather moorland. When the walk was recce'd, there was the constant noise of a helicopter coming and going, bringing in material for the heather restoration.*

Kinder Downfall

Now the path makes its final rocky approach to the Downfall. The cliffs become more and more impressive and the path is forced further and further to the left until the Kinder River is reached, well above the waterfall. *Unless you've ventured to the right and peered over the abyss, you will not have seen the waterfall at all. If you are feeling really brave (or foolhardy), you can scramble down the river to the lip of the fall and gaze over. Best not to try this in icy conditions.*

Cross the river, which is not usually a difficult task as there are plenty of rocks to balance on, and make your way up the other side and onto the Pennine Way again.

From the rocks on the south side you get the best view of the Downfall. In winter it can be a sheet of ice, sometimes hard and thick enough for ice climbing. At other times it can be a mere trickle, or a foaming torrent, but perhaps the most spectacular effect is when there is a stiff wind blowing from the west, funnelling up the valley and blowing most of the water back up the fall to form a rainbow over the moor. The effect is beautiful.

What is the meaning of Kinder Scout? There are various theories but most seem to agree that the name is of Celtic origin. Probably the best suggestion is that the name comes from the Welsh 'Cwm Dwr Scwd', which would translate as the 'valley of the falling water'. In other words the hill gets its name from its most significant feature, which can be seen from miles down the valley at New Mills.

On to Kinder Low

Leave the Downfall with regret and carry on along the Pennine Way, which still hugs the western edge. About 15 minutes after leaving the Downfall, you'll encounter another stream. This is Red Brook. The path swings into the clough to cross the stream and on the far side splits into two main routes. The Pennine Way, and the route of this walk, takes the higher path, but it is possible to cut off some of the distance and ascent of this walk by taking the lower route round through Cluther Rocks to rejoin the main route at the bottom of Kinder Low End.

Continuing along the Pennine Way, you can't go far wrong, even in mist, as it's a broad stony path with steep ground to the right and usually good views on that side too. Only at one point does this change. Here the path bears left along a cairned route onto the summit of Kinder Low. A trig point perched on top of a rock marks the summit. There's also a large cairn. *At 2077 feet/633 metres, the trig point is only 11 feet/3 metres lower than the true summit of Kinder and it is a far better summit both in terms of views and structure. From here you have views in all directions, with only the north-east being disappointing.*

Make your way from the trig point to the large cairn and there pick up the path again. Follow the path, which soon becomes paved with big stone slabs. Where the path forks, keep right, making for Kinder Low End. This path is also paved. You soon come to a fenced off mound, almost at Kinder Low End. *This is Kinderlow Barrow. Unfortunately all of the information boards relating to it are now minus any information at all. The barrow is of a type known as a 'bowl barrow'. This style of burial mound was in use from 2400-1500BC, covering the late Neolithic to late Bronze Age periods. In the late 1990s it was becoming apparent that the monument was suffering erosion because it lay*

Kinder Low: The highest point in the book

on the route of a popular footpath. *To make matters worse, stone from the barrow had been used to construct a cairn alongside the path. The decision was taken to fence off the barrow, re-route the path to the south of the monument, remove the cairn and restore the mound. This was done in 2003, when the flagged path was constructed and the material from the building of the path used in the repair of the burial mound.*

Down to Hayfield

The flagged path ends just beyond the barrow, but continue ahead, through a cluster of rocks, beginning the descent towards Hayfield. *To the left, you can see the Edale-Hayfield 'road' below. It will readily be apparent that the descent to Hayfield is going to be steep and so it proves.* You come to another cluster of rocks and reach the real end of Kinder Low. The ground falls away precipitously and the path wriggles its way down a series of stone steps. These could be very treacherous in icy or wet conditions, but at least they are gritstone and so don't get polished like their limestone equivalents. Descend with care and at the bottom go through the gate on the left. *(This is the point where the lower path from Red Brook rejoins the main route of the walk.)* Bear right, to another gate with a National Trust sign. In this field bear left to a gateway and then follow a broad green path down through a series of fields and gates, making for Tunstead House, which can be seen below. *Look back occasionally to Kinder Scout. At one point you are looking straight up at the Downfall and very impressive it looks too.*

Just before Tunstead House you enter a walled green lane. Skirt round the left of the house and then follow the footpath sign down the driveway to the right. The driveway dips into Tunstead Clough, crosses the stream and turns left. Carry on down to a crossroads and go straight on (not up to Hill House), crossing the River Sett as you do so.

Stroll alongside the brook until the road bends left. *There's a lovely little packhorse bridge just to your right, at the confluence of the Kinder River and the River Sett, which cries out for a photograph.*

About 150 yards/metres further on, you come to Bowden Bridge. *Just over the bridge is Bowden Bridge car park, sited in an old quarry. It was from this spot in 1932 that the Mass Trespass began; one of the legendary events leading*

Kinderlow End from Tunstead House

up to the establishment of National Parks in Britain. There's a plaque commemorating the event on the quarry wall and just in front of it, there's an inscribed memorial seat. Back on the south side of the river follow the path downstream, soon meeting up with the Pennine Bridleway coming in from the left. Shortly afterwards the path becomes a metalled lane and rises away from the river. Carry on along the lane (Valley Road) until you reach the main road through Hayfield village. Turn right here and go down Church Street. *Just past The George Hotel on the left, there's a gap between the properties. There used to be a level crossing here for the railway used in the construction of the Kinder reservoir in the early part of the 20th century. There are some fascinating photographs of this line on the village website.* Continue down to

*Mass Trespass plaque,
Bowden Bridge Quarry*

the church and there turn left, following the Pennine Bridleway signs. Where you come up against the Hayfield by-pass (A624) you have the choice of either using the Pegasus crossing (for the bridleway) or the underpass just to the left. Either way, you'll end up back at the former railway station, with its car park, bus station, information centre and toilets.

Walk 16: Holme (The Fleece)

Start and finish	Holme (The Fleece) GR. SE107058
The route	Holme, Rake Dike, Ramsden Dam, Ramsden Clough, Ramsden Rocks quarry, Ruddle Clough, Snailsden Moor, Snailsden Reservoir, Linshaws Rd, White Gate Rd, Ramsden Rd, Ramsden Dam, Rake Dike, Holme
Length	5.83 miles (9.4 km)
Ascent	1342 feet (409 metres)
Time	Allow 3-3½ hours (exclusive of stops)
Map	OS OL1 (Dark Peak)

Getting there:

By bus. Frequent buses to Holme from Huddersfield and Holmfirth. Seasonal weekend service from Glossop over Holme Moss

By train. Holme never had a railway. The nearest station is Brockholes on the Penistone-Huddersfield line, but Huddersfield station would be a better bet as it's served by a much greater variety of routes and is handy for the connecting bus services.

By car. Holme village is on the A6024 Holme Moss Road from Huddersfield over to Glossop. There is a small car park in the village just east of the pub.

The Walk

Holme to Snailsden Moor

For a description of this part of this walk, **see Walk 2.**

Snailsden Moor to Holme

At the junction of paths on Snailsden Moor, go left. Follow the good track down towards the western end of Snailsden Reservoir, passing over the inlet streams that rise on Cooks Study Moss. *Snailsden reservoir was built by the Dewsbury and Heckmondwike Water Board in 1899, along with Harden and Winscar reservoirs.* The track then goes up Cook Study Hill and bears right through the old quarries to emerge onto Linshaws Road. *The road forms the boundary between West and South Yorkshire. Of course, true Yorkshire folk wouldn't recognise this boundary as to them it would all be the West Riding.*

Turn left along the lane and enjoy an easy, gentle stroll for about ¾ mile/1.2 km, with occasional views eastwards through gaps in the trees. *At the (unmarked) county boundary, the road name changes to White Gate Road, but again, you'd not know it.* At the cross roads, go left, onto a rough walled lane, known as Ramsden Road. *This is still officially a public road and it does see some traffic, though it's main users are farmers and the 'off-roaders'.* There are some deep ruts on this first stretch, but they are easily avoided. *The views eastwards down the Holme valley are magnificent and stretch well over the Vale of York. When the walk was recce'd it was a bright cold day and the plumes of steam from the various power stations could clearly be seen. Beyond them you could make out distant hills, presumably the Yorkshire Wolds. Emley*

View down Ramsden Clough

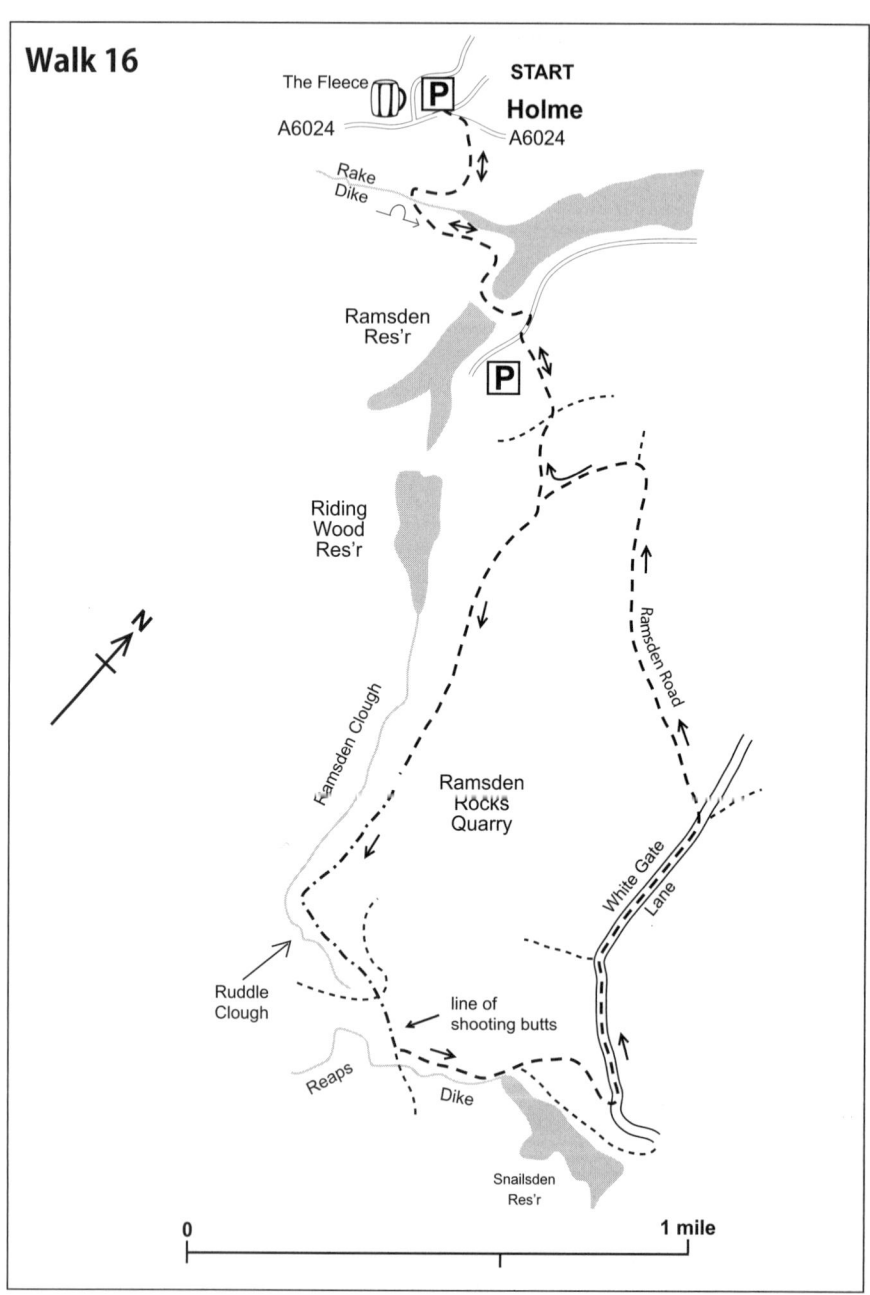

Walk 16

The Fleece
A6024

START
Holme
A6024

Rake Dike

Ramsden Res'r

Riding Wood Res'r

Ramsden Clough

Ramsden Road

Ramsden Rocks Quarry

White Gate Lane

Ruddle Clough

line of shooting butts

Reaps Dike

Snailsden Res'r

N

0   1 mile

Riding Wood Reservoir

Moor mast was prominent of course. You can also see right across the Holme Valley to where the A635 comes sweeping down the hillside from Saddleworth Moor, backed by the prominent top of West Nab.

The lane soon reaches the lip of the upper Holme valley and swings sharp left. *The reservoir that you can see straight ahead is Digley and the small village is Holme, your destination.* The lane descends quite steeply. *Here the erosion caused by a combination of water and motor vehicles has done its worst. There are huge gouges down the middle of the track, making it virtually impassable except for the most dedicated of off-road enthusiasts.* Walkers can descend in relative ease on the right hand side. At the T-junction you rejoin your outward route. Turn right here and continue down the steep, eroded track, over the tram rail cattle grid to the point where the track takes a decisive swing to the left. Go straight on here, following the way-marks, through the posts, down a grassy slope and then right, through a gateway, to pick up another track. Go left and down to the car park, picnic site and road. A quick right and left takes you down to the path across Ramsden Dam.

From the dam, follow the path round and across Rake Dike bridge and up through the fields to the road alongside Underhill. You shouldn't need any further description to get you back to The Fleece, unless you've got an exceedingly bad memory.

The Fleece 990 ft/302 metres
For details of The Fleece **see Walk 2.**

Walk 17: Hurdlow
(Royal Oak and Bull i't'Thorn)

Start and finish	Hurdlow station car park GR. SK126660
The route	Hurdlow (Royal Oak), High Peak Trail, Moscar Farm, The Rake, Monyash, Dalehouse Farm, Blackwell Lane, Hutmoor Butts, Bull i't' Thorn, Hurdlow (Royal Oak)
Length	5.91 miles (9.51 km)
Ascent	602 feet (185 metres)
Time	Allow 2¾ to 3¼ hours (exclusive of stops)
Map	OS OL24 (White Peak)

Getting there
By bus. There's a daily bus service between Buxton and Ashbourne, calling at the Bull i't'Thorn.
By train. Nearest station, Buxton. Alas, train services to Hurdlow station ceased in the 1950s and the line finally closed in 1967.
By car. A515 from Buxton or Ashbourne to Monyash crossroads, then take the road signed to Crowdecote and Longnor. Hurdlow car park (pay and display) is on the left after about ¼ mile.

The Walk

Hurdlow to Parsley Hay (almost)
From Hurdlow station car park, walk down the High Peak Trail towards Hartington. *The High Peak Trail uses the trackbed of a very early railway, the Cromford and High Peak. This railway was conceived in the closing years of*

the canal age and was laid out in canal fashion, with long level sections interspersed by steep inclines in place of flights of locks. It ran from Whaley Bridge, on the Peak Forest Canal, to High Peak Junction, on the Cromford Canal. At its opening in 1830/31 it was the first trans-Pennine railway. In the last decade of the 19th century, the section between Hurdlow and Parsley Hay was rebuilt by the London and North Western Railway as part of a new line between Buxton and Ashbourne. In this guise it lasted until 1967. In the course of the rebuilding the line was widened from single to double track and curves were eased. You'll see some examples of this later in the walk.

The car park stretches a considerable way along the old station site, but a footpath/cycle route keeps first to the right and then the left of the car park access. *In so doing, it is following the alignment of the original Cromford and High Peak line. At the end of the car park the Trail crosses a high arched bridge over the Pilsbury road. You'll notice to your right that the boundary wall of the railway land curves away and then returns towards the bridge. This again is the former C&HP alignment.* This is easy walking on a good firm track. *Indeed the only potential difficulty comes from cyclists many of whom haven't*

Old Cromford and High Peak alignment, Cotesfield

149

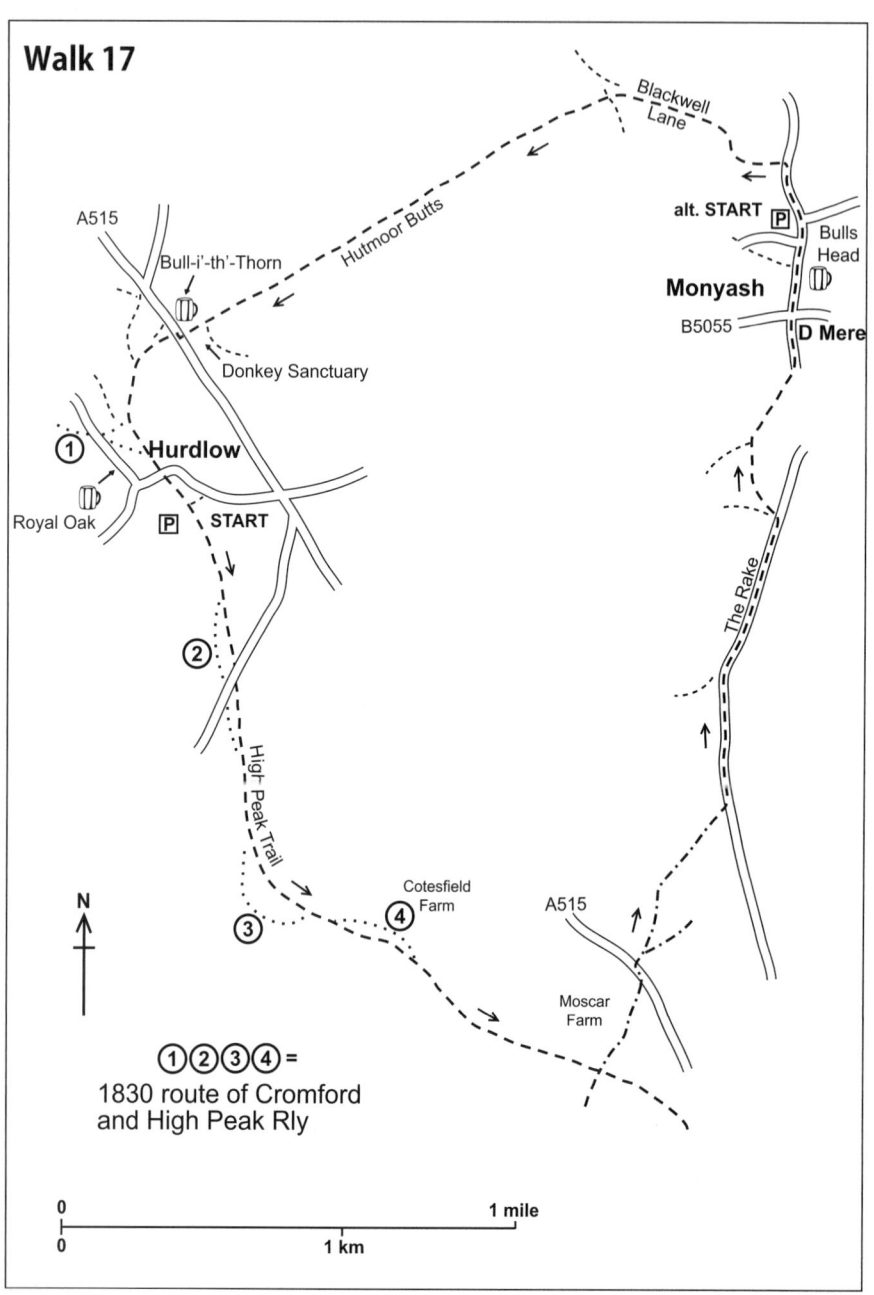

Walk 17

Blackwell Lane

A515

Bull-i'-th'-Thorn

Hutmoor Butts

alt. START [P]

Bulls Head

Monyash

B5055

D Mere

Donkey Sanctuary

① **Hurdlow**

Royal Oak [P] **START**

②

The Rake

High Peak Trail

Cotesfield Farm

A515

③ ④

N

Moscar Farm

①②③④ =
1830 route of Cromford and High Peak Rly

0   1 mile

0   1 km

come across the concept of giving 'early warning of approach' and some of whom seem to regard the Trail as a heaven sent opportunity to try and snatch the world speed record for someone on a pedal cycle. *This line was built as near as possible on the top of the limestone plateau, which is OK for viewing the scenery, but useless for attracting passengers. Only at Tissington was the station close to the place it purported to serve. Some stations, like Hurdlow and Parsley Hay were basically in the middle of nowhere. Looking back from a point just beyond the Pilsbury bridge you can see Cronkston Grange and behind it, Cronkston Low, one of the many tumuli in this area.*

After a pleasant ½ mile/800 metre stroll, the Trail bears left on a gentle curve and enters a cutting. *To the right, the boundary wall continues straight ahead, marking the 1830 alignment.* You pass under a substantial bridge. *It was constructed to allow Cotesfield Farm access to land on the far side of the 'new' railway, but there's no road over this bridge.* As you come out of the cutting, look back and to your right to see the old alignment rejoining. *Here the old route is still in use as a farm access, complete with boundary walls. What is interesting is the difference in levels between the old alignment and the 1890s version and one wonders how the builders of the newer line managed to keep traffic running on the old route, whilst the new route was taking shape.* A short way further on and the old alignment veers off to the left. *It can be discerned quite easily as a grassy embankment separated from the Trail by a narrow field. Take time to gaze around whenever the Trail comes out of a cutting, because the view is a wide one on these occasions. Cotesfield Farm can be seen to the left in its clump of trees. Now the old 1830 railway alignment trails in on the left and at the same level as the 'new' route.*

Parsley Hay is in view ahead. *This isolated station marked the point where the old Cromford and High Peak line diverged from the 1890s Buxton-Ashbourne line. The course of the latter can be seen curving away through a deep cutting. Parsley Hay is now rather busier than it was in railway days as there's a cycle hire centre and car park there and it's possible to get refreshments.*

Parsley Hay is not your objective however. Keep a sharp lookout for a footpath sign on the left. Here you leave the Trail. *If you want to get refreshments at Parsley Hay, carry on to the former station but you'll have to return to this spot.*

Parsley Hay to Monyash

Go over the stile and up the field with the wall on your left, making for Moscar Farm. *As you near the farm, pause for a look back at the extensive view, which stretches over to the gritstone moors beyond Sheen, with Sheen Hill being very prominent, and also the limestone hills near Wetton.* As you near the farm, bear right, skirting to the right of the buildings. Go over a stile and across the farm access, still keeping the buildings and silo to your left. Go round the back of the barns, turning right just before the gate and trough and following the wall up to a stile onto the A515.

Cross the main road and go left. *You now have a view clear across the White Peak to the East Moors, Longstone Edge and Wardlow Hay Cop in one direction and to the gritstone moors beyond the Manifold looking the other way.* There's a stile with two direction arrows on your right. Go into the field and bear left, making for a stile well down the left hand wall, by the second tree. There's no obvious path. Bear right in this next field to another stile, then bear left to locate a further stile. From here the way through the next couple of fields is fairly obvious, with the stiles being in view. The final stile drops you into an overgrown area through which the path wriggles to reach the road. Here go left. *There's quite a surprising view from here looking north to what seem to be the high moors beyond the Hope and Derwent valleys. Chelmorton Low and Flagg are certainly in view and looking east you can see Over Haddon and Manners Wood at the back of Bakewell.*

Go down the road, which is known as The Rake. *There's a curious walled circular pond on the left. Four field walls join onto the circle, but only one field has a gate in the encircling wall.* Carry on down the lane passing underneath a power line. As you approach the next power line there's a gate on the left and beyond it two more gates, both with way-marks. The gate nearest the road should be signed, but the footpath sign was lying in the grass when the walk was recce'd. There is a wooden sign proclaiming that the path is known as Barrowstones Lane. Go through the first gate and at the next two gates, go through the one on the right. There's no obvious path in this field, so head to the right of the electricity pole and then you should spot a stile in the corner of the field. Monyash church is now in view, which is a comforting thought that you can't be far from civilisation.

Once over the stile, go right, into a narrow walled lane. Follow this lane, which is heavily overgrown in places though still passable, until it ceases at a gate and stile. Go down the next field to a stile and then between the houses to emerge on the road just opposite Monyash Mere. Turn left and stroll into the centre of the village, where there's a café and of course The Bull's Head, which features in the *Best Pub Walks in the White Peak* book.

Monyash to the Bull i't'Thorn

Leave Monyash by the Flagg road, i.e. Chapel Street, passing the small car park on your left and the Methodist chapel on your right. Ignore the road leading to Sheldon and carry on along the Flagg road, passing the Pinfold on your left.

Monyash Mere

At Dalehouse Farm, a long line of buildings stretching away from the Flagg road, turn left onto Blackwell Lane. This is a grand walled green lane, easy walking and no chance of going astray – that is until you come to a major junction of lanes with little or no signing. Your route is to the left of the thorn tree, then straight ahead; the continuation of the route you have been on. A further easy 1¼ miles/2km follows, steadily rising on an easy gradient on an almost dead straight walled lane known at Hutmoor Butts. The Bull i't'Thorn can soon be seen ahead, but before you get to it, there's Newton Farm on your left and here you'll probably do a double take as you spot donkeys grazing in the fields. *This is the Donkey sanctuary, so don't be alarmed. The donkeys are all sorts of colours and shapes. At the time of the recce' one of them looked like an ice age version with an incredibly thick woolly coat.*

Just past Newton Farm you reach the A515 again, with the pub just to your right.

The Bull i't'Thorn 1171 ft/357 metres
Telephone 01298 83348. www.bulliththorn.com

The Bull I't'Thorn stands alongside the A515 road. A pub was recorded on this site in 1472, when it was known as The Bull. At this time, the road in use was presumably the one left by the Romans 1000 years earlier (and it remained in use until turnpiked in the 18th century). The pub name changed to Hurdlow House in the 1650s and it is referred to as being near the Hurdlow Thorn. The current unusual name seems to have come about through a combination of the earliest version with the later place name.

The Bulli't'Thorn

The pub's position reflects the fact that this road was the main Manchester-Derby route during the 18th and 19th centuries. During this period the pub was a significant coaching inn. Of course the A515 is still a busy road today and the pub still offers a warm welcome to travellers. The pub offers the usual range of Robinson's Ales, plus guest ales and continental lagers. Bar snacks and lunches are served daily.

On to Hurdlow

Almost opposite the pub there's a footpath sign and a stile. The path goes straight down the field to another stile with another footpath sign. *The High Peak Trail can be seen ahead, and beyond it what appears to be a walled lane up which goes a power line. In fact this is the old C&HP alignment again and is the course of the former Hurdlow incline. This was the first of the inclines to be superseded, when an easier graded alternative was built in 1869. At the top of the incline you can make out the track of the old railway running away to the right. This was the summit level of the line and it held this height all the way round Buxton and right to the head of the Goyt valley and the top of Bunsall incline.* The path now bears left over rough grassland, but it is obvious and easy walking. At the High Peak Trail there's a bridge under the former railway and two pedestrian gates. The left hand gate will take you up onto the Trail where you turn left to reach the former station and car park. The right hand gate takes you under the bridge and then on an ill-defined path up to the lane at the point where the former incline crossed the road. There's no stile here, nor is there a footpath sign to assist. The walls alongside the incline and the road are ruinous, so there's no difficulty in getting onto the road. It's a pity the incline is not walkable (Peak Park take note). Turn left along the road and in less than 100 yards/metres you are at the Royal Oak.

The Royal Oak 1126 ft/343 metres
Telephone 01298 83288. www.peakpub.co.uk

The Royal Oak's website states that the pub's "open fires and hidden corners are a welcoming sight for all tired walkers craving a well earned pint", so that alone is a good enough reason to include the pub in this book. Add to that the pub's well-deserved reputation for reasonably priced good food, plenty of it and a range of cask-conditioned ales and you've got a place not to be missed.

Opening times
Monday to Saturday: 1100 to 2300; Sundays: 1100-2330.
(Open for fresh coffee and hearty breakfasts daily from 1000.)
Food is served every day from 1200 until 2100.

The Royal Oak, Hurdlow

Having drunk your fill and eaten one of their famed meals, cross the road and go down the station approach to the car park, noting that, if you have drunk your fill you should get someone else to do the driving – preferably someone who hasn't had any alcohol at all!

Walk 18: Langsett
(Dog and Partridge)

Start and finish	Dog and Partridge Inn. (Langsett) GR. SE 178011
The route	Dog and Partridge, A628(!) Swinden Lane, Mickleden Edge, Cut Gate Head, Outer Edge, Cat Cloughs Head, Near Cat Clough, Upper Hordron, Hordron Road, Fox Clough, A628, Dog and Partridge
Length	9.4 miles (15.13 km)
Ascent	1500 feet (457 metres)
Time	4½ hours (exclusive of stops)
Map	OS OL1 (Dark Peak)

Getting there

By bus. Despite being on one of the busiest roads in the Peak District, the only bus to use the road is National Express's daily service between Sheffield and Liverpool. It doesn't stop at the pub, but it does serve Langsett three times a day. You have to pre-book tickets. Nearest ordinary bus service is the daily Barnsley-Penistone-Langsett route, which stops at The Flouch a mile from the Dog and Partridge.

By train. Nearest station to the Dog and Partridge is Penistone, which has daily trains to Barnsley, Huddersfield and Sheffield.

By car. The Dog and Partridge is on the A628 trunk road just west of The Flouch roundabout. If you can't find this pub, you certainly shouldn't be contemplating this walk! There is car parking at the pub with permission from the landlord, or there's a large lay-by on the opposite side of the road a little further west. Note that, if you use the lay-by you'll have to cross the road twice – and it's three lanes wide.

The walk

Note that this walk can only be done if the access moors are open. Check before you set out! (If the access moors are closed an alternative circular walk goes along Swinden Lane then through Far Swinden plantation, over the A628 to Swinden Walls and on past Reddishaw Knoll to the Transpennine Trail. Follow the trail back to Dunford Bridge and Winscar where you pick up the final section of Walk 2.)

The description of the Dog and Partridge can be found in **Walk 2** of this book. The first part of Walk 18 coincides with the Dog and Partridge to Cut Gate Head section of **Walk 3**.

Cut Gate Head to Dog and Partridge

At the large cairn at the top of the Cut Gate, turn right onto access land and follow the frequently spongy path along the watershed. After an initial slight descent, the path gradually rises and after about 1 mile/1.6 km you reach the trig point on Outer Edge. *The views east and west are extensive and it's interesting to see what well-known features you can pick out from this less usual vantage point.*

From the trig point the path now takes a more northerly course for about 550 yards (½ km), descending again as it does so. The path then tends towards the north-north west, all the time keeping Harden Grough on the right. Where the grough makes a turn for the north you imperceptibly cross the Sheffield/Barnsley boundary. *There's no fine display of civic pride here in the form of large signs saying 'Welcome to Barnsley' or 'You are now leaving Sheffield'.* The path is now running very much north westerly and you have reached Cat Cloughs Head. Here the watershed is all over the place. Find the first northward heading grough and follow it over rough grass and heather until the slope steepens. *You should then see Hordron Clough in front of you, on the far side of which is Upper Hordron. The A628 can be seen beyond, with its steady procession of lorries.*

With any luck, you are now descending Near Cat Clough and in so doing you'll pick up a path alongside a line of grouse butts. This is not an easy path, but at least it's distinct, with the stream to your left. The slope steepens perceptibly as you descend into Hordron Clough and the path twists its way down to the footbridge over the river. *Further to the east this stream is called the Porter or Little Don, but it's not clear what its name is at this point.* Once over the bridge, climb the broad track up to Upper Hordron, which is used by shooting parties. The track skirts round to the right of the buildings and up to join another track where you turn right.

It's easy going now and you have the chance to admire the view down the

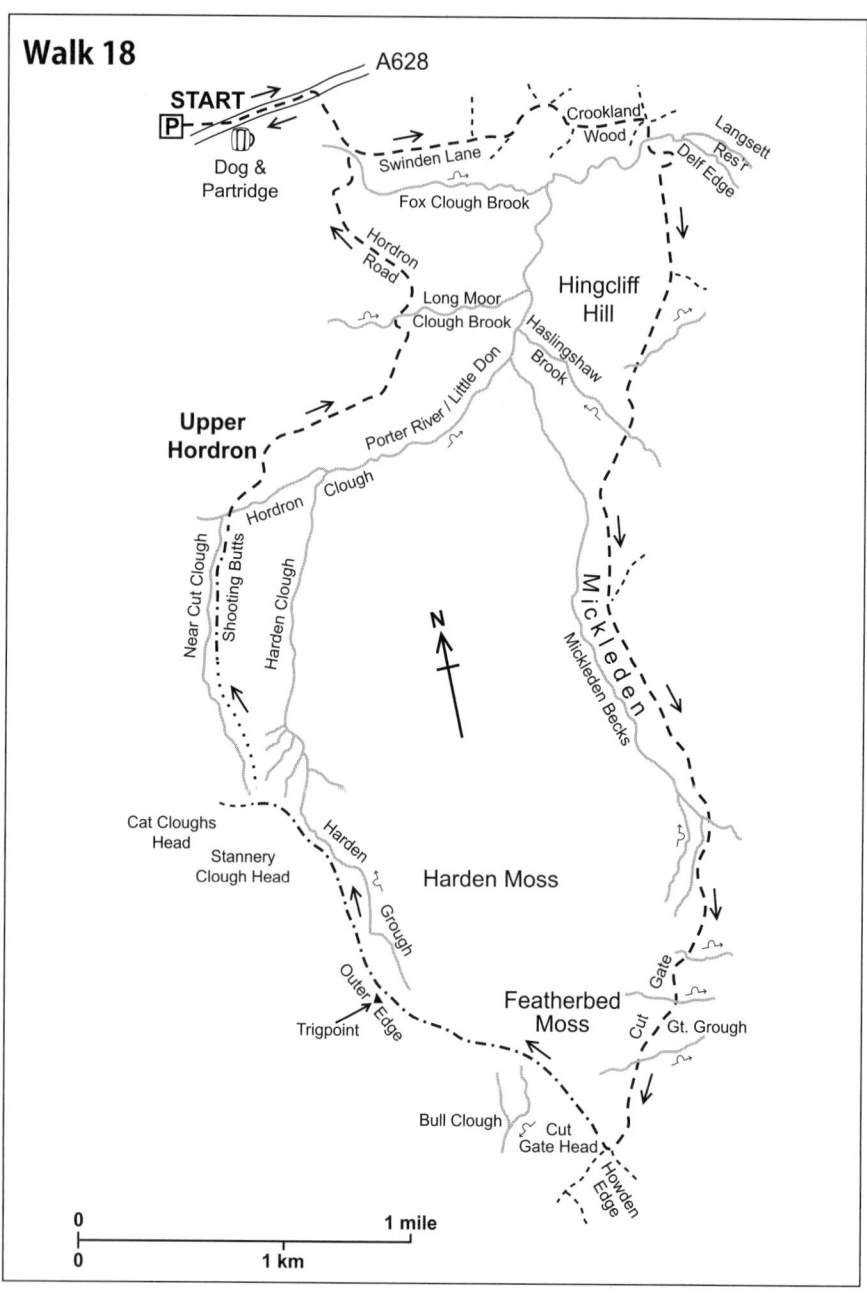

Walk 18

A628

START

Dog & Partridge

Swinden Lane

Fox Clough Brook

Crookland Wood

Langsett Rest

Delf Edge

Hordron Road

Long Moor Clough Brook

Hingcliff Hill

Haslingshaw Brook

Upper Hordron

Porter River / Little Don

Clough

Hordron Clough

Near Cut Clough

Shooting Butts

Harden Clough

Mickleden

Mickleden Becks

N

Cat Cloughs Head

Stannery Clough Head

Harden Grough

Harden Moss

Cut Gate

Gt. Grough

Outer Edge

Trigpoint

Featherbed Moss

Cut

Bull Clough

Cut Gate Head

Howden Edge

0   1 mile

0   1 km

valley towards Langsett and the view back up Harden Clough to the Derwent Moors.

Ignore the track leading off right to Hordron and continue along the Hordron Road, soon swinging left round Little Moor and descending to cross the Longmoor Clough Brook. The track rises sharply on the far side of the clough swinging round another nose of higher land where the Dog and Partridge comes into view. The track then drops again to cross Fox Clough Brook. *These two crossings could be interesting after heavy rain, as neither has a bridge!*

Beyond Fox Clough the track climbs and swings left to join Swinden Lane, which trails in from the right. With any luck, you'll recognise this as your outward route and so you shouldn't need any further details to get you back to the A628 and along to the Dog and Partridge.

Walk 19: Newhaven (Jug and Glass)

Start and finish	Jug and Glass GR. SK156614
Alternative sttart and finish	Friden car park on the High Peak Trail GR. SK172607
The route	Jug and Glass, Hartington station, Tissington Trail, Cardlemere Lane, Green Lane, Pikehall, Long Dale, Friden, High Peak Trail, a different Green Lane, Jug and Glass
Length	9 miles (14.48 km)
Ascent	1121 feet (342 metres)
Time	Allow 4¼-5 hours (exclusive of stops)
Map	OS OL24 (White Peak)

Getting there

By bus. There's a daily bus service between Buxton and Ashbourne calling at the Jug and Glass

By train. Nearest station, Buxton. Hartington lost its passenger services in the 1950s and the line closed in 1967. Friden lost its passenger service in the 1870s (!) and the line closed in 1967

By car. A515 from Buxton and Ashbourne. There's a lay-by just north of the Jug and Glass on the east side of the road. Alternative (free) off-road parking at Friden car park on the High Peak Trail GR SK172607. A515 from Buxton or Ashbourne to Newhaven, then A5012 past Carriages, then left at Y-junction (signed to Friden). Car park is on the right just before the railway bridge.

The Walk

Jug and Glass to Pikehall

From the pub walk up the A515 verge for about 150 yards/metres and then turn left onto a rough green lane. This descends quite sharply and you need to be careful as there is some well polished – and therefore slippery, limestone at the surface. At the Hartington road, go left for about 100 yards/metres to a gate/stile on the right. Go over the stile and follow the wall/fence on the left. *The warning notices and fencing on the right relate to the former quarry, so best not to investigate too much.* Pass through a couple of fields to a gate where apparently there's a concession path off to the left, but this is of no use to you. Your route lies to the right, still following the wall. The path now descends to a stile, with the overgrown quarry workings and tips to your right. The path ahead is obvious, slanting across the small field to a stile. *Unfortunately, when the walk was recce'd there was a large bull in the field and although he was with a number of cows, I decided that discretion was the better part of valour and deviated through the quarry workings to reach Hartington station car park by the 'back door'.*

Assuming the bull is not always there, go across the field and over the stile into an overgrown area, with old workings on your left. The path wriggles through the scrub and high grass – a thoroughly leg wetting experience after rain. Eventually you reach a stile over a wall. A flight of steps then takes you down onto the Tissington Trail, just south of Hartington station. It is worth walking back up the Trail to see the fine job the Peak Park has made of restoring the old signal box. It's just a pity there are no trains to signal nowadays. *By any stretch of the imagination though, this line could never have been a money-spinner. A glance at the map will show how far Hartington station was from the village it purported to serve. Even more optimistic is the station sign now affixed to the signal box, which proclaims that it is the station for Dovedale, Berresford Dale and the Manifold Valley! The line was opened in the final bout of*

Hartington signal box, Tissington Trail

Walk 19

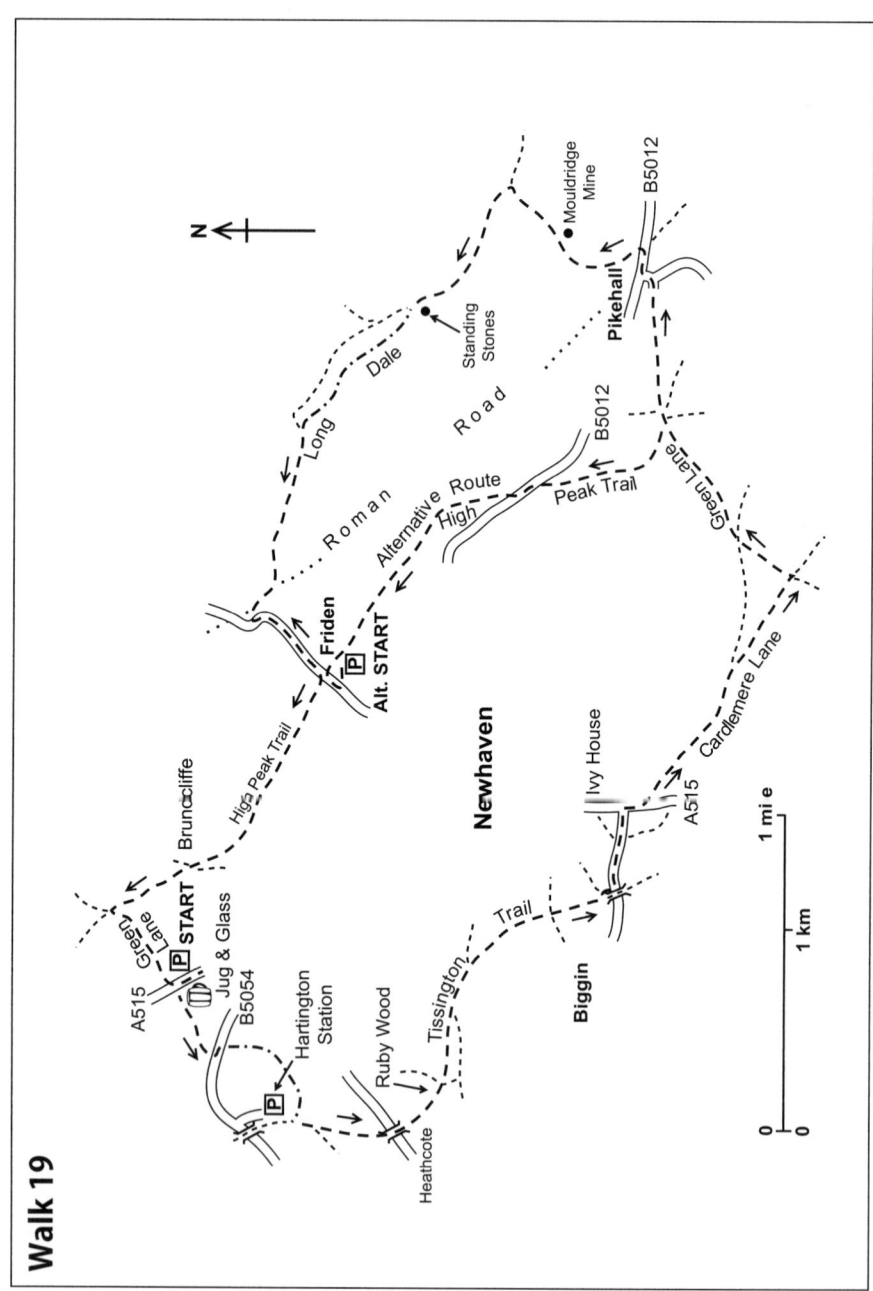

competitive railway construction at the end of the 19th century and for a few years there was even a through coach to London Euston via this route. It says a lot about the lack of traffic that the line was built to accommodate double track, but that only a single track was ever laid. The regular passenger services stopped in the 1950s so you can't blame Beeching for this one. The line finally closed to all traffic in 1967 and was converted into the Tissington Trail in 1971.

Continue down the Trail, passing another former quarry on the left and soon reaching the Ruby Wood, also on the left. *This was laid out to commemorate the 40th anniversary of the designation of the Peak District as a National Park (1951-91).* The view to the right from this point is over Biggin and there's a footpath to the left signed to Newhaven if you've had enough (surely not). Pass under the next bridge, noting the sign on the left hand abutment. *It reads 'Dream of noise and wheels and steam'. Would that it were so, but then you'd probably not be walking here, though given that only a single line was ever laid, there would easily have been room for a footpath. Hmmm, now there's a thought.*

You pass Milepost 3, presumably from a zero point at Parsley Hay where this line left the earlier Cromford and High Peak Railway. Then look out for a signpost on the left indicating cycle route 54. Leave the Trail at this point and drop down the side of the embankment to the Biggin road, just east of the bridge. Turn left. Go up the road on a tarmacked footway to the junction with the A515. The cycleway is signed across the road, then right (along the verge) and then left, up Cardlemere Lane. This is your route.

Cardlemere Lane is a wide walled lane. It isn't surfaced but it is well used by farm vehicles. That being the case it is not a nice green grassy lane. Instead it shows every sign of being well used by the sort of traffic for which it was undoubtedly intended. There are no problems encountered on this stretch and you can bowl along at a steady pace, for about a mile/1.6 km, gradually gaining height. You'll pass a footpath sign on the left directing you across a large field, the other side of which cannot be seen. *At the time of the recce' this field had been ploughed and there was no sign that anyone had ventured across it. In addition, the farmer was busily shooting crows, so it seemed a wise move to stay on Cardlemere Lane!*

As the lane tops the rise you come to a T-junction. The OS map indicates a lane heading north-east towards Pikehall, but doesn't indicate whether or not it is a public right of way. However, at the junction there's a signpost, which points along this lane and simply calls it 'Green Lane'. *It is worth pausing here to have a look round, because the view is surprisingly extensive. You can clearly see the East Moors, whilst Axe Edge is in view to the west. Looking down Green Lane, the belt of trees in the near distance marks the alignment of the Buxton to Derby Roman road.* Turn left here and go down Green Lane. This is much narrower than Cardlemere Lane and sees a lot less use. Stroll easily down the lane, soon reaching a point where two footpaths cross. *Neither is of use to you, but the one on the left is the end of the path across the ploughed field you saw earlier. Here it is also ploughed and here too there's no sign anyone has ventured across.*

Soon you'll see an embankment cutting across the line of the lane. This is the High Peak Trail, the former Cromford and High Peak Railway. The lane rises to meet the railway and crosses it on the level. *You can see tree-crowned Minninglow away to your right. (If you want to cut the walk short you can easily do so at this point by turning left along the Trail and so reaching Friden, there picking up the main route. In doing so you'll miss out on Long Dale, which would be a pity).* Continue along Green Lane, which now descends towards Pikehall. At Pikehall you reach the A5012 Cromford to Newhaven road. *It is one of the few main roads in the Peak District that hasn't got a bus service, so there's no hope of salvation here.*

Pikehall to Friden

Cross the main road and go right, along the verge. You cross the end of a limestone dale on your left and then there's a gate and a path signed to Long Dale. Look across the main road at

this point. *The rough lane on the opposite side is the Buxton to Derby Roman road, still in use here.* Go through two gates and into the dale onto a path by a wall. *The substantial building on your left was probably an inn at one time when the turnpike through Pikehall was part of the main road from Derby to Manchester.*

Leave the A5012 behind and make your way easily down this lovely quiet dale. Keep the wall to your left, ignoring access land signs and gates trying to tempt you away. You soon reach the spoil tips of Mouldridge Mine and on the right is the mine entrance. This is securely gated off. The path picks its way through the

Entrance to Mouldridge Mine

spoil heaps and passes a capped shaft on the left. Continuing down the dale you soon reach the junction with Long Dale. Turn left here, through a gate and make your way up the dale, still with the wall to your left.

Note on the left hand side of the dale a couple of fenced areas containing heather, quite unusual on limestone and clearly this is the reason why they have been fenced. off. A little further on you come to a gate. *On your left here there's a small enclosure with three standing stones. The front one is inscribed with the words, "We meet to create memories and depart to cherish them". Fine sentiments.* Just beyond this point the map shows the footpath bearing right and going up

Stone sculpture, Long Dale

the hillside. You can easily make out the route, but as this is all access land, there seems very little point in climbing out of the dale, just to come back in again a bit further on, so stay in the dale bottom.

About ⅔ mile/1 km further on you come to the end of the access land and there is what passes for a stile, i.e. three planks of wood in the fence. The right of way comes down from the dale top just beyond this stile and there is some indication that you are expected to go up alongside the fence to meet the path and then immediately come down again. It is equally obvious that, having arrived at this point most walkers go over the fence and carry on up the dale.

Having gained the path beyond the access land, continue up the dale with Bolderstone Plantation to your right. Further up the dale, pass through a gate and now there's woodland on both sides, but still a wide-open grassy space between the two. Quite where the path is in this space is a matter for conjecture. The whole width appears to be used, especially by horse riders, for the 'path' is also a bridleway at this point. Keep a lookout for a gateway in the left hand wall, because the route of the path lies through this, then runs parallel with the dale bottom. Having located this gateway, follow the path, which is actually running in a narrow walled lane, though both walls are ruinous. Soon it swings sharply to the left to a gateway and there meets the Roman road. To the left the route of the Roman road can be made out as a trench in the hillside, whilst to the right it forms your route, a walled grassy lane.

Follow the Roman road until you reach a gate at the point where the Youlgreave-Friden road crosses the dale on a substantial stone faced embankment. If you look to the right at this point you can see that the embankment is a newer construction. *The old route of this road came down into the dale bottom and would have met the Roman road more or less where you are standing.*

Go through the gate and then go left, gradually climbing until you meet the road. *It is a pity that the path doesn't follow the boundary wall of the earlier road alignment, as this would obviate the need to walk on the road round a bend where the visibility is not very good.* Take great care. Go up the road and past the cottages, approaching the bridge that carries the High Peak Trail over the road. *Friden brick works can be seen ahead, just beyond the Trail. As you approach the bridge, there's a gate on your right. A narrow gauge railway used to run through this gate en route to various silica sand pits that served the brick works. The railway then went into the road and under the bridge before turning right and into the works.*

There's no access to the trail at the bridge. Go under the bridge and walk past the works entrance, before turning left and going up the ramp leading to Friden car park on the High Peak Trail.

Friden to the Jug and Glass

At the Trail turn left and cross the bridge under which you came a few moments earlier. The Trail now runs alongside the brickworks buildings. *It cannot be said that these are pretty, but to compensate for this, there are two fine information boards and brick murals on the wall, giving details of the brick making process and how it has developed over the years. The two photographs of the railway activity will astonish you as you stand on the Trail today. It is hard to believe that such a hive of industry has passed into oblivion, especially when you read that all the material now required for the works (40,000 tonnes) is brought in by lorry. Friden was the furthest point that 'big' locomotives could venture from the Buxton direction so there was interchange of locos and trains here. South of Friden the C&HP was the preserve of small tank engines.*

Stroll along the Trail which here is almost level. Where the Trail curves to the right, look out for a milepost on the right, an interesting railway survival. Soon you pass Brundcliffe Farm on the right, crossing the farm access as you go. An embankment and cutting follow and then you come to a major crossing of routes. Your route is to the left, signed to the A515. This goes up a narrow walled lane – another Green Lane. *Look in the field on the left hand side to where there is a curious round wall, which probably contains a pond. However, there doesn't appear to be any means of accessing it so its purpose is hard to guess.* Continue up the lane and now the pub comes into view away to your left. Thus you reach the A515. Turn left here to the lay-by and the Jug and Glass. Assuming you are going to the pub, please take care crossing the road. It would be a great shame to lose you having completed the walk and so close to salvation.

The Jug and Glass 1189 ft/362 metres
Telephone 01298 84848. www.jugandglass.biz
The Jug and Glass Inn is a 17th century Inn sited alongside the A515 Ashbourne-Buxton road. It is one of a number of quite isolated pubs along this route and it clearly came into existence primarily to serve travellers rather than locals. It continues to do so to this day and has recently been completely modernised and refurbished. There are usually two real ales on offer, often from local micro breweries.

Opening times
Thursday to Monday: 1200 to 2300; Tuesday and Wednesday: 1800 to 2300. Food is served: 1200 to 2030, Thursday to Monday. Tuesday and Wednesday: 1800 to 2030.

The Jug and Glass

Walk 20: Owler Bar (The Peacock)

Start	Baslow Nether End GR. SK258721
Finish	Owler Bar (The Peacock) GR. SK293780
The route	Baslow, Eaton Hill, Wellington's Monument, Baslow Edge, Curbar Gap, Swine Sty, White Edge, Lady Cross, Barbrook Bridge, Flask Edge trig point, Saltersitch Bridge, Owler Bar
Length	7.7 miles (12.4 km)
Ascent	1328 feet (405 metres)
Time	4 to 4¾ hours (exclusive of stops)
Map	OS OL24 (White Peak)

Getting there

By bus. Daily buses to Owler Bar from Bakewell and Sheffield. Daily buses to Baslow from Bakewell, Buxton, Chesterfield, Matlock and Sheffield

By train. Nearest station, Dore and Totley (Owler Bar and Baslow buses pass station)

By car. Baslow is on the A619 Manchester-Chesterfield road, and on A621 from Sheffield. There's a large pay and display car park at Nether End. There's no public parking at Owler Bar, but you may be able to park at the pub by arrangement with the landlord. The idea of this walk is that you catch the bus from Owler Bar to Baslow, either at the start or end of the walk.

The Walk

Baslow to Curbar Gap

From Nether End car park and bus stops, go across the A619 at the pelican crossing and straight up Eaton Hill. At the T-junction, where Eaton Hill joins Bar Road, go right and carry on up the road until, after the last houses, it deteriorates into a track. Carry on up the track, more steeply now, winding away from the village and up onto Baslow Edge. You soon reach a gate and then you are out onto open moorland, with wide views over to Chatsworth and up the Derwent valley. The track still winds upwards, with long overgrown gritstone quarrying remains to your left and the valley of the Bar Brook to your right.

As the gradient of the track eases, there's a fork. Bar Road continues to the right and if you want to visit Wellington's Monument you should take this route, but note that you'll have to return to this junction eventually. The monument lies only a couple of hundred yards beyond the fork in the tracks. *The monument was erected in 1866 by Dr Lieutenant Colonel E. M. Wrench. It commemorates Wellington's victory at Waterloo and an earlier visit the Duke made to the moor. It was also intended as a counterpoise to the Nelson Monument on Birchens Edge on the opposite side of the Bar Brook valley.*

Wellington Monument

The main track continues on an almost level course, over the moor, making for the Eagle Stone, the 20-foot/6 metre high isolated lump of rock that can be seen ahead. *Legend has it that a man wanting to marry a Baslow girl had first to prove himself by climbing the Eagle Stone. It looks easy from a distance, but looks a good deal less so close up. If you insist on giving it a try, don't blame me for any injuries. Work on the basis that you didn't want to marry a Baslow girl anyway and continue along the path.* The broad path along the top of the moor misses out the drama of the edge itself and it is worth deviating to the left to walk along the rocks. Either way, you'll encounter no difficulties and soon reach the gate that leads down onto the road at Curbar Gap.

It will be a rare day when you find no cars parked here. Frequently they are parked just west of the Gap down the road towards Curbar, completely filling the car park at the Gap itself, plus part way down the road to the east towards the main A621. It's a popular spot. However, most people parking here go up

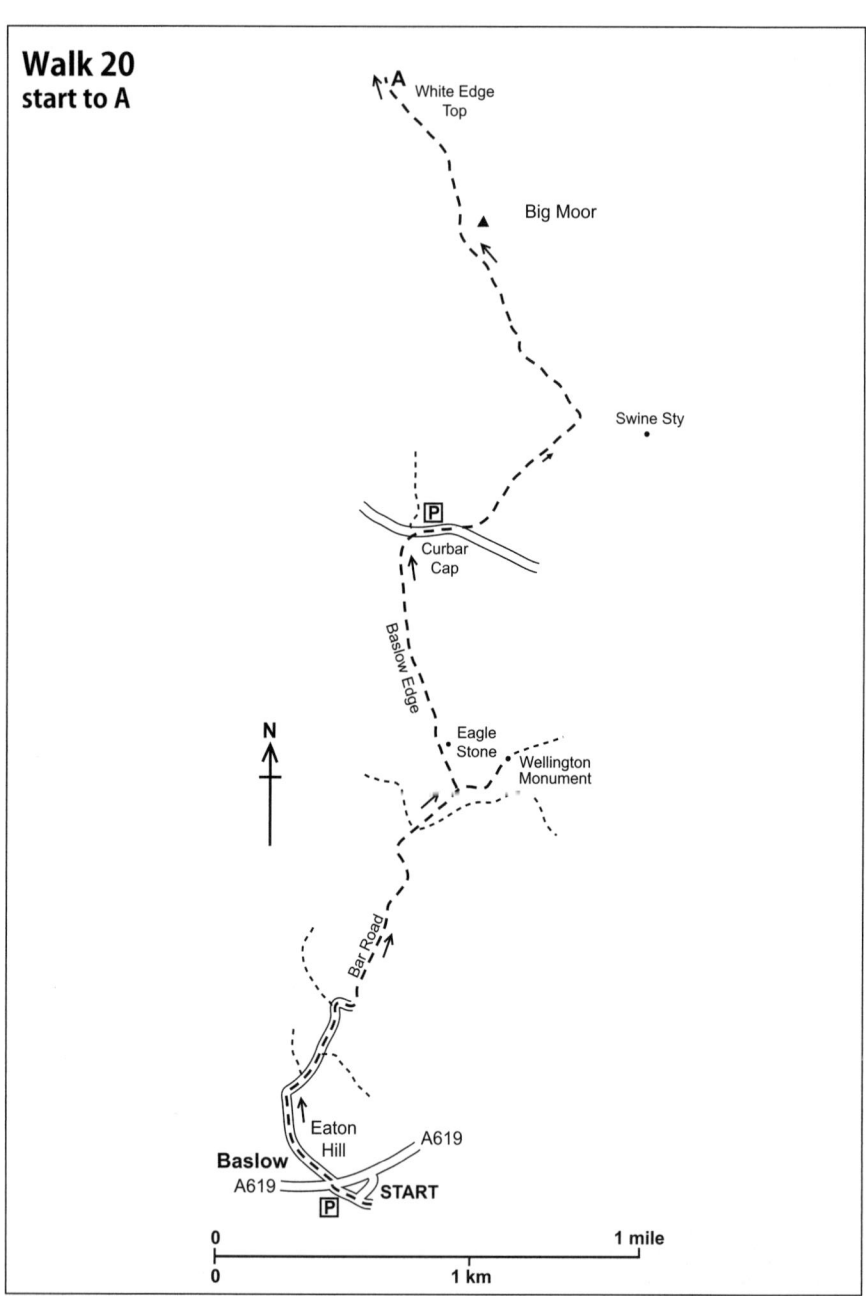

Walk 20
start to A

A
White Edge
Top

Big Moor

Swine Sty

P
Curbar
Cap

Baslow Edge

Eagle
Stone

Wellington
Monument

N

Bar Road

Eaton
Hill

A619

Baslow

A619

P

START

0		1 mile
0	1 km	

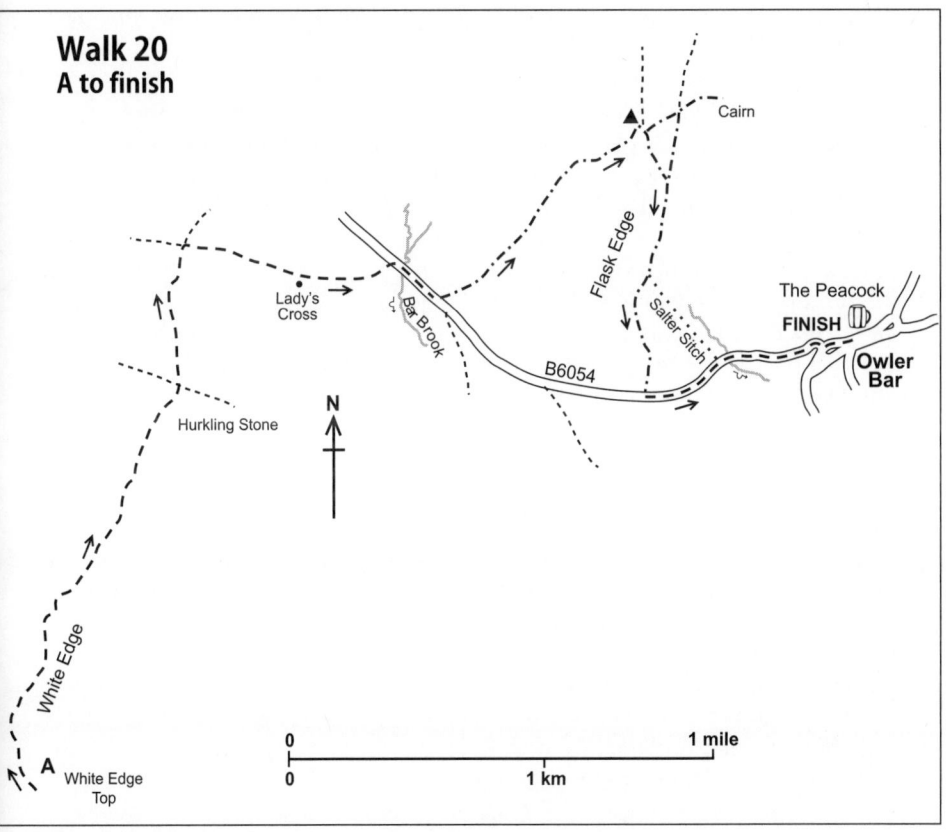

Walk 20
A to finish

Cairn

Flask Edge

Salter Sitch

The Peacock

FINISH

Owler Bar

Lady's Cross

Bar Brook

B6054

N

Hurkling Stone

White Edge

A
White Edge Top

0   1 mile

0   1 km

onto Curbar Edge. Your route is different. Go right at the road and at the vehicle entrance to the car park, go through the gate leading onto the moor. A broad path heads across the moor towards Swine Sty, a cluster of rocks, seen ahead. The path soon dips to cross Sandyford Brook, one of the tributaries of the Bar Brook. This is frequently a muddy experience. Once over the stream the path quickly rises and swings left, skirting Swine Sty Rocks, meeting the path coming up from Clod Hall crossroads and gaining White Edge. On a previous visit we surprised a herd of red deer at this point, so keep a sharp lookout.

What follows is a pleasant stroll along an obvious path with great views on all sides. *White Edge lacks the drama of Curbar and Froggatt edges, but has better views and is a good deal quieter. It is hard to imagine that this moor was once quite heavily populated, but that is the case. There have been numerous Bronze Age settlements found here and they are now well documented.* After around ⅔ mile/1100 metres you reach a trig point. *It's worth pausing here to take in the view. At 1186 ft/365 metres this is not quite the highest point on the edge. That accolade belongs to a cluster of rocks about 760 yards/700 metres further on at 1190 ft/366 metres (old maps put it at 1200 ft).* At that latter point, the path swings towards the north-east. There is an initial descent of a few feet/metres, before the path begins to climb again.

After a mile's tramp you reach a wall. No stile or gate, just a large gap. On the far side of the gap is a signpost. The path to the left would take you to The Grouse, which you can see below. It is not one of the high pubs, missing out by a few feet. Straight on, the path continues towards Longshaw. *There's no direction sign pointing right, though there is a path beside the wall. This wall is a parish boundary and can be followed down to the Hurkling Stone, where three parishes meet. Unless you've a particular urge to see a slab of rock with a wall built onto it, there's no reason to go this way.* Instead, carry straight on along White Edge. The path is well blazed, but can be very muddy. *The views westward are extensive, reaching right up the Hope Valley to Kinder. Mast crowned Sir William Hill is very prominent.* In about 600 yards/550 metres, you'll reach a major crossing of paths. Turn right here and follow the bridleway up and over the moor. The B6054 soon comes into view and the path descends gently towards Barbrook Bridge. *Keep a sharp lookout on the right for the stump of Lady's Cross. It's just off the current line of the path. You'll notice that there are a number of shallow depressions, running down towards the bridge. In all probability these are former packhorse routes. Just past the cross there's also a very deep trench cutting across the line of the path. This may also be a relic of packhorse days. When this walk was recce'd there was a great deal of activity on the moor. Heather was being collected prior to being taken up onto Kinder as part of an attempt to re-vegetate some of the bare peat areas.*

Lady's Cross

There was a broad and extremely muddy track across the moor from Barbrook Bridge as part of this work. Fortunately the path from Lady's Cross wasn't caught up in this activity.

The path joins the road at a stile and gate, just before the bridge. Here you have a choice. The Peacock Inn is about 1.4 miles/2¼km to the right, along the B6054. There is a path (of sorts) on the south side of the road. Without doubt, this is the quickest, easiest and driest route to the pub – but who wants to walk alongside a fast road, when you could be exploring access land? An alternative is to stay on the access land and follow a path south of and roughly parallel with the road, until you emerge onto the road near the gas installation close to Saltersitch Bridge. From then on it's road walking to the pub. This path is so close to the road that you'll wonder why you bothered.

The suggested route of the walk takes you through the gate onto the road and then right, across Barbrook Bridge. *Note the clapper bridge to the right carrying the paralleling footpath.* Cross the road to a small gate leading onto Totley Moss. A distinct narrow path heads north-east across the moor. It is shown on the OS map as a black pecked line, so it's not a right of way. However, as you are in access land, it's OK. The path climbs gently. To the left is a sea of reeds and rushes, that can only mean one thing – bog. *(Having tried to find a way through this area on another occasion I can vouch for the fact that it really isn't worth the effort).* Mercifully, the path avoids most of this morass. There's just about 100 yards/metres of 'damp' ground and then it's firm going again. When the walk was recce'd, I was looking for any routes to the right across the moor. There are various sheep tracks, but none seem to go anywhere in particular, so keep heading gently uphill, until you reach a ruined wall.

Across the moor you'll spot a strange squat tower on a large green mound. This is one of the ventilation shafts of Totley tunnel on the Sheffield-Manchester railway line. It's the only shaft on the moor, because the Duke of Rutland, whose moor it was at the time of the railway's construction, refused to allow any more shafts for fear of disturbing the grouse! You'll often see what looks like smoke or steam issuing from the shaft, but this is not some ghostly steam engine, simply the warmer air from the tunnel rising into the cold air of the moor.

Go right, following the wall. At a large depression, the wall, and its accompanying path, kinks to the left and in another 150 yards/metres you'll spot a trig point on the left. Leave the wall and go left along a narrow path, passing a ruined sheepfold. The trig point stands at 1285 ft/392 metres and is the highest point reached on this walk. As *you reach the trig point a vast view opens up eastwards. Apart from a prominent cairn about 400 yards/370 metres away to the northeast, the ground slopes away before you and Sheffield is spread out like a map. The views stretch beyond the city to the Trent and Don power stations and even beyond that to where you can discern the faint outline of hills both to the north east and due east. It is reckoned that, on a clear day you can see Lincoln Cathedral and the hills beyond York.*

There's a suspicion that the view might be even better from the big cairn, so, in order to test this theory, leave the trig point by one of the many little paths and rejoin the ruined wall. Make your way down hill, across the muddy alignment of the gas pipeline and then up to the cairn. *This must be one of the biggest cairns in the Peak District and it stands at 1252 ft/382 metres. The theory about the view was correct. There's now nothing blocking the view eastwards and Sheffield really is seen in birds-eye fashion, so it's worth the extra walk. You can see the Peacock at Owler Bar too. Unfortunately there's no path direct to the pub from here.*

Return to the pipeline alignment and go left. The first bit is very muddy, but you soon join a good firm track that descends across the moor, skirting to the right of the headwaters of Saltersitch. If you are feeling very adventurous and want to minimise the road walking, keep a sharp look out for a ruined wall on your left; you'll spot a couple of gate posts at least. Where this ends you need to make your way across the pathless moor, braving the tussock grass and 'damp' patches and all the while keeping to the left of the Saltersitch stream. If you achieve this, you should reach the road just east of Saltersitch Bridge and there find a small gate. From there it's only a short stroll of 660 yard/600 metres, along the B6054 to the pub.

Assuming you are not into tussock hopping, bog trotting and blazing trails across access land, carry on along the track, soon reaching a walled enclosure surrounding a gas installation. The track passes to the right of the enclosure to a gate onto the B6054. Cross the road and go left along the verge, following the road for about ⅔ mile/1km to reach the pub.

The Peacock. 1014 ft/309 metres
Telephone 0114 2996219.
www.chefandbrewer.com/pub/peacock-sheffield/s5731/

The Peacock is a former coaching inn, strategically placed at the junction of two important Peak District roads, on what is now a large, elongated roundabout.

There's always a selection of cask ales, including at least three guest ales. Buses to Sheffield stop in front of the pub. Buses to Baslow stop on the opposite side of the roundabout.

The Peacock

Opening times
Monday to Saturday: 1100 to 2300; Sunday: 1200 to 2200.
Food is served Monday to Saturday: 1200 to 2200; Sunday: 1200 to 2100.

Walk 21: Peak Forest (The Devonshire Arms) and Sparrowpit (The Wanted Inn)

Start and finish	Castleton bus station GR. SK151830
The route	Castleton bus station, Cave Dale, Old Dam, Peak Forest (The Devonshire), Old Dam, Perry Dale, Sparrowpit (Wanted Inn), Rushup Farm, Rushup Hall, Rushup Edge, Lord's Seat, Mam Tor slip, Odin Mine, Castleton bus station
Length	9.75miles (16 km)
Ascent	1820 feet (555 metres)
Time	Allow 4¾ to 5¾ hours (exclusive of stops)
Map	OS OL1 (Dark Peak) and OS OL24 (White Peak)

Getting there

By bus. Good daily bus service to Castleton from Sheffield. Seasonal weekend services from Glossop. Sparrowpit and Peak Forest only have a very limited daily service from Buxton and Whaley Bridge.

By train. Nearest station, Hope on the Sheffield-Manchester line, which has daily services. Hope station to Castleton is about 2¼ miles/3.62 km, but is remarkably flat!

By car. A6187 to Castleton from the east. The car park is pay and display and is on the western side of the village. From the west follow the A6 to Barmoor Clough and then the A623 to Sparrowpit. Castleton is signed (for light traffic only) from Sparrowpit via the Winnatts Pass. Alternatively there is a junction on A6 Chapel by-pass signed to Castleton and Edale (again light traffic only) and there is parking either at Mam Nick car park (pay and display) or (free) roadside parking closer to the Blue John cavern on the walk route. Sparrowpit and Peak Forest are on the A623 Manchester-Chesterfield road. There is very limited roadside parking in either place. Both pubs have car parks and it may be possible to arrange parking there by prior arrangement with the landlord, i.e. if you are intending to eat after your walk.

The walk

Castleton

Castleton is one of the Peak District's busiest villages. It has shops and pubs to meet the demands of most visitors. It is particularly famous for its castle, hence the name, its caverns, of which there are four, and for the Blue John stone, which is found only here. The village's origins go back to Norman times, when it was planned as a market town around the castle and as headquarters for the Peak Forest, which was at that time a Royal hunting forest of considerable extent. Parts of the town ditch still survive from the Norman period. When the place is not heaving with tourists it is well worth an extended stay to drink in the history and charms of the place and to uncover some of its lesser known attributes. I am not singling out any one pub here as to do so would be unfair. Suffice it to say that there are six hostelries in the village. They are – in no particular order;

The Bull's Head in Cross Street, The Castle and The George, both in Castle Street, The Peaks Inn and the Olde Cheshire Cheese, both in How Lane and the Olde Nag's Head in Cross Street.

Castleton to Peak Forest

From the bus station go into the centre of the village and up Castle Street into The Square. Go left at the top of the Square as if you were going along the 'Siggate' and keep a sharp look out for a narrow opening, denoted by a footpath sign indicating the Limestone Way and leading between houses into Cave Dale. The change from village to countryside is abrupt. Here you are in a deep, steep sided limestone dale that used to form the main way into Castleton from the south. *As you progress up the dale you'll notice on your right the walls of Peveril Castle perched on the very edge of the cliffs and dominating the dale below. Near this spot there was a mass gathering of ramblers in 1946 addressed by Hugh Dalton. The subject was freedom of access and the need for National Parks.*

The path through the dale climbs relatively gently, but over bare limestone, much polished by the passage of thousands of feet. This can be treacherous when wet so have care. As you reach the top of the dale the path levels out and Mam Tor comes into view on the right. Soon there is a major junction of paths and you want the one to the right. *This probably formed part of the prehistoric*

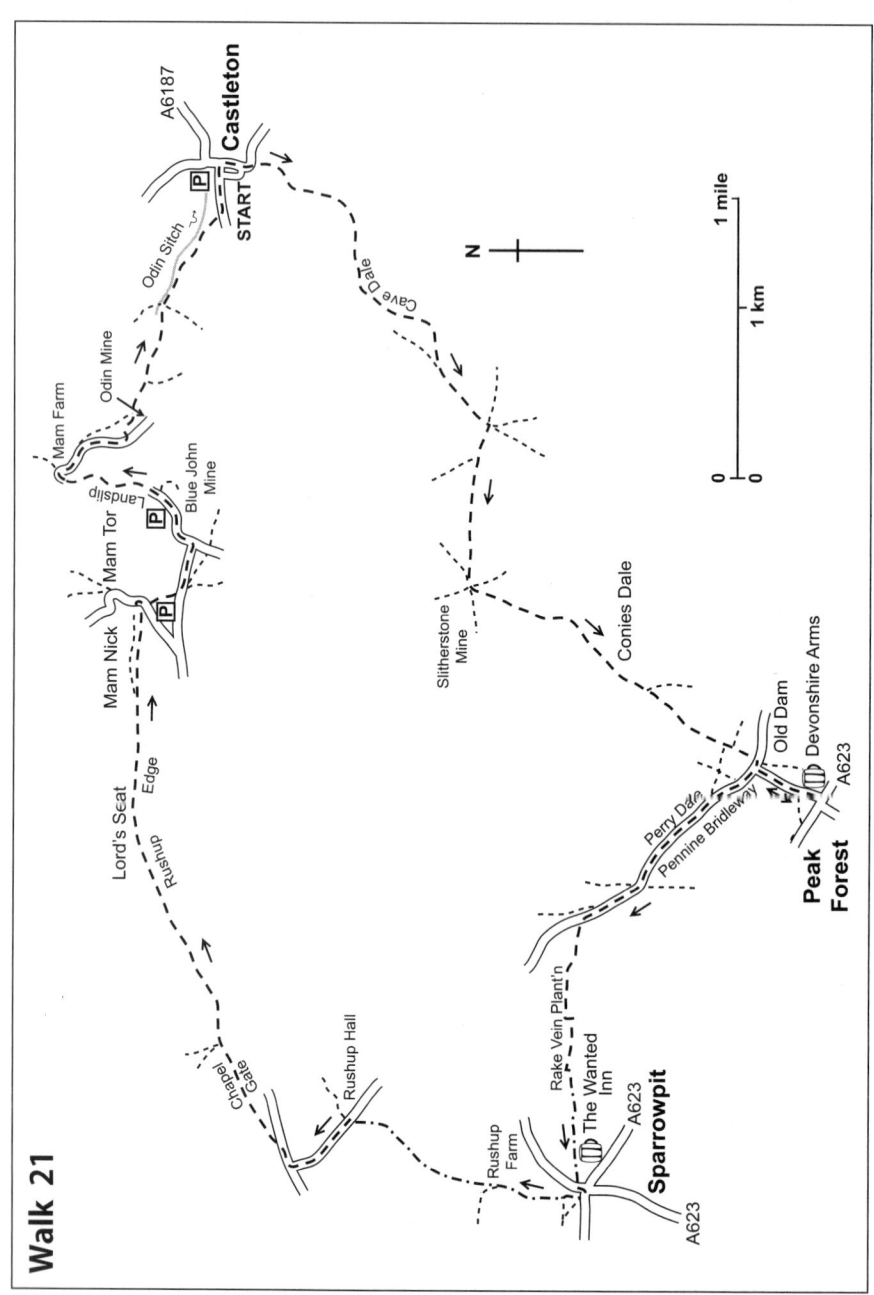

Walk 21

START Castleton
A6187
P
Odin Stitch
Odin Mine
Mam Farm
Odin Mine
Landslip
Blue John Mine
P
P
Mam Nick
Mam Tor
Lord's Seat
Edge
Rushup
Chapel Gate
Rushup Hall
Rushup Farm
Rake Vein Plant'n
The Wanted Inn
A623
Sparrowpit
A623
Rushup
Perry Dale
Pennine Bridleway
Old Dam
Peak Forest
Devonshire Arms
A623
Slitherstone Mine
Conies Dale
Cave Dale

N

0   1 km
0   1 mile

route linking communities on the limestone plateau with the Mam Tor hill fort. Its Saxon name was the Portway and it is still known as such today. This route has remained in use ever since and even today is shown on the OS 1:25000 map as a public road, albeit one used only as a footpath. After about 200 yards/metres the Portway heads off to the right, making for Rowtor Farm and Mam Tor. Your route lies straight ahead, another historic trackway, this time coming up Pindale from the Hope Valley and going across to Sparrowpit via Perryfoot. *In the 1970s and '80s there was a serious proposal to upgrade this track into a motor road as an alternative to the Mam Tor road which slipped catastrophically in the 1976/7 winter and never properly reopened. Fortunately for the peace and tranquillity of this area, the scheme*

Peveril Castle

never came to fruition. After about ½ mile/810 metres you reach a gate where there is another crossing of paths. *Portaway Mine lies away to the left and Slitherstone mine is to the right in the next field. This whole area is honeycombed with old lead mine workings, long defunct, though some have been reworked for fluorspar and barytes in modern times. The remains of these old workings are fascinating and the old tips are a haven for lead tolerant plants, but it is best not to stray too far from the paths, for although most of the shafts are now capped, they have been known to collapse without warning. It would be a shame to lose you at this stage, without you being able to complete this walk!*

Go through the gate and turn left. Go over a stile and bear right, following an obvious path in a south-westerly direction. After a few yards the track forks. Keep right here. The remains of lead mining are all around and the path descends to pass through a line of trees that mark an abandoned lead rake. Conies Dale can be seen below to the left. Bear left at a fork in the path and now the village of Peak Forest can be seen ahead. Descend towards Peak Forest, through a series of fields and stiles to a narrow lane that drops you into Old Dam. When you reach the road from Peak Forest, continue straight ahead, into the village. The Devonshire Arms is on the main road just left of the traffic lights.

The Devonshire Arms 1016 ft/310 metres
Telephone 01298 23875. www.devarms.co.uk

The pub stands alongside the main A623 in the picturesque village of Peak Forest. As you might expect, given its position on this main road, the Devonshire Arms was once a coaching inn, but today is a pub/hotel with an enviable reputation for staff service, real ales, food and accommodation.

The Devonshire Arms

Opening times
Daily: 1100 to 2300.
Food is served: Monday to Saturday: 1200 to 1430 and 1830 to 2130; Sundays: 1200 to 2130.

Peak Forest

Peak Forest is named after the Royal Forest of the Peak, which despite its name was an open area used as a Royal hunting park rather than a forested area. One of the courts of the Royal Forest, the Swainmote, used to meet at nearby Chamber Farm.

The most the majority of people see of Peak Forest is a straggle of houses as they pass through on the A623 Chesterfield-Manchester road. However the village has a number of interesting features, one of which is the church. This has the unusual dedication to Charles, King and Martyr. Even more unusual is the fact that it received this dedication during the Commonwealth period. At the time it was an 'extra parochial' church and enjoyed the right to marry people without the usual residence qualifications and publication of banns. It was the Peak District's answer to Gretna Green, but unfortunately for would be elopers, that right ceased many years ago.

Eldon Hole (one of the seven 'Wonders of the Peak'), a deep chasm in the ground, is situated on the side of a gentle hill about a mile and a half to the NW of the village. Inevitably it was reputed to be bottomless and legend had it that a goose fell into the hole and emerged later singed by the fires of Hell.

Peak Forest to Sparrowpit

Once you have explored the church and then possibly indulged yourself in a 'thirst after righteousness' in The Devonshire Arms, return up the lane to Old Dam and there go left, following the Pennine Bridleway along Perry Dale. *Perry Dale is a dry dale, by which is meant it hasn't a regular stream along it. It does not mean it is always dry underfoot, though being a surfaced road is a big help.* Follow the narrow road for about ⅔ of a mile (about 925 metres) until you come to a belt of trees on the left, marking another lead rake, this one being called Rake Vein, which is a classic example of tautology. Go through the stile on the left and then steeply uphill inside the belt of trees. This is not as shown on earlier OS maps, but the path up Rake Vein plantation is clearly waymarked. The path continues just inside the wood, crossing a couple of narrow walled accessways. At length, you'll encounter a gate, stile and signpost on the left. Go through this into the field. In the field, bear right and make your way alongside the wood and then across towards the plantation seen ahead. (There seems to be a path right along Rake Vein to a stile in the end wall, but you are not directed to use it, so rely on the waymarked route.) Turn right when you reach the plantation, along a short 'lane', at the end of which you are back in fields again for the final romp to Sparrowpit. Bear left and head towards the right hand end of the pub. Negotiate a couple of stiles before ending up on the Sparrowpit-Castleton road. The pub lies just to your left.

The Wanted Inn 1216 ft/371 metres
Telephone 01298 812862. www.wantedinn.com

In 1618 there is a reference to Sparrow Pit House, which seems to relate to what is now The Wanted Inn, though it was then a farmhouse. The house was situated on the old road from Chapel to Peak Forest via Blackbrook. This formed part of an ancient saltway from Cheshire to Sheffield and Chesterfield. Both these towns have street names referring to the salt routes. In 1700 the farmstead became an inn known as the 'Three Tuns' and was fortunate enough to be sited on one of the new turnpike roads. The

The Wanted Inn, Sparrowpit

Manchester to Chapel-en-le-Frith road was turnpiked in 1724 and in 1749 the turnpike was extended east to Peak Forest via Sparrowpit. The link from Sparrowpit to Sheffield via the Winnatts and Castleton was not promoted and authorised until 1758. In 1839 the name of the Inn was changed to The Devonshire Arms and it remained so until 1956. The inn was owned by Chatsworth Estates. When the 10th Duke died in 1950, there were massive death duties to pay, so the Inn was put up for auction. It remained unsold (and 'unwanted') until it was eventually purchased at a second auction in 1956 by a couple from Whitehough. They renamed it The Wanted Inn. The pub is a Robinson's house and sitting outside quaffing a pint of their best bitter and watching the traffic negotiate the notorious Sparrowpit bend is entertaining, especially on a lovely sunny day.

Opening times
Mondays, Wednesdays, Thursdays and Fridays: 1200 to 1500 and 1730 to 2300; Tuesdays: 1730 to 2300; Saturdays, Sundays and Bank Holidays: 1200 to midnight. Food is served: Weekdays: 1200 to 1430 (except Tuesdays) and 1800 to 2100; Saturdays: 1200 to 2100 and Sundays: 1200 to 1930.

Sparrowpit to Castleton
On leaving the pub, turn right. Cross the Castleton road with care, as the visibility is not good and then turn left, into a farmyard, following the signs for Rushup and Castleton. At the end of the farm buildings, there's a gate on the right, whence an obvious path leads towards Rushup Farm. As you approach the farm the path is fenced on both sides, eventually passing through the garden of the farmhouse and onto the farm access road. The way ahead is clearly signed, bearing left by a barn and then following the waymarked path left and up the hill to a stile. Once over the stile, go straight ahead, descending slightly to a stile and always heading towards Rushup Hall, which can be seen about ⅔ mile/1km ahead. *In the first field there is a part completed memorial on the left dedicated to 'Ronny', a young man of 20.* Beyond this, the path passes through a series of fields, one of which is extremely wet. In the final field, bear left, following the waymarks and so reach Rushup Lane (which here forms the Pennine Bridleway), right opposite Rushup Hall. Go left and follow the lane uphill to the main road. Cross the main road, go through the gate and turn right, following a path parallel to the main road, until you reach a gate giving access onto the Chapel Gate. Go onto this broad path and enjoy the stroll up onto Rushup Edge. The Chapel Gate 'road' bears away to the left just after a gate, but your path carries on climbing gently to Lord's Seat.

The view from Lord's Seat is extensive. Southwards you are looking over the limestone plateau. The scar of Eldon Hill quarry, once so prominent, is rapidly mellowing since closure and is a fine example of restoration. However, most people's eyes will be drawn northwards, to the Vale of Edale and the long length of Kinder Scout, with Jacob's Ladder, Crowden Clough, Grindslow Knoll and Ringing Roger featuring prominently. Ahead of you on the ridge is Mam Tor. The tumbled ground on your left as you approach Mam Tor is nothing to do with mining or quarrying this time, but the result of natural forces and the unstable combination of inter-bedded gritstone and shale. You'll see a more spectacular version of this phenomenon shortly.

Mam Tor

At the end of the ridge the path drops down to Mam Nick. It is best to take the right hand path, which reaches the road on the south side of the Nick. This avoids a steep and rough descent, and also avoids you having to negotiate the road through the Nick, where there's no footway or verge. You now have the choice of making an ascent of Mam Tor or simply carrying on down to Castleton. *If you decide not to go up Mam Tor you can console yourself with the fact that, having come over Lord's Seat you've been on a higher summit in any case (and you've avoided the crowds).* From Mam Nick go down the path signposted to Castleton, soon reaching the old main road, close to the junction for the Blue John Cavern. Go down the road to the cavern, where a grand view of the Hope Valley opens up, with that finest of guide stoops the Hope Cement Works chimney being a prominent feature. Continue down the road to the turning circle and marvel at the sight of chaos and destruction that greets you. *Until the winter of 1976/7 this was the main road west out of the Hope Valley. Ever since it was built in about 1812, the road had given trouble. Mam Tor is not known as the 'Shivering Mountain' for nothing. It takes a particular form of engineering 'genius' to build a road across the face of an active landslip, twice! The result was that the road was in a constant state of*

Kinder and Edale from Rushup

repair from Day One. The increased weight and volume of 20th century traffic didn't help matters and you can see the successive layers of tarmac as you gaze on the shattered remains of the road below you. The summer of 1976 was very hot and dry for a long time and the following winter was very wet. The result was predicted by the then Assistant County Surveyor who remarked that he was certain that 'Mam Tor will go'. Go it did, in spectacular fashion, the road falling a metre in one night and continuing to slip thereafter. Attempts were made to reopen the road, but it was never fully repaired and after a series of reports Derbyshire County Council decided to abandon the route.

Walk down the old road, examining the landslip and gazing up at the face of Mam Tor. *The interleaving beds of shale and gritstone can be clearly seen and are the root cause of the problem. As the blocks of gritstone and shale slide down the face they turn and are pulverized, so that, by the time they reach the lower part of the slip they are almost totally inverted and crushed to very fine particles that can be almost fluid. The road crossed the slip twice. The top crossing is the more spectacular of the two. The road over the lower crossing is still open to give access to a farm, which fortunately is not built on the landslip.* Go round the hairpin bend and over the lower slip onto firm ground where the road comes off the shales and grits and onto limestone. *To your right is the Odin Gorge and to your left the remains of Odin Mine, with its crushing circle and unusual oval shaft. The workings stretched back westwards almost to Mam Nick.*

Go down the path on the left, to the mine site, passing to the left of the crushing circle before descending again to a bridge over Odin Sitch, which was the drainage level for the mine. The well-blazed path continues beside the stream for about 800 yards/740 metres, turns right to pass between houses and so reaches the main road. Turn left to reach the car park, information centre and the bus station.

Walk 22: Pomeroy
(Duke of York)

Start and finish	Pomeroy (Duke of York) GR. SK119675
The route	Pomeroy (DoY), Pasture Barn, Flagg, Rockfield House, Taddington, Sough Top, Chelmorton, Highstool Lane, Blinder House, Pomeroy (DoY)
Length	7 miles (11 km)
Ascent	988 feet (301 metres)
Time	Allow 3¼ to 4 hours (exclusive of stops)
Map	OS OL24 (White Peak)

Getting there

By bus. Daily bus service to Pomeroy from Buxton and Ashbourne. Daily bus service to Taddington and Chelmorton from Manchester, Stockport, Buxton, Bakewell, Matlock and Derby.

By train. Nearest station is Buxton, which has an hourly service from Stockport and Manchester. The bus connections call at the railway station.

By car. Pomeroy is on the A515 between Buxton and Ashbourne. The only parking is at the Duke of York, so ask permission first. Taddington is just off the A6 and there is limited on-street parking in the village

The walk

Pomeroy and the Duke of York

Pomeroy is a curious name that appears to be of French origin. However, it doesn't appear on any maps before the 20th century and then only in relation to a group of cottages built between the late 1890s and 1920. Burdett's map of

1791 refers to the area as Over Street, which relates to the Roman Road and the various 'street' names given to farms and properties in the area, e.g. Street Farm. As a place it consists of little more than Street Farm, Pomeroy Cottages and of course, the pub. The A515 slices between the pub and the other parts of the hamlet, closely paralleling the Roman road alignment at this point. Details of the Duke of York are given in **Walk 8.**

Pomeroy to Taddington

On leaving the pub, go through a sign-posted stile on the left. Bear right in the field and head to a gateway, then bear left to a stile in the middle of a wall. At this point you can see Flagg ahead. Make for the far right-hand corner of the field to a stile. This is followed in quick succession by another stile on the left. Negotiate this and bear right, passing a pond in the middle of the field. Head for the clump of trees and then skirt to the right of Pasture Barn to a gate. The path then runs beside the wall to reach Pasture Lane and here turn left. In about 100yds/metres go right, into fields and follow the right hand wall. Go straight ahead, through a number of fields, making for the sharp bend in Mycock Lane. Note the lead mine spoil heaps in the fields nearest the lane. Follow Mycock Lane up to the T-junction, passing the nursery school on the left. *Flagg no longer has a pub, The Plough having closed some years ago. However, Flagg does have its claim to fame with the annual Flagg Races. These are held on Easter Tuesday and consist of a series of point-to-point races over the numerous dry-stone walls.*

At the T-junction go straight ahead, up the access track for Flagg Hall Farm, which boasts some very fine old buildings, one barn having a date-stone 1681.

Past the farm the path runs along a track and then passes through a clump of new(ish) trees and alongside a pond, before entering a long field. Keeping the wall to your right go through this field to reach Flagg Lane. Here turn right. After only about 100 yds/metres on the road, go left, beside Rockfield House. This path follows a broad green lane. *Given the various lead mine hillocks and shafts in the surrounding fields, this is almost certainly an access track to the mines. Under the Derbyshire lead mining laws, a miner had the right of access to his mine from the nearest public highway. The width of the access was limited to that of a cart.* The path bears right and makes its way across the former workings, eventually passing through a gate to clip the corner of the next field. In the next field bear right to reach Whitefield Lane, here no more than a broad green track. Head straight up the shallow valley to a stile in the middle of the top wall. Now bear right, making for the top right-hand corner of the field, then diagonally right, across the next field to a lane, known as The Jarnett, at its junction with Moor Lane. Follow the road signed to

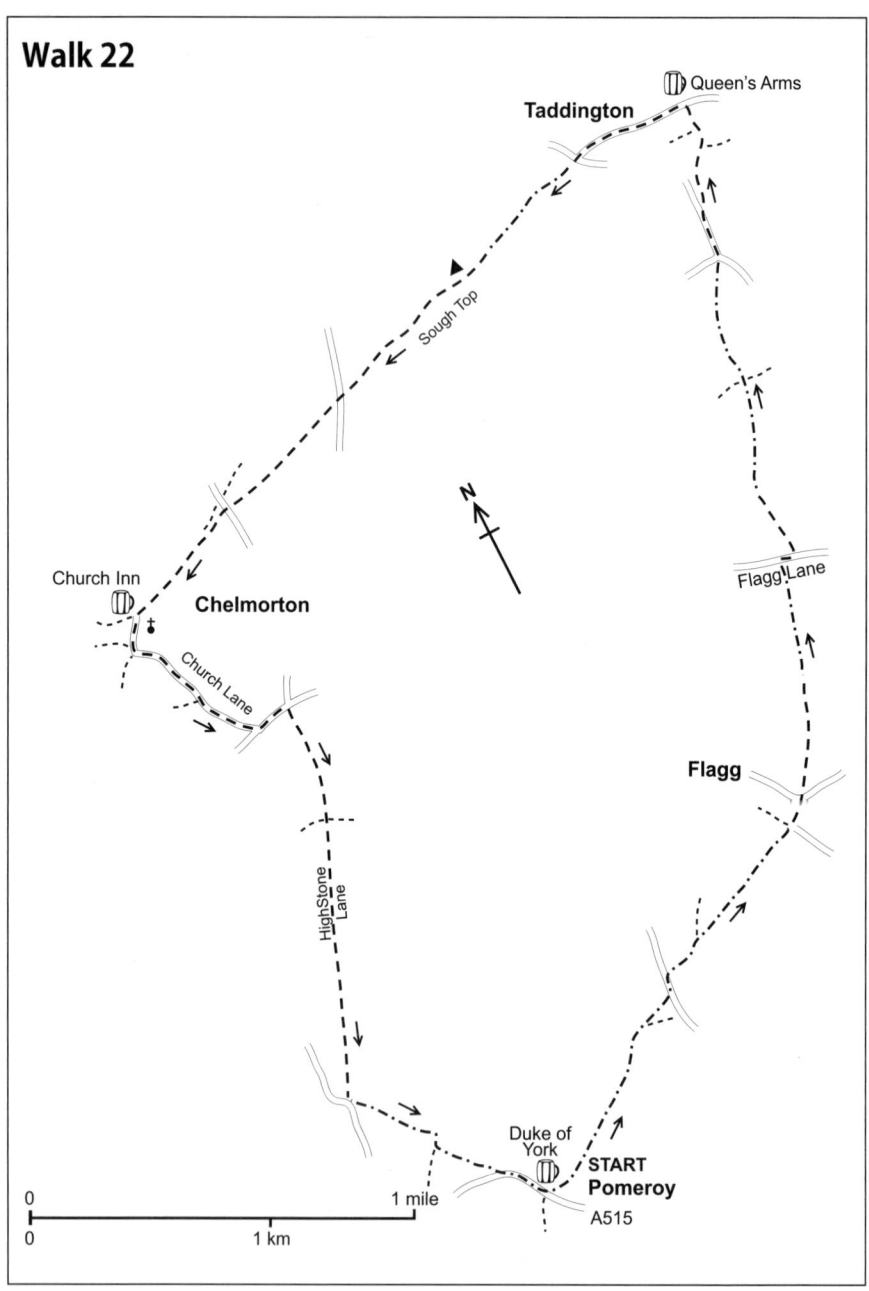

Walk 22

Queen's Arms

Taddington

Sough Top

Church Inn

Chelmorton

Church Lane

HighStone Lane

Flagg Lane

Flagg

Duke of York

START
Pomeroy

A515

N

0   1 mile
0   1 km

Taddington, but in about 200 yds/metres, bear right into a narrow green lane. This drops steeply down into the village, emerging by the chapel. The Queen's Arms lies just up the main street. Details of the Queen's Arms are given in **Walk 6**.

Taddington to Pomeroy

The second part of this walk is described in **Walk 7**, including a description of the pub in Chelmorton.

Walk 23: Reapsmoor (Butcher's Arms)

Start and finish	Longnor Market Place. GR. SK089649
The route	Longnor, Manifold east bank, Lower Boothlow, Hill End, Slate House Farm, Sheen, Brund, Brund Mill, New Road, Knowle Farm, Reapsmoor (Butcher's Arms), Blake Brook Ford, Boosley Grange, Bank House, Shining Ford, Hardings Booth, Fawside, Gauledge, Longnor
Length	9.8 miles (15.8 km)
Ascent	1318 feet (402 metres)
Time	5-5½ hours (exclusive of stops)
Map	OS OL24 (White Peak)

Getting there

By bus. Daily bus service to Longnor from Buxton and Ashbourne. Also demand responsive service (Moorlands Connect), bookable in advance. (Reapsmoor only has the Moorlands Connect service.)

By train. Nearest station, Buxton. The Ashbourne-Longnor-Buxton bus service calls at the station.

By car. Longnor is on the B5053 road from Brierlow Bar (A515 Buxton-Ashbourne road) to Bottom House (A523 Ashbourne-Leek road). There is parking in the Market Place and some on-street parking in the village, but please park considerately.

The Walk

Longnor to Lower Boothlow

From the Market Square, head east for about 220 yards/metres and then turn right at the second footpath sign, just past The Cheshire Cheese. Go down to the farmyard and turn left, through a gate. Bear right to a stile and follow the sign saying 'Brund via riverside' descending the field to reach the infant Manifold. Now go left.

Continue through a series of fields each with a waymarked stile, following the Manifold Trail. There's no difficulty in route finding on this stretch, though the path is not always distinct. At least the next stile can be seen ahead. Eventually the path diverges from the river, to cross the track between Waterhouse and Over Boothlow farms. You'll spot the waymark post by the side of the track. Go straight on. The next stile is not obvious but keep to the left hand side of the large patch of rushes or risk a serious case of wet feet – believe me. The path now bears left, making for Lower Boothlow Farm. Pass through another stile and continue towards Lower Boothlow. Just before the farm, there's a footpath sign on the left. Here you have a choice. The route of the walk goes left, over this stile and makes for Sheen.

You can reduce the mileage and the ascent considerably by carrying on along the Manifold Trail, through the stile you can see ahead. You'll rejoin the main route of the walk at Brund Mill and you'll have saved 1.6 miles/2.5 km and 380 ft/117metres of ascent.

Lower Boothlow to Sheen

Go left, over the stile and up the field, leaving the Manifold Trail. At the top of the field there's a stile by the gate. *There's a good view back up the Manifold Valley from here, with the limestone reef knolls in Dovedale overtopping the Longnor ridge.* Skirt the farm, passing the usual array of semi-derelict farm machinery and turn right, passing through another stile, onto a track. *When the walk was recce'd we'd had one of the wettest spells of weather for ages – and it showed. The passage along the path near the Manifold was a constant squelch, so to get on firm and almost dry ground was a delight.* Follow the farm access track down and across a cattle grid, then up again to a road. Here turn right. Go down the road for less than 100 yards/metres, then go left, over an unsigned stile, just opposite the start of a line of pine trees. There's no obvious path here, but follow the wall on the left until it kinks left. Go straight on along a sketchy path through rushes, making for a line of trees. Keep alongside the remnants of a hedge bank on your right and soon come to a steep drop to a stream. The boundary fence of the field forces you left, but in so doing you'll locate a stile that has been hidden until this point. Go over the stile, which is quite an awkward one and drop steeply to a plank bridge that was devoid of a handrail when I recce'd the walk. The path climbs the far bank with a series of steps and bears right to a stile. Once over the stile, turn left and follow the wall up the field, making for Hill End Farm, which

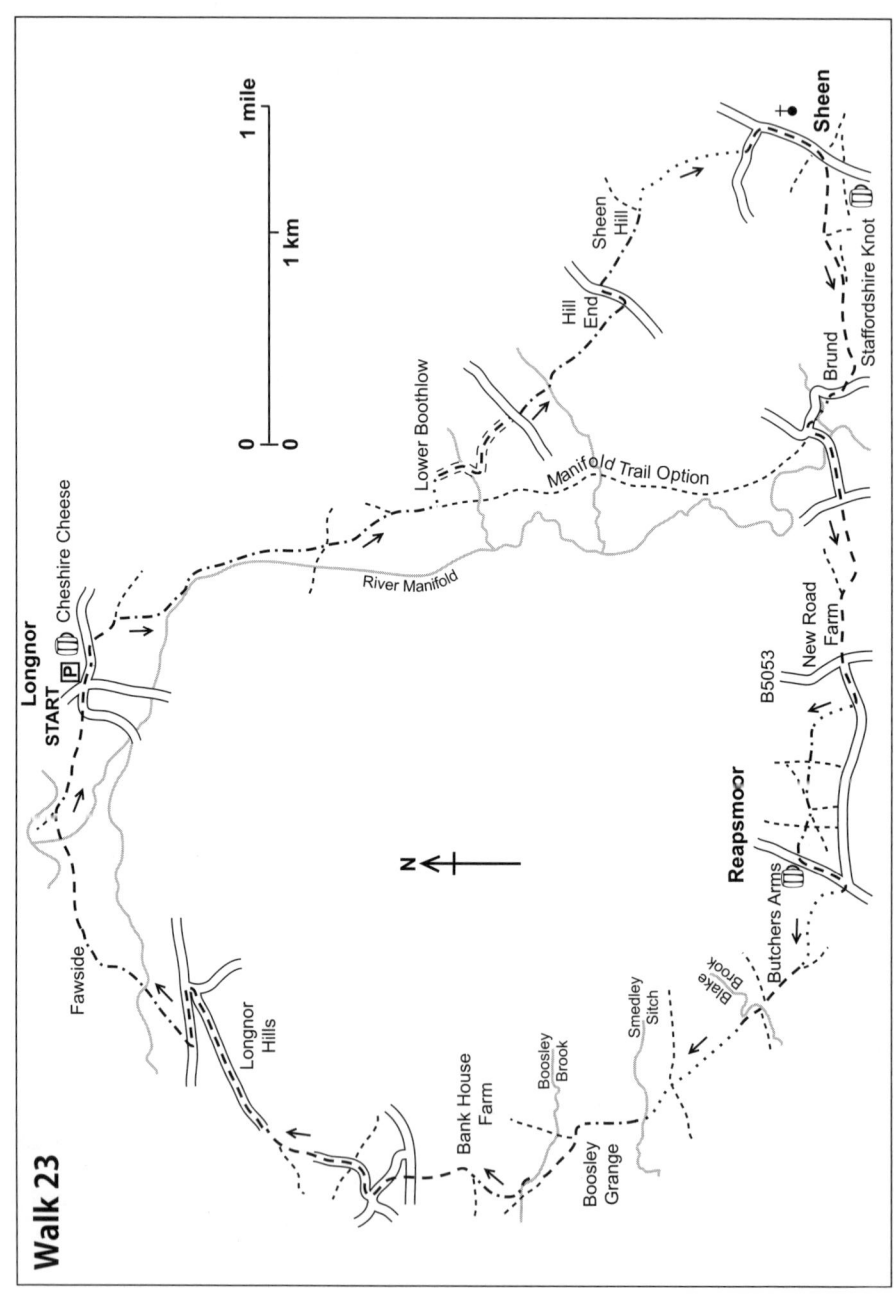

Walk 23

Longnor
START
Cheshire Cheese

Fawside

Longnor
Hills

Bank House
Farm

Boosley
Brook

Boosley
Grange

Smedley
Sitch

Blake
Brook

Butchers Arms

Reapsmoor

New Road
Farm

B5053

Staffordshire Knot

Brund

Sheen

Sheen
Hill

Hill
End

Lower Boothlow

Manifold Trail Option

River Manifold

N

0   1 km   1 mile
0

you'll see ahead. In the next field the path allegedly keeps alongside the wall, but this is clearly not the walked route, which bears right to join a farm track and in so doing avoids a boggy area. Go left at the track and up towards the farm. Just before the farm gate, bear right to a stile and skirt round the buildings to another stile on your left, leading out onto the farm drive. Go right and up to the road.

For some time, Sheen Hill has been in view on your left, an unusually rocky tor in this otherwise gently rolling landscape. Oddly it isn't access land, which is great pity, as it must have a magnificent view from the summit. You'll get a flavour of that view shortly. At the road, turn left. Go up the hill until you reach a footpath sign on the right. *Pause here to look back at the view, which is extensive, taking in the reef knolls of the Upper Dove and right up the Dove and Manifold valleys to Axe Edge.* Now tackle the stile, which is about the best bit of rock scrambling you'll get on this walk. The path is not obvious, but goes straight up the hill, alongside the right hand wall. You join a tarmacked drive and approach a gateway. It is not clear from the map, or on the ground, whether the right of way goes through the gate, past the house and through a gate on the far side, or whether it goes around the boundary wall. A few

Sheen Hill

waymarks would be useful here. *I went around the boundary and it was obvious others had done the same.* Beyond the house, pick up the wall-side path again and pass through a gateway (no gate). *Sheen Hill rises steeply to your left, but there's a grand view across the Manifold valley even from this point.* The path leaves the wall and rises up the side of the hill. A myriad of paths trace their routes along the hillside. Most are made by large cloven feet, but the uppermost ones have occasional imprints of boots. The path swings left, away from a tempting gateway, to a stile in the wall on your right. *Ahead you can see the summit of Sheen Hill, temptingly close and crowned with a trig point. To your right you can see the cluster of hills beyond Hulme End, where the Manifold enters its limestone phase.*

Go through the stile. You'll spot another stile in the wall ahead and to the left, but this isn't the one you want. Your stile is in the bottom wall of the field, also to the left. Go through this stile and then down the next field to a stile in the bottom fence. You are heading for Sheen church, the tower of which you can see ahead. In the next field the stile is hidden, but continue to head for the church and you'll find the stile in the bottom fence/hedge. Here you cross a ditch and then up the bank to a small gate. Now head for an obvious gateway, diagonally up to the right. Here you'll join a narrow lane. Go left to a T-junction. Go right here and enter Sheen village.

Sheen church

'Twixt Sheen and Brund

After the rural nature of the walk so far, Sheen seems like an urban metropolis. There's even street lighting and a roadside footway! Walk along the road, passing St. Luke's church and the village cross. You'll pass a footpath sign pointing right, but ignore this first one. Another footpath sign on the right actually points to a path on the left, so you don't want this one either. About 200 yards/metres beyond the church there's a third footpath sign, pointing right and signed to Brund. This is your route. *(If you are intent on visiting Sheen's pub, The Staffordshire Knot, you need to go a little further along the road and then return to this stile. The Knot is not one of the high pubs, only managing a mere 893 feet/272 metres).* Go over the stile and head across the field, keeping to the right of the barn, thus reaching a gateway and stile. In the next field the path is obvious, straight ahead to a small gate with its own footpath sign. Straight on in the next couple of fields, then bear left towards two new(ish) concrete gateposts, one of which appears to be waymarked. On closer inspection the 'waymark' turns out to be a sign saying 'No through route'. Don't go through the gateway, but keep in the field you are already in and follow the wall on the left. You'll soon reach a fine green lane. This descends towards the Manifold at Brund. As the lane swings right, there's a good view of Brund hamlet.

When you reach the road at New House Farm – a fine looking building, go right for about 100 yards/metres, before turning left at the footpath sign. Bear right across the field to a short, but steep, drop to a stream. Descend and cross the stream (no bridge) then onto the road again at a stile, bearing left now to Brund Mill. *(If the weather has been wet you would be well advised not to use this path, but instead simply carry on along the road which will bring you down to a T-junction, where you turn left, signed to Hulme End and Longnor).*

Brund Mill

Anyone who decided back at Lower Boothlow that they'd stay on the Manifold Trail and not go up to Sheen will rejoin the main walk here.

Brund to Reapsmoor

Pass the restored mill and go over the bridge spanning the Manifold. Continue along the lane to a T-junction and go straight ahead, through a stile. Follow the fence up, alongside the course of an old road. *Look back at this point. Sheen Hill is in view and so too is Wetton Hill and the limestone ridge beyond Dovedale. The factory you can see is Belle Engineering, makers of a wide range of construction machinery, including concrete mixers. Doug Blackhurst, the late owner of the factory, was a keen railway enthusiast and built a $\frac{1}{3}$ scale replica of one of the Leek and Manifold Railway engines. He had a line laid from his garage to his office at the factory and claimed, with some justification, that he* *was the only person in the Staffordshire Moorlands to commute to work by narrow gauge railway.* At the end of the second field, go right, to a gate. Follow the wall up to New Road Farm and pass through the farmyard to the B5053 road. *There are buses back to Longnor from here.*

Go up the lane opposite to reach Field Head Farm and go right, over a stile just past the farm, and then to another stile a few yards further on. There is no obvious path in this next field, nor can you see any exit stile. What looks like a stile in the fence/hedge diagonally left turns out not to be so. Head straight across the field towards the house and thus locate a hidden stile. *On the far side it is well guarded by some evil looking mud, whose source is best left to the imagination.* Now head uphill, bearing left of the house to a small gate, which is waymarked. Cross the driveway, bearing left to a gate and stile and then go alongside the right hand fence, leaving the farm track to your left. At Knowle Farm, follow the rough path to the right of the barns, passing through a couple of gates. Cross the farm access, which at the time of the recce' seemed to be home to half a dozen elderly ice cream vans, then pass through a small gate into fields again. Follow the left-hand wall/fence through a couple of fields, noting that Longnor is now in view to your right, but that you seem to be heading away from it. You'll reach twin stiles in a wall ahead. Both go into the same narrow field passing Old Ralph's Farm on the right.

At the end of the narrow field, go through the gate and then bear right, following the wall on the right. The Butcher's Arms can now be seen ahead. Ignore the waymarked gate on the right and continue ahead towards the pub, passing through a decrepit gate/stile then following the left hand hedge to a stile that gives out onto the road almost opposite the pub. *(The driveway from Old Ralph's Farm comes out right opposite the pub and is just to the right of the stile.)*

Reapsmoor and the Butcher's Arms. 1034 feet/315 metres
Telephone 01298 84477. No website
Reapsmoor is only a scatter of farms and cottages; certainly not a village, so, given how many village pubs have closed down recently, it's little short of a miracle that The Butcher's Arms still exists. The pub is walker-friendly, no frills but with an enviable reputation for good-value food in walker-filling portions. Fast food it is not! There are regular real ales from local micro breweries and guest beers change frequently. One commentator remarked that he and his party left the pub *"two stone heavier and almost two hours later"*and that, like Brigadoon, *"it's the sort of place that if you went back to look for it - it wouldn't exist!"* However, exist it does and it has done so since at least the late 1820s. It was recorded as the Butcher's Arms in 1834 and

even boasted a Friendly Society that lasted until at least 1940.

Opening times

In theory the pub is open daily from 1000 to 2300, but when I recce'd this walk it was certainly not open at lunchtime and there were no opening times displayed anywhere obvious. Best to telephone first.

Reapsmoor to Longnor

Butcher's Arms, Reapsmoor

On leaving the Butcher's Arms go right, down the lane for about 300 yards/275 metres, to a road junction. Just before the house on your right, look out for a footpath sign and go right, then immediately right again through another stile and into a field. Bear left to the wall corner, then bear left to a stile in the wall. Follow the right hand fence and wall to a stile in the field corner, not the more obvious gateway on the right. Continue alongside the ditch, fence and wall to a barn. There's a stile of sorts just beyond the gateway to the barn. Go over this and then over another dilapidated stile a few paces ahead. Now go left and follow an obvious path down the field to the bottom, where there are two stiles, side by side on opposite sides of the dividing fence. Go over your stile and onto a track. Follow this down towards the Blake Brook and where the track veers right, go straight ahead alongside the wall to locate the footbridge. Immediately over the bridge, there's a stile on your right. Go over this and make your way up the field alongside the wall. This leads to a gate, which has one of the small footpath gates alongside it. However, this is securely fastened with barbed wire, so you have to use what passes for a stile just to the right. Continue ahead, still with the wall to your left until you reach another gate and a waymarked stile, leading you into a large field in which there is no obvious path. *The OS 1:25000 map indicates a number of field boundaries, but they are long gone, with only a few remnants to mark where they were.* Head up the field to a line of stunted trees, probably the remains of a hedge. There's a ditch between you and the trees and there's no bridge over it. Cross it as best you can and then follow the former hedge until it peters out. There's still no obvious path, but to your left is Smedley Sitch Farm and to your right there's a barn. Keep straight ahead, midway between the two, until the far corner of the field comes into view, with Boosley Grange up on the hillside to your right. In the field corner you'll find a gate and a culvert over the Smedley Sitch. Then go up the field to a small gate, which leads you into a paddock beside Boosley Grange. Cross the paddock to another stile in the right hand top corner and then follow the way-marks to the left, around Boosley Grange onto a track.

Boosley Grange is something of a mystery. The word 'grange' usually implies a monastic farm. However, no monastery or abbey is known to have owned land in the area, so the name may relate to some seasonal dairying usage. The site is obviously of considerable antiquity as in the late 14th century there are references to Boothesley Grange and the Bank or Over Boothesley. The present house at Boosley Grange was probably built in the mid 1600s and it retains much 17th-century stonework. Fawfieldhead, in which Boosley Grange is situated, formed part of a Royal Forest known as the Forest of Alstonefield. It is known by this name in 1227 and seems to have existed much earlier. The forest was also known as the Mauban or Malbank Frith (Forest) and this name persisted until the late 16th century. Tradition has it that one of the forest's keepers lived at Boosley Grange.

Go along the track to a gate and stile and continue along the track for about 300 yards/277 metres until it forks. You'll need to keep a sharp lookout for this, as there's no signpost or waymark. You'll spot Bank House on the opposite hillside and that's your next objective. A cart width terrace bears right, down the bank side to the stream. There's no bridge or obvious stepping-stones, so cross where you can and then go left, alongside the stream, to a decrepit gate and stile, leading into a field. According to the map, the path describes a graceful arc left then right, up the field to the gate and stile that you can see at the bottom of the clump of trees fringing Bank House. Needless to say, the path is not obvious on the ground, so make your way up to the gate/stile. Follow a farm track upwards, passing three stone troughs on the left and then through a gate onto the farm access. Follow the farm access up the hill to the road. Cross the road and go straight ahead, down a narrow track to another lane, where you turn left.

At the crossroads, a little further on, turn right, along the lane marked with the 'No Motor Vehicles' sign and with a variety of hand-painted signs suggesting that there is no route this way for Longnor Wood caravan site. Go along the lane, enjoying some firm and relatively dry ground under your feet. As you approach Lane Head Farm the lane forks. Keep straight on, through the gateway, passing the main farm buildings on your left. Just beyond the farm the tarmacked lane ends abruptly at a gate. Beyond the gate is a very narrow, sunken lane, possibly just wide enough for a farm cart – if it was cleared of vegetation, but otherwise only wide enough for a packhorse. *Now you see the reason for the 'No Motor Vehicles' sign and the hand-painted signs.*

Being sunken, the lane is regarded by any surplus water as a heaven-sent route down which to run! Just beyond the gate, there's a stile on the left. There is no corresponding path marked on the map, but this may be one of those instances where the main 'vehicular' route was regarded as so wet and muddy that a parallel path was established on higher ground. There are a number of examples elsewhere in the Peak District, but alas, not here – at least, not officially. Go up the lane, which soon emerges from its defile and widens out where it joins the driveway to Hillend Farm. *There's a footpath sign here, pointing down the driveway, but this doesn't correspond with any path paralleling the lane either.* Go along the now tarmacked lane, soon passing the entrance to the caravan site on your right. *There's a lovely view up the Manifold valley from here, almost up to the source of the river near Flash Bar.* As you go along the lane the distinctive conical shape of High Wheeldon hill comes into view ahead. Longnor Wood is to your right. Continue alongside the wood down to a T-junction, where you turn left. Almost at once you reach another T-junction and turn left again, despite the signpost directing you to the right to Longnor! Go down the road, through the trees, keeping well to the right and prepared to squeeze into the bank-side as there's little or no verge. At the bottom of the hill you come out of the trees and soon reach a gate on the right, signed as the Manifold Trail. Turn right here.

Follow the path diagonally across the field, making for Fawside Farm, which can be seen on the far hillside. Cross the Manifold by the footbridge and go up to Fawside, noting that Longnor church is now in view ahead. Follow the waymarks past the farmhouse, through a couple of gates and onto the farm access. Where the track goes left, go right, as signed and then follow the wall on the right, to a small gate. Pass through the new(ish) planting to another gate and thus into fields. Keep the wall to your right to yet another stile, with Longnor now clearly in view ahead and with a fine view down the Manifold valley to Sheen Hill. Go down the field to a bridge over Hollinsclough Brook, defended on both sides by a quagmire. Once over, go straight up the field to a stile at the top and then bear right to a stile in the corner. Follow the left-hand wall past Gauledge Farm. You soon reach a lane, which leads unerringly into Longnor village. The Market Square, its café, shop and pubs lies only a short distance further on.

Walk 24: Royal Cottage
(Royal Cottage and Winking Man)

Start and finish	The Winking Man GR. SK026638
Alternative sttart and finish	Gradbach car park. GR. SJ998662
The route	Royal Cottage/Winking Man, Hazel Barrow, Summerhill, The Roaches, Doxey Pool, Roach End, Back Forest, Lud Church, Gradbach, Bradley Howe, Sniddles, Little Hillend, Adders Green, Gib Tor, Royal Cottage/Winking Man
Length	8.43 miles (13.57 km)
Ascent	1497 feet (456 metres)
Time	Allow 4-5 hours (exclusive of stops)
Map	OS OL24 (White Peak)

Getting there:
By bus. Daily bus service between Leek and Buxton stops at the Winking Man
By train, Forget it. Nearest station, Buxton
By car. The Winking Man is on the A53 Buxton-Leek road. It has a large car park, but seek permission from the proprietor if you want to park there. If parking at Gradbach use the A53 from Leek or Buxton to just south of Flash Bar then through Flash village and follow the lane and signs down to Gradbach car park (GR. SJ 998662). From A54 from Congleton to Allgreave then right on minor road to Gradbach. The car park at Gradbach is just in Staffordshire, signed to the right (a very sharp turn) down an even more minor lane.

The Walk

Winking Man to The Roaches

From the Winking Man, go across the main road and at the crossroads turn right, down the lane towards Hazel Barrow. *Gaze back to the moors behind the Winking Man for a glimpse of The Mermaid, which would have been one of the 'high' pubs in this book had it not ceased to trade. Great shame, but a sign of the times. At the junction by the Corner House – which may or may not still be doing teas and cakes, there's an access land sign on the right and this is where you would emerge if you started from Gradbach and chose to avoid the road walk from Gib Tor to the Royal Cottage.* Bear left at the junction by the Corner House, soon passing Hazel Barrow Farm on your right. *It was up for sale when the walk was recce'd.* A couple of hundred yards/metres further on, keep right at the next road junction and carry on along the lane for about another 400 yards/370 metres. At this point, with the ridge of The Roaches rising before you, there's a footpath sign and stile on the left alongside a track and a cattle grid. *One glance at the stile and the jungle beyond it will convince you that the cattle grid and track is the better option and indeed it seems that the only reason for the stile is to avoid the cattle grid and the track is actually the right of way.*

Go up the track with widening views to the left. The track reaches a crossing of paths. Go straight ahead here and at the next fork in the track bear right, now on a footpath, though it has obviously seen greater use than foot traffic in the past. As you top the rise there's a grand view to Morridge, Hen Cloud and Tittesworth. Leave the path here and bear right, following the line of a derelict wall. There's a sketchy path that soon dips to cross a stream, then proceeds towards a ruined barn. Pass to the right of the barn and follow sheep tracks up the slope to an outcrop of rocks then making your way to the left to pick up a broad path, which leads onto the top of The Roaches.

Along The Roaches

Whence came the name 'The Roaches'? It is apparently a corruption of Norman French 'Rocher', simply meaning 'rocks'. It occurs elsewhere in the Peak District, e.g. near Bradfield in South Yorkshire. The walk along The Roaches is a real delight. *The views to the west are stunning; not just the nearby views of Tittesworth Reservoir and Bosley Minn, but much wider views to the Shropshire and Llangollen hills and the Clwydian range. Eastwards the Staffordshire Moorlands and the limestone Peak roll away seemingly endlessly.* The going is easy, but don't let your concentration slip because this is no paved path. It can be quite rough underfoot and it's always well to remember that to your

Walk 24

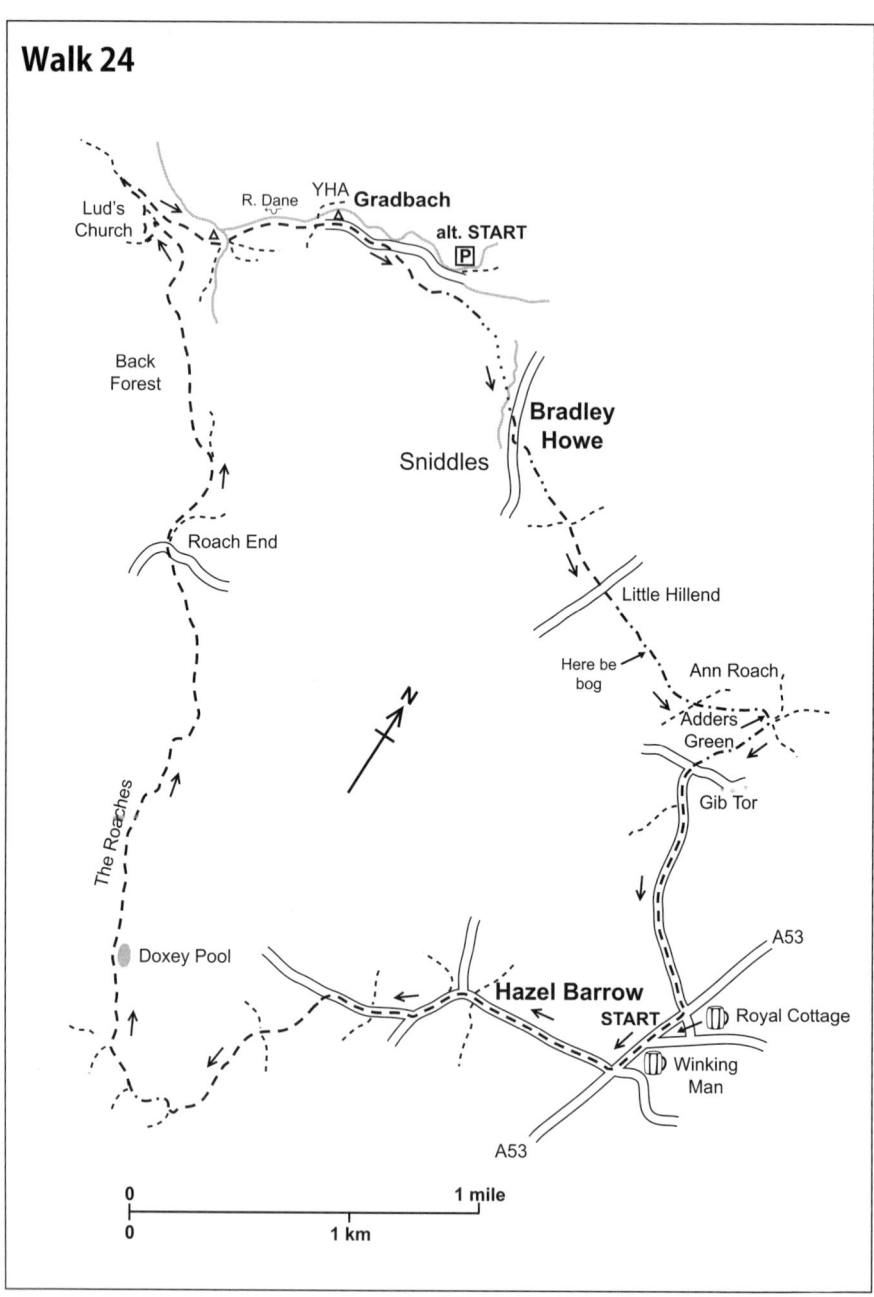

Lud's Church

R. Dane

YHA **Gradbach**

alt. START

Back Forest

Bradley Howe

Sniddles

Roach End

Little Hillend

Here be bog

Ann Roach

Adders Green

Gib Tor

The Roaches

A53

Doxey Pool

Hazel Barrow

START

Royal Cottage

Winking Man

A53

| 0 | | 1 mile |
| 0 | 1 km | |

The summit of The Roaches

left is a precipitous drop. There could also be the occasional rope lying across the path, because this is one of the Peak District's most popular climbing areas. The path along the top is always busy, in complete contrast to other parts of the Staffordshire Moorlands where walkers tend to be few and far between. You soon pass the lovely Doxey Pool and its attendant bizarre rock formations, then it's a steady stroll of about ¾ mile/1¼ km to the trig point at the highest part of The Roaches. Then it's downhill all the way, but with a cracking view ahead to Shuttlingsloe, Croker Hill and the Cheshire plain. The path reaches the road again at Roach End.

In search of the Green Knight

Go over the road and through the stile. Turn right, down the path signed to Gradbach and Danebridge, not the path signed to Lud's Church. The path drops steeply and roughly towards the valley of the Black Brook and soon reaches the outskirts of Back Forest. As the path dips to cross a small stream, look out for a path leading away to the left and signed to Lud's Church. Follow this path through the woodland for a little over ½ mile/850 metres until you reach a junction. The path to the left is signed to Lud's Church and The Ridge.

Follow this path and where it forks again, keep straight ahead, signed to Lud's Church. You soon reach a hole in the ground, on your right. At busy times you'll usually hear voices emerging from the hole, possibly followed by human beings. This is the back entrance to Lud's Church and it is a tricky descent over slimy rocks. If you don't fancy this route, carry on along the path for a short distance and you'll find a flight of steps, which are much easier, though not such a challenge. *If you were expecting a church, you'll be disappointed, but not for long. Dissenters from the established religion used Lud's Church as a place of worship.* It is a mysterious place; a great fern clad cleft in the rocks that

Top entrance to Lud's Church

wriggles its way down to an exit onto a good path. *Part way down, on the right hand side look out for the Green Knight, his giant face frozen in stone following his fight with Sir Gawain.*

You emerge, blinking into the broad daylight onto a good path and turn left. The path soon reaches a junction signed to Danebridge (straight on) and Gradbach (to the right). Turn sharp right and pass a rock outcrop, then follow the broad descending path through the trees, with the noise of the river down below growing steadily louder. As you near the valley bottom there's a signpost pointing left to Gradbach. Go left here, leaving the track and dropping down a short flight of steps, past a large tree and a ruined building to a footbridge over the River Dane. Once over the river, the path bears away to the right, rising sharply. However, in just a few paces, there's a stile on the left. Go over this and bear left onto a track. This track soon degenerates into a footpath, but runs easily and on the level to reach Gradbach youth hostel, where, if you are lucky, the café will be open.

*(It is possible to combine this walk with **Walk 14** from this point. This makes for a lengthy hike, but it does take you to The New Inn at Flash and it also avoids the bogs between Little Hillend and Adders Green.)*

Gradbach to Royal Cottage and Winking Man

Go up the lane from the youth hostel and through the gateway. Another lane trails in from the right and almost immediately another lane branches off right. This is unsigned, but it is a public footpath, so go up the track towards Greensitch Farm.

(If you are starting from Gradbach car park you can either walk towards the youth hostel and then make a sharp turn left onto the track described above, or turn left at the car park entrance, go along the road for about 100 yards/metres then go right at a signposted stile. Bear right up the steep bank to a footbridge, then left to the driveway of Greensitch Farm.) As you approach Greensitch Farm, the path is signed to the right to a footbridge and then round the right hand side of the farm complex before dropping onto a track at the far side.

Continue upwards alongside the wall, noting that Gradbach car park is just below you at this point. At the waymarked stile, which also boasts a television aerial(!) continue ahead, with the wall to your right until you reach the wall corner. Here bear right and go down to a gate and stile, then down again to cross a stream. As the path rises up the bank on the far side of the stream it becomes less and less distinct, finally vanishing altogether in a mass of rushes, which can only mean 'bog'. Ahead you'll see Bradley Howe Farm, so make a beeline through the rushes for the electricity pylon just to the right of the farm. In this way you'll come through the reeds onto more open ground and be confronted by another stream. The map indicates a crossing close to the wall and there is a stile at this point, but for once, sheep prove more sensible and the easiest crossing is the one they've chosen; use it, then go right, to reach the stile. *When the walk was recce'd there had been torrential rain the day before and the area beyond the stile was a real quagmire. It is doubtful whether it ever really dries out, so be warned.* Bear left up the field – no obvious path, to a stile onto the road, just to the right of Bradley Howe Farm.

Go up the road for about100 yards/metres, just before the delightfully named Sniddles, there's a stile on the left, into fields. Go over the stile and up the field to another gate/stile in the wall ahead. *Pause here and look back to where Croker Hill is now in view, crowned with its telecommunications mast.* Bear right and follow a sketchy path across the rough field, making towards a clump of trees. *Ramshaw Rocks and the Roaches are now in view ahead and to the right.* The path becomes a well-defined track between walls and soon skirts a range of semi-derelict buildings that are un-named on the OS map. At the far end of the buildings go right and then left, through a gate and onto a good hard track, which leads you to the road opposite Little Hillend.

A signpost points up the driveway of Little Hillend. Up you go and through a gate at the far end, onto open moorland. The best that can be said for this next stretch is that the path is obvious. *At the time of the recce' it was also excessively wet. Wellington boots would have been an advantage as in places the water and mud were over the tops of my hiking boots.* Follow the path upwards to a gate and stile, well guarded by quagmires either side. On the far side of the stile there's a gate in the wall on the left and a sign denoting access land.

(Although I didn't explore this option, it seems from the map that you could go onto the access land, skirt round the back of Ann Roach Farm and pick up the path from Flash to Adders Green, thereby avoiding the next boggy section. Of course, the access land may be equally boggy, but I rather doubt it.)

Continue on what is now a broad track with the wall to your left, with Adders Green Farm in view ahead and also a distant view to the traffic on the A53. At the wall corner there is another morass and a mass of rushes and reeds through which you make your 'damp' way. Then, in front of you and only separated from you by a ditch, is a hard, surfaced track. Wonder of wonders, there's a bridge of sleepers across the ditch and now you are on dry land. *There's a sign here too, and it reads, "No right of way along the farm road. Private".* Here follows an unprintable expletive. Ahead lies more bog trotting as you carry on towards Adders Green, finally bearing right along a broad green swathe of grass to reach the farm. Turn right just before the farm buildings and go through a gate, where again a sea of rushes and reeds confronts you – and you know what that means. There is a waymark post some way into this 'jungle' but apart from that, there's no obvious indication that anyone has ever passed that way. *Temptingly, just to the right is the farm track you saw earlier (and were warned not to use). I'll leave it up to your conscience whether you plough through the bog or use the track. Suffice it to say that I've now passed this way three times and never got wet feet.* The path emerges from the rushes close to a cattle grid and gate. Here too there's a waymark post. Go over the cattle grid and onto the road. *Note that the name of the farm has changed from Ann Roach to Anroach and that it is now not a farm at all but an acupuncture clinic*

Go down the road towards Gib Tor, passing the camp site on your left. Follow the road up towards the A53. *The land to your right is mainly access land and can be reached either via a path on the right opposite Gib Tor or from a lay-by part way up the lane, just where the road bears left. Unfortunately, if you do go on the access land, there's no reasonable way of getting off until you get to the Corner House at Hazel Barrow, which then necessitates another road walk back to the Winking Man. The advice is to leave the access land for another day.* Carry on up the road, passing the Blackbrook information point on the left. You reach the A53 almost opposite the Royal Cottage, but unless you are on the right day and at the right time, it'll not be open. Go right (there's a wide verge on the right hand side of the road) and in about 300 yards/275 metres you'll be at The Winking Man and the end of the walk.

Royal Cottage. 1480 feet/451 metres
Telephone ? No website.

The name derives from the legend that, during the Jacobite Rising of 1745, Prince Charles Edward Stewart (Bonnie Prince Charlie) slept there on his march south (or on his march back). It is more likely he slept in Leek. Indeed there is some doubt whether the property known as Royal Cottage existed before the Leek-Buxton road was turnpiked in the 1760s. The building was certainly an inn by 1805 and by 1833 was known as the Royal Cottage. It eventually formed part of

The Royal Cottage

the Harpur-Crewe estate and passed into the hands of the Peak National Park Authority along with large portions of the Warslow Moors in lieu of death duties. It is still open for business, though apparently only on Friday, Saturday and Sunday evenings, so you'll need to pick your times. Apparently there are occasional 'folk' nights at the pub. The North Staffs Folk diary records these as being held on the last Friday of the month, at least during June to August.

Inn sign, Royal Cottage

This is a real survivor, an ultra traditional pub. It's a member of a dying breed of farmhouse pubs. They act as almost a social service, giving the farmer a bit of company and also being a place to meet for the few local residents. Given the proximity of The Winking Man and the Royal Cottage's opening hours there's probably minimal passing trade. You need to make a special effort to visit this pub but it does come highly recommended. As for the beers – well, there only seems to be draught ale when there's a folk night, otherwise it's bottled beers only. Would you be surprised to learn that the pub doesn't do food and has no intention of starting? Visit the Royal Cottage while ye may.

Opening tmes
The Royal Cottage opens 'about 20.00' but the landlord (Cliff) has always said that you can knock if you're in the area earlier and he'll let you in.

The Winking Man. 1464 feet/446 metres
Telephone 01538 300361 or 07779 300361. www.winkingman.com

The Winking Man

A few hundred yards down the road from the Royal Cottage is the Winking Man. This takes its name from the rock formation on the opposite side of the road a bit nearer Leek. One of the rocks has a hole through it, which, as you pass by on the road, appears to wink as other rocks obscure the hole. The Winking Man is a traditional Free House country pub, offering Coors beers and regularly changing guest beers, Usually there are three real ales on offer, these being changed regularly. There's a large beer garden to the rear of the pub.

The website gives details of a minibus service to get punters to and from the pub. This can pick up locally (and that includes Leek and Buxton). A minimum of 8 passengers is required before the service can run.

Opening times
Tuesday to Friday: 1200 to 1500 and 1800 to late; Saturday and Sunday: 1200 to late. Closed on Mondays, except Bank Holidays.
Food is available from 1130 to 1430 and 1800 to 2100 Tuesday to Friday, all day Saturday until 2100 and all day Sunday to 2000. Food is also available on Bank Holiday Mondays 1200 to 1900.

Walk 25: Strines (Strines Inn)

Start and finish	Strines Inn GR. SK222906
The route	Strines Bridge, Foulstone Delf, Back Tor, Dovestone Tor, Strines Edge, Moscar, Sugworth Hall, Strines Reservoir, Strines Bridge
Length	7.9 miles (12.7 km)
Ascent	1532 feet (467 metres)
Time	Allow 4 to 4¾ hours (exclusive of stops)
Map	OS OL1 (Dark Peak)

Getting there:

By bus. There's a daily bus service from Sheffield and Castleton along the A57 and there's a stop at the end of the Strines Road. The nearest point from there to the walk route is about 1060 yards/970 metres

By train. Nearest station, Sheffield.

By car. There's parking at the pub assuming you get permission from the landlord first. Otherwise there's limited roadside parking near Strines Bridge. The pub and Strines Bridge are best reached from the A57, Sheffield-Glossop road, then along the Strines Road, just west of Moscar Lodge.

The Walk

Strines Bridge to Back Tor

The Oxford English Dictionary defines the word 'strynds' or 'strinds' as a rivulet or a stream. The place name is first recorded in this particular location in the 13th century when it was mentioned in the Sheffield Court records, with reference to the stream flowing down Bradfield Dale.

From the car parking area at the bottom of Foulstone Delf, go up the rough track alongside Foulstone Dike. *The Foulstone Road, so called, gives access to*

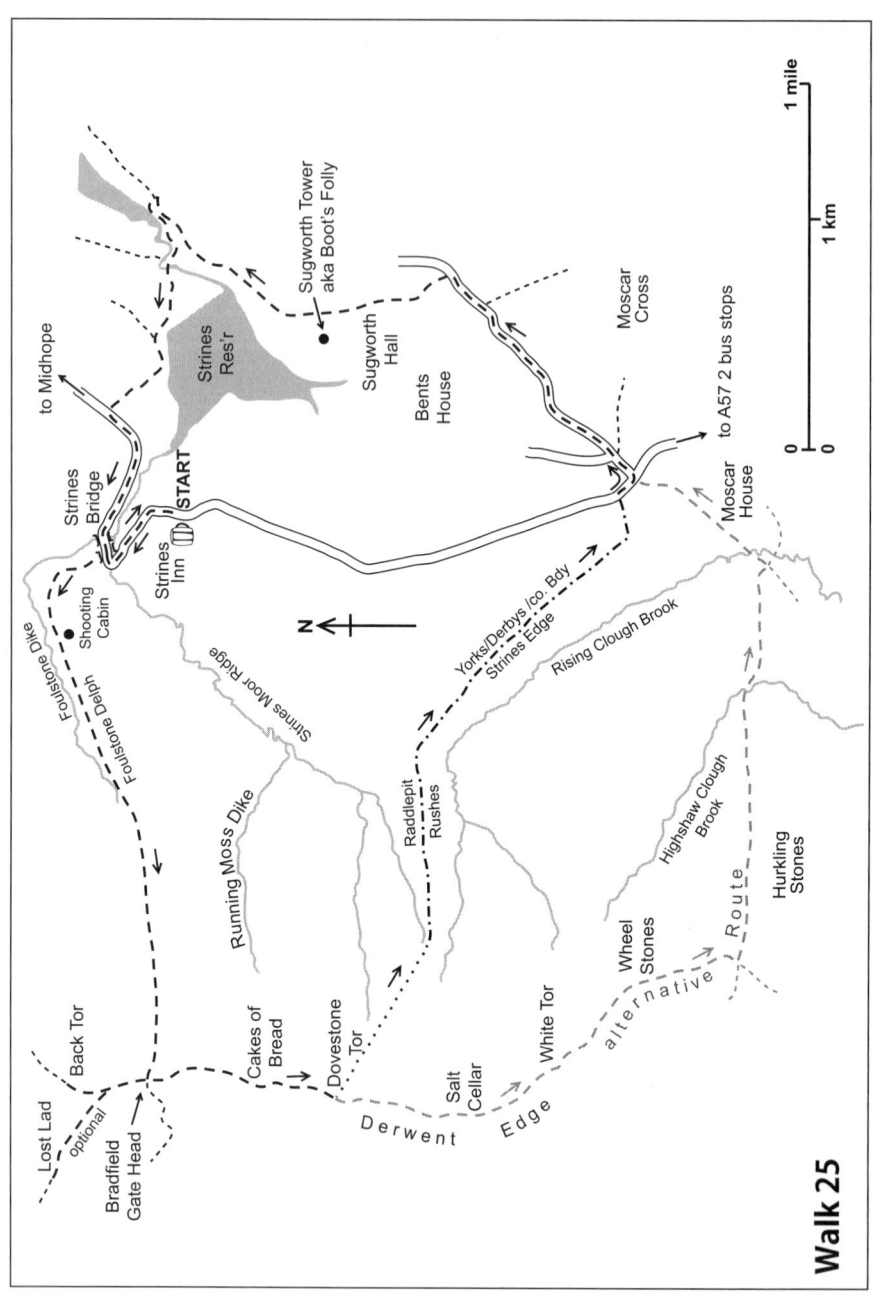

Walk 25

a shooting lodge and to the grouse moors belonging to Wentworth Estates. It is also a right of way and amongst the easiest and safest routes onto the Derwent Moors. Initially you pass through a conifer plantation, which was being clear felled when this walk was recce'd. *One hopes that any subsequent planting will incorporate native, deciduous trees rather than the 'serried ranks of conifers'.* After about 800 yards/740 metres, you reach a gate, giving out onto open moorland. *The shooting lodge of Foulstone Delf lies just to the left, perched above the main track. The moorland is still managed for grouse shooting, but is now all access land.* Nevertheless, there is no reason to stray from the track, so carry on upwards, with Foulstone Dike down to your right.

The path crosses a line of shooting butts and there were occasions in the past when attempts were made to stop walkers using the path during a shoot. *I've not heard of this recently and in any case the landowner is not supposed to interfere with the use of the public right of way or endanger users on it. It is worth pausing occasionally to look back at the widening view down towards Bradfield and Sheffield's 'Lake District'.*

Ahead you begin to discern the rock formations on Derwent Edge and the higher you climb, the more dramatic they look. You soon reach a major crossing of paths. *The view ahead has been constrained by higher land in front, but now, at this crossing of paths there is a sudden dramatic widening of the vista, taking in all the highest hills of the Peak District. It's a vast expanse, including, Kinder Scout, Bleaklow, the Axe Edge moors beyond Buxton and down to Sir William Hill and Minninglow. The upper Derwent valley is spread out below you and its southern continuation can be seen snaking away, with the gritstone edges guarding its eastern side.* You have reached Derwent Edge at Bradfield Gate Head, marked by a large standing stone. *The 'gate' element of the place name is nothing to do with your average garden gate, but is an old word for a road or route. Hence Bradfield Gate is the route to/from Bradfield.*

Approaching Back Tor

211

Turn right and go up the paved path to Back Tor, a magnificent viewpoint. *On a previous visit it was clear enough to see across to Lincoln Cathedral and the Yorkshire Wolds. There'll be few people who can resist the temptation to climb on the rocks to get to the trig point, but don't blame me if you find it harder to get down than get up! (You may also wish to go out and back along the paved path to the delightfully named 'Lost Lad', which is another good view point, complete with viewfinder. This adds about ⅔ mile/1 km to the walk and a further 110 feet/33 metres of ascent.)*

Back Tor to Moscar

From Back Tor, follow the broad paved path southwards along Derwent Edge. After only a couple of minutes you come to the standing stone that you passed on your way up. Continue along the path with extensive views both left and right. *Left you are looking far out across Yorkshire, well beyond Sheffield, whilst to the right you are looking into the heart of the Peak District, with Kinder, the Losehill/Mam Tor ridge and Win Hill being prominent. The curious shaped rocks on the moor on your left are the Cakes of Bread.* The path rises slightly to reach Dovestone Tor. Here you have a decision to make.

If the access moors are open, the weather balmy, the visibility good or your navigational skills with a compass efficient, then bear left at Dovestone Tor, following an obvious stream course that runs in a roughly south-easterly direction (about 120 degrees east of north). Keep company with this watercourse for around 430 yards (400 metres), at which point it swings to run decisively east. Leave the stream and continue on the same bearing for another 430yards (400 metres) at which point you should – if your navigation skills were as good as you thought – pick up a good track heading almost due east (85 degrees E of N). *Oddly enough this track is not marked as such on the OS map. This is the Yorkshire/Derbyshire County Boundary and from here on it is well marked with boundary stones and accompanied by a good track. Your route from Dovestone Tor was also along the boundary but there it is not so well defined.*

The track goes steadily down hill, crossing an area shown on the map as Raddlepit Rushes, which gives you a fair idea of the nature of the terrain if you stray too far off the track. The track and the boundary run down the watershed between the headwaters of the Strines Dike to the left and the Rising Clough Brook to the right. At the saddle you cross a stretch of quite 'moist' ground before the track rises slightly onto Strines Moor. Here the path takes a turn to the south, but you'll not miss it, even in mist, as the track is obvious and still well marked by boundary stones as it progresses along Strines Edge. *As you proceed there are glimpses left to Strines and Dale Dike*

Reservoirs and Sugworth Hall with its attendant tower, Ahead is Stanage and to the right a view opens out towards Ladybower Reservoir, with Win Hill and Lose Hill beyond.

After a little over ⅔ mile/1km, you'll suddenly notice that the boundary stones no longer accompany the track, but have veered away to the left. A faint path follows the line of stones over the brow of the hill until the gate leading onto the Strines road comes into view. Make a beeline for the gate. If you miss the path it doesn't matter greatly as the track carries on to join the old coach road just NE of Moscar House Farm and here go left, up to the gate.

Boundary stone, Strines Moor

Alternative route to Moscar from Dovestone Tor

If the weather is against you or the access moors closed, continue along the well-beaten path south from Dovestone Tor for about another mile/1.6km, passing the Salt Cellar, White Tor and the Wheel Stones, until you reach an obvious crossing of paths. Here go left and follow the path across Derwent Moor, for about a mile/1.6km, keeping company with lines of grouse butts, until you meet the old coach road, just a few hundred yards south-west of Moscar House Farm. At this point turn left and follow the coach road, up, through the farmyard and on to the gate at the Strines/Ughill road junction (GR. SK 224885), there

Bridge over Strines Dike

213

rejoining the main route. (This option adds nearly a mile/1½ km to the walk, plus about 220 feet/67 metres of ascent.)

Moscar to Strines Bridge

If time is pressing or you've just had enough, you can turn left here and simply follow the road along to The Strines Inn (1.4 miles/2.3km) and then down to the car park near Strines Bridge. The best thing you can say about this option is that it is nearly level or downhill all the way. The views down the valley over Strines and Dale Dike Reservoirs aren't bad though.

Public transport users will start the walk at this point having got off the bus at the junction of the A57 with the Strines road. It also follows that public transport users will finish the walk at this point and wander down the Strines Road to the A57, hopefully in time to catch their bus back to Sheffield or Castleton.

Head along the lane signed to Ughill and Dungworth. Follow this lane, which doesn't see a lot of traffic, with grand views away to the left over Strines reservoir and back towards Derwent Edge. In about 0.8 mile/1.3 km, you'll come to the entrance gates to Sugworth Hall on your left. There's a stile and gate alongside the main gates and a signpost reassuring you that this is indeed a public footpath. Go over the stile and down the drive for a short way (about 100 yards/metres) until you come to another footpath sign on the right. This takes you away from the drive and onto a path which skirts round the outside of Sugworth Hall gardens, at one point passing through a veritable tunnel of bushes and scrub, before finally emerging through a fancy gate into open fields again. Here the path bears right and Sugworth Tower can be seen ahead. *The tower is also known as Boot's Folly or Strines Tower. The tower was commissioned in 1927 by Charles Boot of Sugworth Hall, with the intention of providing work for Sugworth Hall's workmen during the Great Depression. Apparently there was originally a staircase to the top but this was removed after a cow got in and got stuck on the stairs! There's no public access to the tower.* Look out for the marker posts in the field, as the path isn't clear. It goes well to the right of the tower, eventually swinging right and heading in a north-easterly direction towards Strines Reservoir, which can be seen below. Soon you leave the well maintained fields around Sugworth Hall and enter an area of rough pasture. The path descends more steeply now and can be quite muddy. You may need to utilise some of the alternative routes that have been blazed in an effort to find drier ground. The path swings left at a wall corner and drops sharply downhill before swinging right again. At the bottom of the slope there's a stile on the left, which requires considerable agility to get over with any dignity. This drops you down onto another path, coming up from Dale Dike Reservoir.

Dale Dike reservoir collapsed on 11th/12th March 1864 sending a catastrophic flood down the valley into Sheffield. 240 people were killed. Where the path forks, bear left and cross the wooden bridge. Follow the path across an area of flat (and damp) land, soon crossing the outfall stream from Strines Reservoir. The path now rises through trees, eventually emerging into the open, close to Strines dam. *In the 1850s the Sheffield Waterworks Company obtained powers to build four reservoirs in Bradfield Dale to cater for the increasing demand for water from the burgeoning city. Strines Reservoir was completed in 1869. Originally it had been intended to construct Strines last, but Dale Dike dam was not completed until 1875, following its earlier collapse in 1864. Strines dam is 1083 feet (330 metres) long and 95 feet (29 metres)high. The reservoir holds 452,900,000 gallons of water. With the exception of some small streams draining off the Ughill Moors, all the water for Strines Reservoir comes off the Derwent Moors via two main streams, Strines Dike and Foulstone Dike.*

Follow the path steeply up to Brogging House, then go right to reach a track. Brogging House predates the reservoir, having been in existence certainly since 1715 and probably earlier. The water company used the property to house their reservoir keeper. Go left at the track and follow it up to the road. Go left and follow the road downhill again to Strines Bridge. You would be well advised to walk on the left hand side of the road, especially at the right hand bend as the visibility there is not good and it would be tragic to lose you now. *Oddly, although the OS 1:25000 map clearly names this first bridge as Strines Bridge (and the OS has done so on all the maps from the 1850s onwards), it doesn't span the Strines Dike. Instead it spans a stream of indeterminate name, which might be the Hollingdale Brook, or the Foulstone Dike, or maybe the Brogging Moss Dike, or even the Rushy Flat Dike.* Just beyond Strines Bridge is the car parking area and the entrance to the Foulstone Road. If you are walking up to the Strines Inn, carry on along the road, crossing another bridge (which does span Strines Dike) and go up the hill. Take great care at the right hand bend at the top as it is very narrow and has poor visibility. If you are visiting the pub and are only part way through the walk, you'll need to retrace your steps down to the start of the Foulstone Road.

Strines Inn. 1044 feet/318 metres
Telephone 0114 2851247. www.thestrinesinn.webs.com
The Strines Inn sits in splendid isolation on the picturesque minor road between Moscar and Langsett. It has a fine view down Bradfield Dale to Strines Reservoir and beyond. Despite its isolated position, it's a very popular pub

for either a casual drink or food. As one recent visitor from Canada said: "The meals are great, the views from the forecourt terrific, and they probably serve the best coffee for miles. The Kelham Island Pale Rider Ale is pretty good too! Highly recommended."

The pub is a Marston's house with their usual range of beers, but also regular guest ales, often from local micro breweries. There's also a beer garden.

Opening times

Opening hours are the same throughout the week: 1030 to 2300 in summer. Check website for winter opening times.

Food is available, all of it described as 'homemade'. No booking is required, but this pub does get busy so booking might be advisable. Food availability times are the same throughout the week; 1200 to 1430 and 1730 to 2100.

The Strines Inn

Walk 26: Taddington (The Waterloo)

Start and finish	**The Waterloo Hotel GR. SK131714**
Alternative sttart and finish	**Millers Dale station GR. SK138733**
The route	**Taddington (The Waterloo), Priestcliffe Ditch, Blackwell, Blackwell Mill, Mosley Farm, Wormhill, Cherryslack, Monksdale House, Limestone Way, Millers Dale, Moor High Mines, Priestcliffe, Taddington (The Waterloo)**
Length	**8.1 miles (13 km)**
Ascent	**1727 feet (526 metres)**
Time	**Allow 4-5 hours (exclusive of stops)**
Map	**OS OL24 (White Peak)**

Getting there:

By bus. Daily bus services from Bakewell, Buxton, Derby, Manchester, Matlock and Stockport to The Waterloo. Daily bus services to Millers Dale from Buxton, Chesterfield and Sheffield.

By train. Nearest station, Buxton. The bus services mentioned above call at the station.

By car. The Waterloo Hotel is on the A6 Derby-Buxton road, just west of Taddington village, so you should need no further instructions. There's parking at the pub, with permission from the landlord. Otherwise there's parking in lay-bys on both sides of the A6 about ¹/₃ mile/½km west of the pub. There's also pay and display parking at Millers Dale station on the Monsal Trail, just off the B6049

The Walk

From Waterloo to Blackwell Mill

From the front door of The Waterloo, turn left along the A6. This is not the most pleasant start to a walk as for ¹/₃ mile/½km you have to walk alongside the road to the lay-by on the Buxton bound side. Keep on the left hand verge, which is wide enough and even enough for comfortable walking, though there's no beaten path. *(It is possible to avoid the road walk by turning right just outside the pub and following the Limestone Way up the rough lane for about ¹/₃ mile/½ km, then turning sharp right onto a field path and descending again to emerge on the A6 at the lay-by mentioned above. This adds ¹/₃ mile/½ km and 90 feet/28 metres of ascent, to the walk.)* At the lay-by, note the small spinney on your left and the sign pointing out that this is one of 16 paired spinneys on this road. *Apparently they were meant as guidance for travellers using the route in bad weather. There's another one on the opposite side of the road.* Cross the A6 to a stile, well hidden in the undergrowth, but properly signposted. Drop into the field and go down beside the spinney on your left. There's little or no path visible, but the route lies straight ahead through a gap in the bottom wall of the field. Similarly through the next field. In the third field the map indicates a right of way near the left hand wall. It also shows a pecked line bearing right and this is the walked path. Pass just to the right of the left hand electricity pylon and a stile/gate comes into view, just to the left of the house on the south side of the Priestcliffe Ditch road. At the road, go left, noting the nice stone trough.

At the crossroads with the B6049, go straight ahead, up the lane signed to Blackwell.

Go through this small hamlet, with Crossroads Farm to your left and soon pass the entrance to the Farming Life Centre on your right. *The Centre opened in June 2005. It was set up by a group of interested individuals, all of whom have a professional or personal commitment to Peak District hill farming. It is based in a converted barn at Blackwell Hall Farm – a working dairy and sheep farm situated between the market towns of Buxton and Bakewell in the Peak District National Park. The Centre develops and hosts a range of health, social and economic activities which promote the well-being of Peak District farmers and rural communities, and celebrate farming past, present and future.* Continue up the lane, passing the caravan site on the right and then, where the lane turns left, go straight ahead, following the Pennine Bridleway signs down a rough track. Continue along this track, which is easy walking, until you reach a junction at a gate. Ignore the track leading right and continue on the Pennine Bridleway, through another gate. The bridleway now runs along

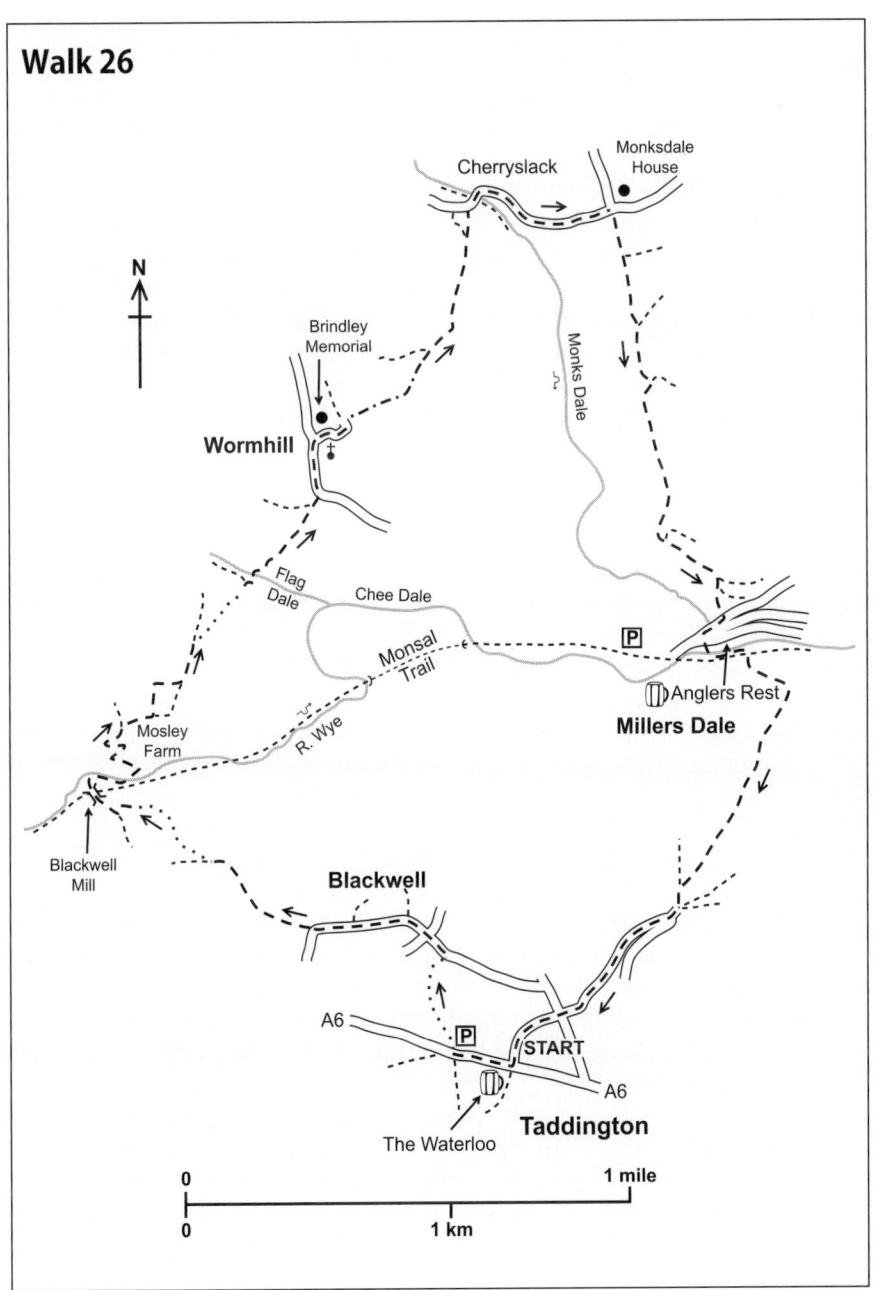

Walk 26

N

Cherryslack

Monksdale House

Monks Dale

Brindley Memorial

Wormhill

Flag Dale

Chee Dale

Monsal Trail

P

Anglers Rest

Millers Dale

Mosley Farm

R. Wye

Blackwell Mill

Blackwell

A6

P

START

A6

The Waterloo

Taddington

| 0 | | 1 mile |
| 0 | 1 km | |

the hillside, with a view over Chee Dale and up to Tunstead. *Tunstead Quarry is huge. It reputedly has the biggest limestone quarry face in Europe. You'll see it at closer quarters later.* Where the bridleway begins to turn to the left, bear right, down the rough slope to a stile in the bottom wall. If you make for Tunstead you'll find the stile. There's no path and no signs.

You need to bear in mind that this path has a sting in the tail as it descends into Chee Dale. It's steep and underfoot it's polished limestone, very slippery when wet and quite un-nerving. In these sorts of conditions it may be better to ignore the footpath and continue on the bridleway, which soon swings into the head of the dale and descends in a rather more genteel fashion to the Monsal Trail.

Once in the field, ignore the tempting gateway to your left and make your way down beside the wall, thus locating a stile, almost at the bottom of the field. Neither of these stiles accords with the OS 1:25000 map. Bear right across the next field to another stile, which takes you over into the Chee Dale Nature Reserve. The path twists its way through the vegetation until you suddenly come to the lip of a steep slope. The A6 can be seen across the dale. The path goes steeply down, sometimes zig-zagging and at one point dropping down a small rock step. You reach the dale bottom at a stile, where you rejoin the Pennine Bridleway and here you turn right. Go down the dale to the bridge over the Monsal Trail. *If time presses, or you've just had enough, you can reduce the length of the walk considerably and the amount of ascent, by going onto the Trail and following it to Millers Dale, picking up the main route description there. This entails walking through three of the recently opened tunnels, including the long Chee Tor tunnel, which is lit, and crossing four viaducts. You may also have to contend with horses and you'll certainly have to mix it with cyclists, some of whom have yet to discover the meaning of the words 'give audible warning of approach'. Personally I can't see the point of walking through any tunnel when there's such magnificent scenery outside. The tunnels were built for trains, and that is what they should be used for.* Ignoring the blandishments of the Monsal Trail and maybe bemoaning the loss of the Derbys-Manchester railway, go over the bridge and follow the Pennine Bridleway down to Blackwell Mill. *There's a cycle hire centre here, opened in 2011. It does hot and cold drinks and snacks and is a welcome addition to the area.*

Blackwell Mill to Wormhill

Blackwell Mill cottages were built by the Midland Railway Company to house their staff and their families, for what was then an important junction on the main line to Manchester. The cottages had their own little station on the Buxton branch. The platforms and the tiny waiting shelter still exist, just waiting for

Blackwell Mill cottages

someone to reopen the line. *Doing so would give a good means of access to the Monsal Trail from Buxton and would not impinge on the use of the Trail itself.* Go down to the river and across the bridge to Blackwell Mill cottages and there go right. Note the sign on the bridge warning of difficulties using the riverside path if there has been heavy rain. This mainly relates to the passage of Chee Dale. Your route should be OK unless there is obvious sign of flooding near the bridge. If this is the case, retreat to the Monsal Trail and use that. Stroll along beside the river with the former railway route up to your left. *This was built by the Midland Railway in the 1860s and formed their main line to Manchester. It was closed in 1968 in the aftermath of the Beeching Report, though its closure was never envisaged in that infamous document.* The path forks. Keep left, following the Pennine Bridleway signs. The path now climbs away from the river and passes under the railway to a gate. There follows a grand series of well-graded zig-zags, up the hillside, with ever widening stunning views down Chee Dale and up Wye Dale. Just beyond the first hairpin bend there's an access onto the Monsal Trail, so anyone who was thwarted by flooding at Blackwell Mill could rejoin the walk route here.

At the top of the zig-zags, the path enters a short, walled lane. At the gate, the lane clearly originally continued ahead, but the expansion of Tunstead Quarry into Old Moor has put a stop to this. Instead the Pennine Bridleway is signed to the right, through the scrap infested Mosley Farm. Look out for the PBW signs part way through the farm complex and there go left. *(The OS map shows a path continuing through the farm complex, but this is not signed and the PBW route goes to the same place in any case, so it doesn't matter.)* You are now in a narrow walled lane, heading for a belt of trees. These trees form a screen round the Old Moor Quarry site and were one of the conditions of the planning consent from the National Park.

The bridleway does not pass through the obvious gap in the trees, but turns right, passing through a gate into a field and running alongside the wood to another gate. This exits onto a tarred lane, which you cross and go through another gate, opposite. Go left along the bridleway, noting that the path you 'missed' at Mosley Farm is signed here. The bridleway runs alongside the lane for a short distance. Just before it rejoins the lane, you need to look out for a sign-posted gate on your right. Leave the bridleway here, go through the gate and into the field. There's no obvious path in the field and the far boundary cannot be seen. Make your way diagonally across the field, heading towards Hassop Farm, which can be seen on the far side of Flag Dale. You should also be able to discern the path leading up to the farm so if you make for this you'll come across a ruined wall, in which there are the remnants of a stile. Still no obvious path and no sign of the end of the field, but bear right, making for a gate and stile that can be seen, as before, on the far side of the intervening dale. You'll soon spot a gate and stile in the fence/wall ahead. Go through this into Meadow Wood and descend into Flag Dale down a steep twisting path. In the bottom of the dale, keep straight ahead and up the other side to the gate and stile you saw earlier. Follow the path diagonally across the field to Hassop Farm. Go into the farm yard and turn right along the farm access to the road, where you turn left. Stroll up the road to Wormhill.

Wormhill to Millers Dale

As you enter Wormhill, there's a lane on the right leading to the parish church. This is your route, but before you take it, go a little further on to the village green where there's a set of old stocks and large drinking fountain. *This is the Brindley memorial. James Brindley, the great canal pioneer, who engineered the Bridgewater Canal, was born in the parish and is rightly celebrated in this fine water feature. Brindley was the civil engineer for over 300 miles of canals. In 1733, when he was 17 he was apprenticed to a millwright. By 1742 he had started his own business in Leek and was already becoming well known for his engineering expertise. In 1759 he was engaged by the Duke of Bridgewater to construct the Worsley to Manchester canal (the Bridgewater Canal). Incredibly, the whole project was opened for business in 1761, including aqueducts and tunnels. The price of coal, on which the great manufacturing city of Manchester depended, dropped dramatically. Not surprisingly, Brindley became much sought after. He is, without doubt, Wormhill's most famous son. Wormhill sits on top of the limestone plateau so the presence of a regular and unceasing supply of water must have been the reason for the village's existence. There are seats here and it's a pleasant place to stop and have a rest.*

Brindley memorial, Wormhill

Now go down the lane signed to the church. Follow the lane until it degenerates into a track, just past Holly House. The path is signed to the left, by the side of Holly House, to a stile and into a field. Ignore the tempting stile opposite and instead go right, following the far wall up this long field to a signposted gate by a solitary tree. Bear left here, making for a gap in the wall ahead. *Looking right, you can see the curious shaped hill known as Knot Low, overlooking Millers Dale. Looking ahead, you can make out the telecommunications mast on Sir William Hill and The Barrel Inn at Bretton.* The gap in the wall turns out to be the entrance to a very narrow walled lane. Go down this lane with Tideslow and Wheston now in view ahead. *The hills in the distance are Mam Tor and Rushup.* At the T-junction you rejoin the Pennine Bridleway and go right. The narrow, walled lane continues and soon swings left to begin its descent into Monks' Dale, which can be seen below. The angle of descent steepens and you are now looking straight up Peter Dale. Where the walled lane comes out into open fields, there's a PBW waymark pointing left and a footpath waymark pointing straight down the hillside. Follow the footpath steeply down to the Wormhill-Tideswell road at Cherryslack and go right.

Footpath signs to the left and right indicate routes up Peter Dale or down Monks' Dale. Theoretically, the Monks' Dale path offers a potential short cut and avoids some climbing. However, it is not recommended, especially after

223

heavy rain, where the path doubles up as the riverbed. *I recall one walk from Peak Forest to Millers Dale where the road embankment on which you are now standing made an effective dam and there was a sizeable lake in Peter Dale. The river then ran down the length of Monks' Dale and the gymnastics required to avoid a wetting would have done credit to the Olympics. That, coupled with the fact that one had to walk bent double for a mile or more to get under the trees/bushes, rather put me off Monks' Dale!*

Suitably discouraged, go up the road towards Tideswell and leave Monks' Dale Nature Reserve in peace. Carry on up the road for about ½ mile/800 metres until you reach Monksdale House, where there is a crossing of routes. Go right here, along the Limestone Way, leaving the Pennine Bridleway to pursue its course northwards.

This section of the walk should be easy. There's no chance of getting lost. The route is confined between dry-stone walls and there are good views down into Monks Dale and ahead to Millers Dale and Knot Low. *When the walk was recce'd, there'd been heavy rain and there were some monumental puddles in the ruts made by farm vehicles. Marginally easier than the passage of Monks' Dale though.* There's a T-junction of tracks about half way along this stretch and here go right. Ignore a footpath sign trying to entice you into Monks' Dale and continue down the track until you reach Monksdale Farm, where there's a barrier and a gate, both of which open. Skirt round the farm and then down the signed route of the Limestone Way to the right. Again, ignore a footpath sign enticing you into the lower reaches of Monks' Dale and continue on the bridleway, which now swings left and descends to join the old road from Tideswell to Millers Dale. Go right here and down to the B6049, emerging almost opposite The Anglers' Rest. *There are buses to/from here for Buxton, Chesterfield, Sheffield and Tideswell.*

Go along the main road towards Millers Dale church, to look at the bottom of Monks' Dale. *When the walk was recce'd there was a substantial stream flowing at this point, so choosing not to go down the dale was the correct decision.* There's a flight of steps on the opposite side of the road, leading down onto the Litton Mill road. The route of the walk goes down these steps.

Millers Dale to The Waterloo

From the bottom of the steps go left and then almost at once, go right and cross the twin footbridges over the Monks Dale stream and the River Wye. *Of course you may have been distracted by the close proximity of The Anglers' Rest, which features in the 'Best Pub Walks in the White Peak' book. Can't say I blame you and if this is the case, rejoin the walk at the footbridges.* Once over the river go up the steep and rough limestone path to the Monsal Trail.

(Anyone who has parked at Millers Dale station should turn right here and follow the Trail back, over the magnificent 1860s viaduct to the former station. Likewise anyone starting from Millers Dale station should go over the viaduct and on the Trail towards Bakewell until you reach this crossing of paths and then go right, signed to Priestcliffe).

Cross the Trail and go up the path signed to Priestcliffe. The path climbs steeply away from the Trail,

Anglers' Rest, Millers Dale

up steps, then bearing left below overgrown waste tips and skirting the edge of the disused Millers Dale quarry. *This is now part of a nature reserve and is a haven for a number of rare plant species, including various orchids. When the walk was recce'd, spiders had done their level best to garrotte any passing walkers by spinning their delicate threads across the path just at neck height.* The steepness of the path increases as it rounds the end of the quarry, and this can be quite tricky in wet weather when the well-polished limestone is slippery. Console yourself with the knowledge that there's a fence between you and the quarry! Where the gradient eases, look back for a view over Millers Dale and up Monks' Dale. *There are a couple of signs on the fence warning you of 'cliffs', which is surely so obvious that one wonders why they were thought necessary.* The path now moves away from the quarry edge to a stile on the left and thus out into open fields. Go straight on, across the field on a sketchy path. *To your left there are extensive remains of lead mining activity. This was Moor High Mine, though it also had other names, which were a corruption of the real one, More Eye and Morey apparently being two of these.*

Go over another stile and follow the wall on your left, with a view down High Dale. You'll be delighted to know that all the stiles from here to Priestcliffe are well marked by yellow paint. The next stile is in the corner, marked by a thorn tree. Continue straight ahead to a stile half way down the field in the left hand wall. Cross the stile and continue, now with the wall to your right. Another stile and the path tops the rise, with the first houses of the metropolis of Priestcliffe now in view. Another series of well-marked stiles takes the path into the field nearest the farm. Bear right here to a signposted stile, leading out onto a rough lane. Go left to the farm and at the 30 mph signs(!) and the junction of lanes, go right. Musing on the bureaucracy that requires the installation of 30mph signs (and more particularly, 'de-restriction' signs) on lanes like this, go up the road, keeping to the right where it forks. Pass Holme Grange and Priestcliffe Hall on your right and go up the road to the crossroads. Go straight across, following the sign to The Waterloo and noting that it does 'good food and ale'. As the road swings left there's a last glance across to Tunstead quarry in the distance and then, ahead of you The Waterloo comes into view. *Don't make a mad dash for the front door. Remember that there's the A6 between you and salvation! It would indeed be a shame if you met your fate now.*

The Waterloo Hotel. 1187 feet/362 metres
Telephone 01298 85230. www.thewaterloohotel.robinsonsbrewery.com
As the name suggests, the pub has been on this site since just after the Battle of Waterloo in 1815. Initially it was a coaching inn on this important turnpike road. It is still a convenient stopping point on the A6, being the only pub on the main road between Buxton and Bakewell. Before 1815 it was known as Sough Farm, a sough being a tunnel for draining the local lead mines. The beers are from Robinson's of Stockport and certainly a combination of a pint of Unicorn real ale and one of the pub's homemade steak pies is a real treat.

Opening times
Sunday to Thursday: 1200 to 2300; Friday and Saturday 12 noon to midnight. Food is served: 1200 to 1500 Monday to Friday, 1800 to 2030 Tuesday to Friday (kitchen is closed on Monday evenings), 1200 to 2100 Saturday and 1200 to 1700 Sunday. Traditional Sunday lunch is served between 1200 and 1430. Drinks and snacks are available all day.

The Waterloo Hotel

Walk 27: Tideswell (The Anchor)

Start and finish	The Anchor GR.SK159763
The route	The Anchor, Castleton Lane, Poyntoncross Barn, High Rake, Great Hucklow, Grindlow, Silly Dale, Wardlow Mires, Cressbrook Dale, Tansley Dale, Litton, Litton Edge, The Anchor
Length	6.5 miles (10.5 km)
Ascent	840 feet (256 metres)
Time	2½-3 hours (exclusive of stops)
Map	OS OL24 (White Peak)

Getting there:

By bus. Daily buses to The Anchor from Bakewell, Buxton, Castleton, Chesterfield and Sheffield.

By train. Nearest stations, Buxton (Buxton-Sheffield/Chesterfield bus services pass the station). Hope (Manchester-Sheffield Hope Valley Line). Castleton-Bakewell bus service passes station entrance.

By car. The Anchor Inn lies on the main A623 Chesterfield-Manchester road. If you can't find this, you really should seriously think whether you are sufficiently geographically aware to safely do these walks. There's no public parking at The Anchor, but you may be able to park at the pub if you ask for permission from the landlord. Alternatively, there's limited on-street parking in Litton and Great Hucklow.

The Walk

Anchor Crossroads to Great Hucklow

From the front door of the Anchor, turn right, along Castleton Lane. This was the old road to Castleton, before the existing road through Bradwell was constructed. The lane sees little traffic and is a pleasant stroll. Soon after leaving the Anchor you pass Tideswell cemetery on the left. As you stroll along the lane look right. *There's a view right through to the Eastern Edges, with the cliffs of Curbar Edge being particularly clear. Ahead of you and to the right rises Hucklow Edge. Watch out for gliders from the airfield above Hucklow. To the left is mast-crowned Tideslow.* You pass the access to Rising Sun Farm on your left and then, on your right there is a triangular shaped field. *The late RWP Cockerton did a lot of research into the medieval Portway and surmised that it came up this field en route to Tideslow. No trace now remains, though there is a curious shallow depression running across the field that could be the route – or maybe just a natural feature.*

You have gradually been climbing as you walked along the lane, though you'd scarcely notice it. However, at Poyntoncross Barn you top the rise and begin to descend along the delightfully named Wash House Bottom. *These two place names cry out for some explanation. What was the Poynton Cross (and where was it) and where was the wash house? Any answers would be gratefully received.* Now to the left you can see the tumbled nature of Tideslow Rake. *This extensive lead mining site has lain untouched for many years and so contains some fascinating examples of early lead mining practices.* As you go down the hill you'll come to stiles on either side of the road. Your way lies to the right, but it is worth going over the stile on the left to examine the lead mining remains at closer quarters. *There are examples of early open cut workings and buddling ponds where the lead ore was separated from the waste materials. Take great care when poking around these sorts of sites.* Return to the stile, cross the road and go over the stile on the far side. *This is High Rake, another lead mining site, now almost completely overgrown with trees. It is in the ownership of the National Park.* The path wriggles its way through the trees until it suddenly emerges into an open area; the site of High Rake Mine. *The site has been excavated and the remains of the buildings*

High Rake Mine

exposed. Well worth looking round and reading the excellent information boards. Like many such mines in the Peak District, this one failed to live up to expectations and cost the investors many thousands of pounds. It was first sunk in 1768 but ran into problems with water. There was considerable investment in the 1830s and 40s to tackle the water problem, including the installation of steam driven pumps. However, the miners failed to locate a workable body of lead ore despite driving a shaft to a depth of 720 feet (220 metres). They had bottomed out the limestone and reached non-mineral bearing rock (toadstone). They attempted to drive through this to the limestone beneath but failed. It has been suggested that they were very unlucky and the toadstone through which they were driving was in fact a volcanic plug. If this was the case they would never have got through it. However, the nearby Milldam Mine in Great Hucklow also had the same problem with toadstone and they too never managed to break through to limestone below.

The path now joins a track and soon reaches a lane. *There's a grand view from here, down Bradwell Dale to Win Hill and Lose Hill.* Carry on along the lane to Windmill. *There's no windmill here now, but on an 1880 map there is a curious circular building to the west of the hamlet, which may be a windmill. Later maps don't show it as a building but as a circular feature. Modern maps and aerial photography don't show it at all. Burdett's map of 1791 (originally surveyed in 1767) shows the place name as Wind Mill, but unlike elsewhere on his maps he doesn't show a windmill symbol.*

Still musing on the non-existent windmill, go through the hamlet to the main road. Take great care here. Despite this only being a B road, it is well used by lorry traffic, to and from the cement works in Hope. The visibility is not good, especially to the left where lorries are coming up the hill. You need to cross smartly and go up the lane signed to Great Hucklow. Once across, make your way towards the next crossroads. Just before you get there, there's an unsigned path on the left. This runs parallel to the road to Great Hucklow and is infinitely preferable to walking along the road. *The path runs through more lead mining remains and there's another excellent information board describing the various mines along this rake.* The path rejoins the road at the Great Hucklow boundary stone. Carry on along the road – there's a semblance of a footway on the right hand side, towards the village. *As you near the village, there's a lane off to the left. This is (or was) the access to the latest mining venture, the re-opening of Milldam Mine. Following the 1979 cessation of mining at Ladywash, at the eastern end of Eyam Edge, the mine owners, Laporte Minerals sought alternative, cheaper means of access to the Hucklow and Eyam Edge veins by driving an adit from Great Hucklow. (Ladywash had been worked by a shaft 730 feet/222 metres deep, with underground haulage*

Walk 27

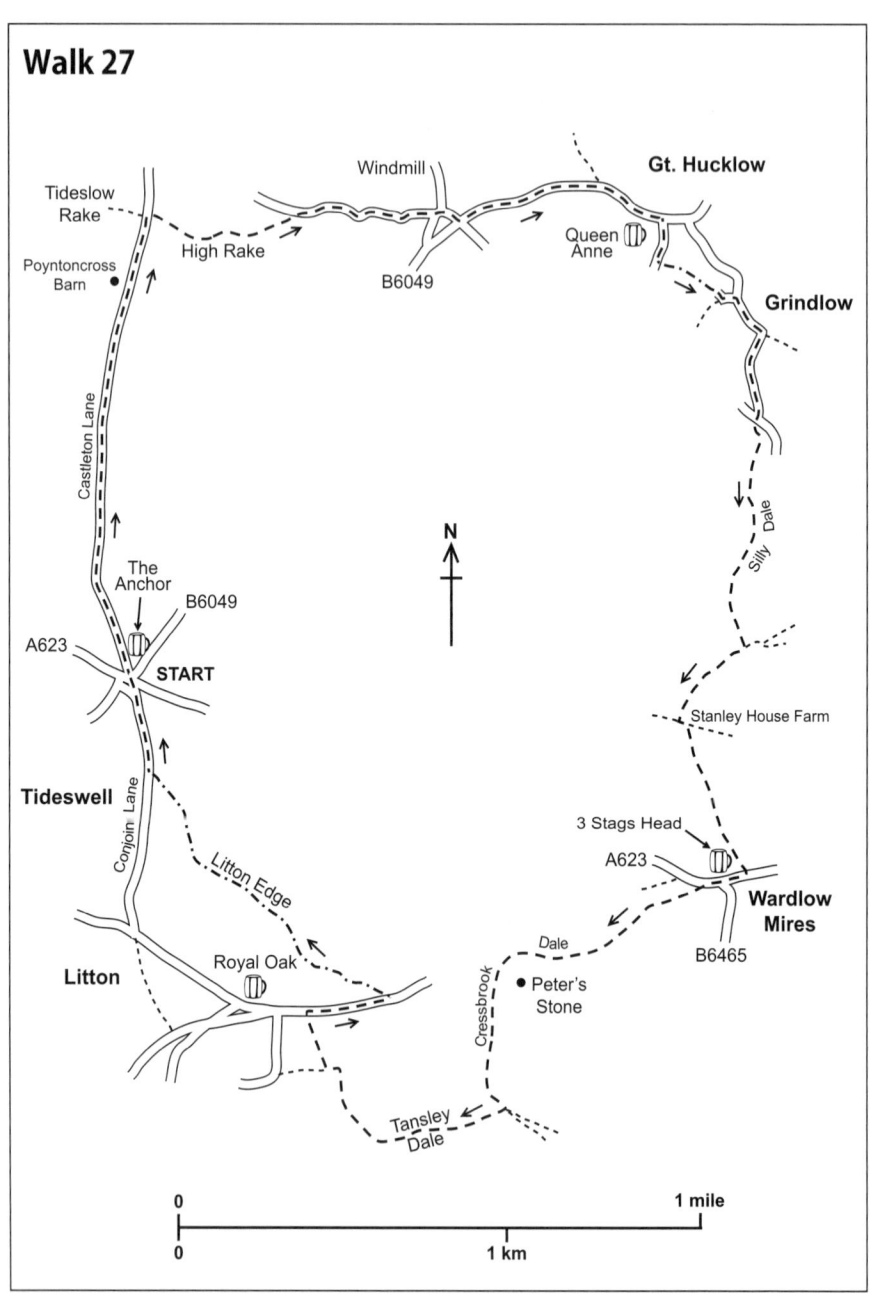

Tideslow Rake

High Rake

Poyntoncross Barn

Castleton Lane

The Anchor

B6049

A623

START

Tideswell

Conjoin Lane

Litton Edge

Litton

Royal Oak

Windmill

B6049

N

Gt. Hucklow

Queen Anne

Grindlow

Silly Dale

Stanley House Farm

3 Stags Head

A623

Wardlow Mires

B6465

Dale

Cressbrook

Peter's Stone

Tansley Dale

| 0 | | 1 mile |
| 0 | 1 km | |

by an 18inch/450 mm gauge railway system). The new venture envisaged an adit with a gradient of 1:8, which would allow the use of modern machinery. Planning consent was granted in 1987 and the mine was re-opened in 1991. Changes in the price of fluorspar and a change of ownership saw the mine close again in 1999 and it is now on a care and maintenance basis. The mine compound is almost completely invisible from the village, but interestingly the landscaping made use of surplus concrete panels from the Carsington Reservoir tunnelling project. Some of the rolling stock from the former Ladywash Mine found its way to the Steeple Grange Light Railway at Middleton by Wirksworth, where it is still in use. Carry on along the main road into the village. The Queen Anne pub (1024 ft/312 metres), is on your right as you enter the village. This pub features in 'Best Pub Walks in the Dark Peak', also published by Sigma and needs no further description here, except to say that it's well worth a visit, the food being particularly good.

Great Hucklow to Wardlow Mires

Go through the village, passing the Nightingale Centre and the Old Manse on the right. Turn right at the T-junction, just beyond the Methodist chapel and go down the lane. As you pass the fine old building that is the Unitarian church, there's a stile on the left. Go over this and follow the footpath beside the wall, through a series of fields, and over the various step stiles – some easier than others, until you reach a lane at Grindlow. Go left here and then after only a few yards/metres go right at the T-junction.

Pass through Grindlow. At the barn, follow the road round to the right, ignoring the tracks and paths leading straight on. Stroll down the lane, with a view ahead down Silly Dale and beyond to Wardlow Hay Cop and Longstone Edge. When you reach the Eyam-Windmill road, there's a track straight ahead. This is your route. It skirts to the left of the bungalow, then swings right into a narrow walled green lane. Follow this down Silly Dale. Unusually for a route down a dale, it does not run along the dale bottom, but well up on the right hand side. There doesn't seem any obvious reason for this, though there is evidence further on of former lead mining activity, where an overgrown rake crosses. The dale deepens and there are a few small limestone crags, then the dale ends abruptly and beyond stretches the broad, open and almost flat area in which lies Wardlow Mires. The last word of this place name is the clue to this area and it must once have been a difficult place to get across. At the T-junction of tracks, go right. Here you join the route of **Walk 6**. If you've already done that walk the next section should be familiar to you (and the description the same). You soon reach Stanley House Farm, which now has a number of holiday cottages. Just beyond the farm, the track swings right and there's a footpath sign and stile on the left by a gate. A notice warns you to 'Beware of the bull'. Having ascertained that there's no bull in the vicinity, go over the stile and bear right, making for a gate and stile by a trough in the bottom wall of the field. *Wardlow, Wardlow Mires and the head of Cressbrook Dale can be seen ahead with Peter's Stone prominent.* In the next field keep by the right hand wall to a gate leading into the farm complex. Continue ahead, with the barns on your left and a fence to your right, to another gate, into the farmyard. Go left, through another gate and then right, out onto the A623.

New bridge in Cressbrook Dale

Wardlow Mires and the Three Stags Heads. 791 ft/241 metres
The Three Stags Heads lies just to your right and a description appears in **Walk 6**. Suffice it to say this pub is legendary.

Wardlow Mires to Litton
Cross the road and go right, keeping an eye open for ferocious guinea pigs! Cross the road leading to Wardlow and then go along the new roadside path

to a small gate. Turn left here and pass round the back of the garage into a broad green lane, where you turn right. You are now in Cressbrook Dale National Nature Reserve. *The walk down the dale is delightful. You pass below Peter's Stone, the top of which can be visited, if you have a mind to.* The best ascent is to go round the back and scale it from there. For details of Peter's Stone, see **Walk 6**.

Three Stags Heads, Wardlow Mires

Continue down the valley, to the new (2012) bridge where a path diverges right to Tansley Dale and Litton. Turn right, cross the bridge, go over the stile and enter Tansley Dale. Climb steadily up the dale, noting the spoil heaps from past lead mining ventures and soon reach the head of the dale. Here the path bears right, up the hillside, alongside more lead mining remains, to a stile in the wall corner. Go over the stile and bear right, making for the Peak and Northern sign at the angle of the wall, then straight on to a stile by a gate. This gives out onto a narrow walled lane. Litton is in view across the fields. Go left, but in less than 50 yards/metres go right, over an unusual (and unsigned) stile into fields again. Bear left across the field on an obvious path to another step stile and P&N sign in the far left hand corner. Here you reach Litton's main street.

This walk is centred on The Anchor, but readers of 'Best Pub Walks in the White Peak' will recall the ringing endorsement of The Red Lion at Litton. (988 ft/301 metres) This excellent pub lies about 300 yards/280 metres to the left. Temptation indeed.

Litton to The Anchor

If you are resisting temptation, turn right at the main road and go up the street to the last houses. At the brow of the hill, just before the driveway to the B&B on the right, there's an unsigned rough track on the left. Go up this track to a gate and stile.

Here a good view begins to open up to the right. Indeed, the walk along Litton Edge does have some great views in all directions. Go up the field to a gateway in the top right hand corner and then follow the left hand wall. *Win Hill, Losehill and Kinder are in view to the right, as is Hucklow Edge. The view west stretches to the hills beyond Buxton and southwards you've got the distinctive outline of Wardlow Hay Cop.* The map shows the path keeping close to the wall, but beyond the next stile, the route bears right to a gateway, then bears left again, skirting to the left of an old pond to another stile alongside the low crags of Litton Edge. *The map shows some very narrow fields coming up to the Edge from Litton and you'll spot these as they breach the crags and provide access from the village onto the grazing land.* Continue by the wall now, climbing gently and passing through a series of fields and stiles, where the path is not at all obvious. At the brow of the hill, don't go straight on towards the obvious gate, but leave the wall and bear right, heading towards Tideslow, marked by the telecommunications mast. The stile out onto Conjoint Lane is in the far corner, just to the left of Bank Farm. Once in the lane, go right. The lane bends to the left to make a junction with the B6049, but just before it does so, there's a path on the right, through the fringe of trees, to the A623. The Anchor lies just the other side of this busy road. Take care crossing. It would be tragic to lose you now.

The Anchor. 1019 feet/311 metres
Telephone 01298 871371. www.anchorinntideswell.co.uk

The Anchor, Tideswell

The Anchor is a former coaching inn, which is not surprising considering its situation on the main Chesterfield-Manchester road. It has its origins in the 15th century as a farmhouse, opening officially as an alehouse in 1699. It is highly likely that prior to the place becoming an inn, the farmer brewed ale and sold it to travellers as a means of supplementing his income. This was a quite common practice. Almost inevitably, given the age of the pub, there are tales of ghostly happenings. A young man called William Swindell is still said to haunt the pub. He died in 1825 aged only 15.

Robinson's beers are the staple fare, but consuming too much of Robinson's Old Tom will probably cause Master Swindell to appear before your very eyes. The pub is open Tuesday to Sunday.

Opening times
Tuesdays to Saturdays: 1130 to 1430 and 1800 to 2300; Sundays 1130 to 2100. Food is served lunchtimes and evenings.

Walk 28: Uppermill
(Cross Keys and The Church)

Start and finish	Greenfield station. GR. SD 991046
The route	Greenfield station, Huddersfield Narrow Canal, to Diggle, Diglea, Running Hill Head, Pob Green (pubs), Dolefield, Fur Lane, Pennine Bridleway, Chew Valley Road, Greenfield station
Length	6.64 miles (10.7 km)
Ascent	954 feet (291 metres)
Time	3-3½hours (exclusive of stops)
Map	OS OL1 (Dark Peak)

Getting there:
By bus. Daily bus services to Greenfield station from Ashton, Manchester, Oldham, Stalybridge and Huddersfield
By train. Daily train service to Greenfield station from Manchester and Huddersfield.
By car. There's limited parking near the railway station and on-street by the two pubs (**see Walk 1** for description). There are public car parks in Uppermill and at the tunnel mouth at Diggle.

The Walk

Greenfield to Diggle
From the railway station, go down the road past the Railway Inn and round the hairpin bend onto Shaw Hill Bank Road. There's no footway on the left hand side of the road beyond the hairpin bend so best to keep on the right

hand side. At the bottom of the hill, just beyond the junction with Chapel Road, you cross the Huddersfield Narrow Canal. Go down the steps onto the towpath and begin your stroll along this delightful waterway. Immediately on your right there's The Kingfisher, a new canalside pub, part of the Marston's group. Too early for refreshment at this stage, so carry on along the towpath, soon encountering the new Frenches Wharf marina on your right. *There's a fine modern example of a lifting bridge taking the towpath over the access to the marina. A plaque commemorates the opening of the marina on 23rd May 2008.* You pass under the first of many bridges, this one being No. 79, and then reach the first lock. *This one is numbered 20W, denoting the fact that it is the 20th lock on the western side of the Pennines, measured from the junction of the Huddersfield Narrow with the Ashton Canal. The canal keeps close company with the River Tame to the right and as you pass a weir on the river, look out for the remains of a mill-race, which once provided the water for the erstwhile Frenches Mill.*

Bridge 78 is High Street Bridge and this was rebuilt in 2001 as the plaque explains. *This was one of the many bridges that had to be reconstructed in order to reopen this canal. Many people must have thought it was a lost cause, but the Huddersfield Canal Society thought differently – thank goodness.* There's no towpath under this bridge, so go up to the main road and cross it with care. In crossing the road, you also cross the canal and the towpath is now on the left hand side. Here is lock 21W.

Stroll along the towpath, noting to your right the Saddleworth Museum and the mooring for the trip boat. *The trip is worth the ride, especially if you've never experienced going through narrow locks. If you want to visit the museum or have a ride on the trip boat leave the canal at the next bridge (77) and go into the town, rejoining the walk later. The obelisk that you can see on the summit of Pots and Pans is the Saddleworth area war memorial, visited on* **Walk 13** *in this book. Every Remembrance Day there is a service at the memorial. It is a very moving experience to see hundreds of people, young and old, climbing the hill from all directions to attend the service.*

At Bridge 77 you cross the canal again and continue along the towpath on the right hand side. In a short while, look out for the stepping-stones across the river on your right. These lead into Uppermill park and are a favourite with children (of all ages). (*Note that, on a visit in February 2013 the last stone had been displaced and a flying leap was required. If you need the public toilets in the park you've been warned.*) Lock 22W soon follows, and then the canal curves to pass beneath the great stone viaduct that carries the Manchester to Leeds railway line. *It was the construction of this line in the mid 19th century that brought about the downfall of the canal. Lock 23W is right underneath*

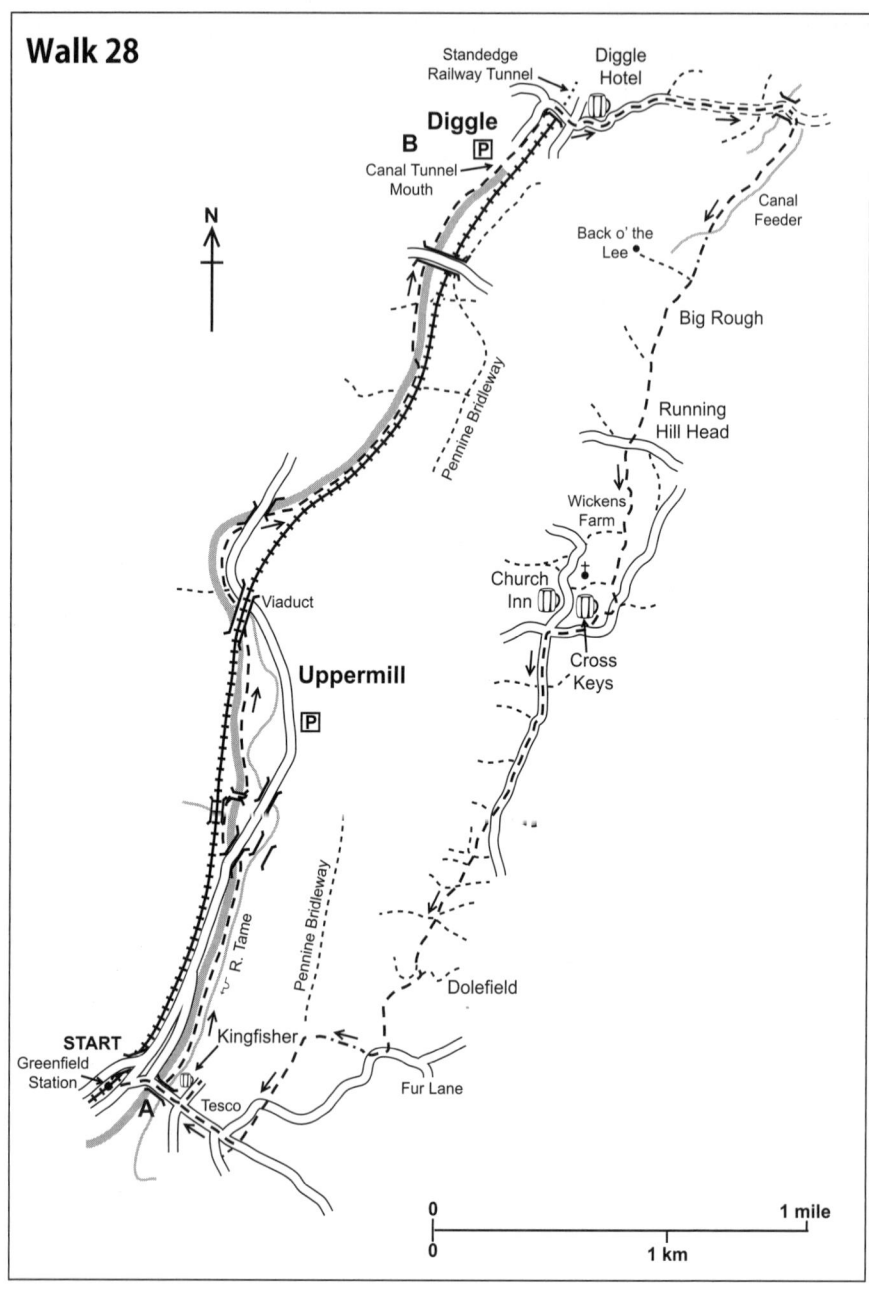

Walk 28

N

Diggle

B

Standedge Railway Tunnel

Diggle Hotel

P

Canal Tunnel Mouth

Back o' the Lee

Canal Feeder

Big Rough

Running Hill Head

Pennine Bridleway

Wickens Farm

Church Inn

Cross Keys

Viaduct

Uppermill

P

Pennine Bridleway

R. Tame

Dolefield

Kingfisher

START
Greenfield Station

A

Tesco

Fur Lane

0   1 mile

0   1 km

Uppermill viaduct and Huddersfield Narrow Canal

the biggest arch of the viaduct and involves quite an awkward manoeuvre with a 70 foot narrow boat! Ignore the path to the left and carry on along the towpath, crossing the river as you do so. Almost at once you reach the Brownhill Information Centre and the Limekiln café (open daily from 0900 to 1900 according to the notice board). *Information boards give you details of the canal and the public art sculpture trail.* You now pass under the Dobcross road bridge, beyond which there's a very narrow section of canal; so narrow in fact that there's no way two boats could possibly pass one another. This carries on for about 100 yards/metres. *Here the canal broadens out into a winding hole and wharf serving the Woolroad transhipment warehouse. This is where the trip boat turns round and where, from 1799 to 1810 goods were transhipped from canal boat to carts for a journey over the Pennines to Marsden and thus onto the canal again.* The towpath deviates from the canal bank for a short distance and passes through a car park, at which point there's a slipway on the left for trailed boats. Resuming its canalside position the towpath now passes the restored transhipment warehouse and then goes under a new road bridge. *There's a rather fine mural on the far wall of this* bridge, depicting the first and last boats to pass along the canal in its first incarnation. Just beyond the bridge is lock 24W and a flight of steps leads up beside it.

On the opposite side of the canal are the remains of another wharf and a mill. If you look closely you'll spot the tell-tale curved walls in the canal bank that indicate that there was once an arm of the canal into the mill itself. Long gone now of course, though the 1893 map shows it intact. Carry on along the towpath. Locks 25W and 26W come in quick succession and now you get a feeling that the hills are crowding in on you, with the valley narrowing appreciably. 27W and 28W also come quickly. The towpath keeps to the right hand side, but there is a path on the opposite side that can be accessed at any of the locks. Just after 28W there's Shaw's Mill on the left, complete with the remains of a wharf, but the skew bridge over the canal was once a railway siding as the 1893 map shows. Locks 29W and 30W quickly follow and then Bridge 66. It is possible to leave the canal here and go up the road to the right. Ward Lane, High Stile Lane and Church Lane will lead you unerringly to St. Chad's church and its near neighbour, The Church Inn.

Locks 31W and 32W complete the series of western locks and you are now at the summit level of the canal. The competing railway is just over the fence to your right and you'll regularly be assailed by the noise of passing trains because this line has a passenger train every 15 minutes in each direction and is soon to be electrified. Just past Lock 32W there are seats on the left hand side of the canal. There's also a series of stone blocks made into a type of 'snakes and ladders' game with key dates of the canal inscribed on them and forward or backwards moves to suit the type of event. From these stones you learn that the first boat through the tunnel was called 'Lively Lady' and the last through trip (in 1948) was by a boat named 'Ailsa Craig'. You also learn that the last commercial traffic through the tunnel was in 1921 and that the tunnel was reopened on 3rd September 2001. Carry on along this final bit of the towpath to the tunnel entrance at Diggle.

The Standedge tunnel took 16 years to construct (1794-1810) and cost rather more than originally anticipated – now there's a surprise! However, when you consider that the work was going on at a time when Britain was at war with France it's perhaps surprising that the tunnel was built at all. There's a plaque at the tunnel mouth commemorating Thomas Telford whose engineering skills rescued the original tunnel project from the brink of financial disaster. This is a strange place. It doesn't look as if you need to tunnel here at all, until you read the information board and realise that you are not looking at the original tunnel entrance. When the railway was widened and a third railway tunnel built in the 1890s, it proved necessary to extend the canal tunnel to

Locking up to Diggle, Huddersfield Narrow Canal

accommodate the new railway. *There was never a towpath through the tunnel. Horses had to go over the moor on a specially built route and the boats were 'legged' through as the design of the tunnel gates makes clear. Nowadays, boats are taken through with an electric tug.*

Diggle to Pob Green

Leaving the canal behind, go up through the car park to the road and bear right, alongside the railway line. *There are buses back to Greenfield from here, and also to Ashton, Huddersfield, Manchester, Oldham and Stalybridge should you need to avail yourself of public transport.* At the T-junction, go right, passing over the railway line. *Take the opportunity to look over the parapet on your left to see the 'new' railway tunnel of 1890s vintage (and still in use) and the two older railway tunnels to the right (1849 and 1871) and now disused. The original entrance to the canal tunnel was between the 'new' railway tunnel and the original ones. The railway builders used the canal to ferry spoil out of their tunnel workings, which was ironic to say the least. Even today there are apparently cross-cuts into the railway tunnels from the canal tunnel.*

Once over the railway, bear left by the Diggle Hotel, up the lane signed 'To Diglea only'. The lane climbs away through some very attractive stone buildings of typical Pennine design. *As you emerge from the cluster of buildings, look up to the left to where you can see the traffic on the A62 almost at the top of the Pennine ridge. The prominent building on the skyline was once The Floating Light pub, but is now a private house. Apparently it got its name from the fact that, seen from the valley bottom at night its lamps seemed to be floating in mid air. No doubt it was a very welcome sight to anyone crossing the moors.* The road now reaches another cluster of buildings and forks. Bear right. It's signed as 'Private Road', but it is a public footpath. Carry on along this road, ignoring the bridleway sign on the right, until you cross a substantial stone bridge. *There's a sign on the left indicating that swimming here is dangerous, but from the looks of the stream it would seem to be more true to say swimming is impossible. Just after the bridge there's a curious statue on the right. It's Victorian and apparently this has a gruesome tale attached to it. It represents Jeptha, a Jewish leader mentioned in Judges, who, in the midst of battle vowed that, if he were victorious, he would sacrifice the first living thing he met on his return home. Alas, this proved to be his young daughter and the statue apparently shows him in the act of sacrificing the girl. Rather a grim tale to be commemorated by a statue and why here? It is only fair to point out that the Biblical tale is the subject of much controversy and is thought to be a classic example of mistranslation.*

Just beyond the statue, go right, over a stile, which is signed, and into fields. The path follows an embankment, with a watercourse on the left. *This is a canal feeder from Diggle Reservoir, built in 1799 as one of a number of reservoirs required to keep the canal 'in water'. The feeder marks the boundary of the National Park at this point.* The map shows the path bearing away to the left, but this is not possible until you reach a sleeper bridge over the feeder. It's best to avoid the first of these and cross over the second one, just before the feeder bends to the right. Make your way up the pathless and, at the time of the recce', very wet, rough pasture, to a stile by the right hand corner of the wall. *A lot of the field boundaries shown on the 1:25000 map seem to have been removed, which doesn't make navigation any easier. Throughout this section of the walk there are good views across the valley and back the way you've come. The head of the valley is particularly impressive.*

Having located this stile go straight up the next field, by the wall, to another stile, complete with signpost. Straight on again, still following the wall, up to a gateway into a narrow walled track leading from Back o'the Lee Farm through the fields and onto open moorland at Big Rough. Cross this track and continue up, beside the wall, avoiding some very well disguised boggy sections, to a gate in the top right hand corner. Go through the gate and turn left, still alongside the wall until you reach a track. Go left, through the gateway, following the track, but in the next small field, look out for a stile just to the left of the point where the track goes through another gateway.

Go over the stile and up a path, hemmed in by a wall on the right and a fence on the left. This path gets narrower as it passes between two gardens, the hedges of which are bidding fair to close the route entirely. Assuming this doesn't happen, you'll end up on the lane at Running Hill Head. *St Chad's church can be seen ahead.*

Cross the lane and go through a kissing gate, signed as the Oldham Way. Another gate soon follows and then the route follows the top of a deep cut V on the right, soon bearing left and dropping steeply into a shale gully to cross a stream. No bridge or stepping-stones. Follow the way-marked path up the other

St Chad's, Saddleworth

side and pass to the right of the house, on steep sideways ground, to a well-hidden stile in the field corner. Follow the path down to the plank bridge across the stream. *The plank was rotten when I tried to use it and it is easier (and probably safer) to avoid it altogether. The stream isn't very wide in any case.* Over another stile and up the other side of the stream onto a path hemmed in by fence or hedge on either side. This carries on through a series of gates and stiles until you reach a tarmacked driveway. *There are no waymarks here and you could certainly do with them. The map clearly indicates that the driveway is a public footpath in both directions, so here you have the ultimate choice; which pub to visit first?*

If you go right, down the drive and through the yard you'll come to a gate and a steep narrow path alongside the churchyard. This lands you on Church Lane, less than 100 yards/metres from The Church Inn. If you go left, up the drive, you'll come to Running Hill Gate and there turn right. After only a few paces, there's a footpath sign on the right and a narrow path drops down beside a hedge to a stile. Go left here and you'll end up in the beer garden of the Cross Keys.

The Cross Keys and The Church

*Details of these two pubs appear in **Walks 1 and 13**. Although neither pub is in the National Park, they are both within spitting distance of the Park boundary. To exclude The Church because it's slightly lower and further from the boundary would be a crying shame, especially as it has its own brewery! Both are very popular pubs and on the occasion that a similar walk to this was recce'd – on a Sunday afternoon in January – it was impossible to get into The Church and only just possible to get into The Cross Keys. The latter managed to fix us up with meals for 15 hungry souls so all credit to them. Best to book!*

Back to Greenfield station

From The Church Inn make your way up Church Lane to the crossroads and go straight on into Gellfield Lane. From the Cross Keys go down Running Hill Gate to the crossroads and turn left into Gellfield Lane. *The first few yards of Gellfield Lane are quite narrow and there's no verge or footway, so do take care. Saddleworth cemetery is to your right and you don't want to end up there.* The lane dips to cross a stream and then climbs again to pass the substantial property known as Kirklea to your right. *The left hand wall of the lane marks the National Park boundary. There's an extensive view to the right, across Uppermill towards Delph. The big railway viaduct that you passed earlier is quite prominent and even from this distance you can hear the trains clearly, especially those working hard on the upgrade to Standedge tunnels.*

The lane forks and is marked by a street nameplate indicating Higher Cross Lane to the right and Knowl Lane to the left. Keep right, along what is little more than a rough track. This passes Higher Cross Farm on the right and then dips sharply to a junction. It is possible to drop down to the right here, straight into Uppermill for buses back to Manchester etc, but the route of the walk continues straight on, through the next farm complex and out onto a rough lane. *The view to the right opens up again, with mast crowned Wharmton Hill being particularly prominent.* Where the lane bears left, there's a stile in the fence ahead. Go over this stile, preferably showing rather more agility than the author in doing so, as I got tangled up with one of the fence posts. Go down the field and bear left in a distinct groove to a stile and stream in the bottom. No bridge (of course) and then up a flight of steps leading up to a tarmacked lane, with Dolefield to the left. Here you go right, down the lane, following it round the hillside until you pass alongside a house and down their drive past Fur Lane Farm to Kinders Lane.

Go down the lane to the right, noting the large anchor in the field on your right (!) and in less than 50 yards/metres, go right again at a footpath sign and through a stile into fields. Keep alongside the right hand wall until you top the brow and then follow the right hand wall steeply down, through another field to a bridge that spans the former Micklehurst loop railway line, now part of the Pennine Bridleway. *The railway was opened in 1885, in order to provide extra capacity on the Manchester-Leeds main line between Stalybridge and Diggle. It's primary role was as a freight route, but a passenger service was provided, albeit briefly (it ceased in 1917). The line closed in 1966 and key engineering features like the viaduct at Greenfield were demolished in the 1970s. The route became part of the Pennine Bridleway in the 1990s and probably sees more 'passenger' use now than it ever did when train services operated.* Just before the bridge, go left and follow a distinct path along the top of the cutting, taking care not to stray too far to the right, or you'll end up tumbling down to the bridleway below. Eventually the two routes merge and you go left, following the sign to Greenfield. When you reach the road called Higher Arthurs, carry on along the Pennine Bridleway to Chew Valley Road (for buses to Ashton, Manchester, Oldham and Stalybridge). Turn right and follow the main road past the Wellington Inn, the post office, Tesco and The Kingfisher, back over the River Tame and the canal and up to the railway station.

Walk 29: Wildboarclough (Stanley Arms)

Start and finish	Wildboarclough (Stanley Arms) GR. SJ980724
The route	Wildboarclough (Stanley Arms), Forest Chapel, Macclesfield Forest, Shuttlingsloe, Wildboarclough, Clough House, Danethorn Hollow, Cat and Fiddle, Chest Hollow, Torgate Farm, Bottom of the Oven, Wildboarclough (Stanley Arms)
Length	7.82 miles (12.6 km)
Ascent	1779 feet (542 metres)
Time	3½-4 hours (exclusive of stops)
Map	OS OL24 (White Peak)

Getting there:

By bus. There's a daily bus service from Macclesfield to Buxton via the Cat and Fiddle. Alight at the Cat and pick up the walk from there.

By train. Nearest stations, Macclesfield and Buxton. The bus service above serves the railway stations.

By car. A537 from Macclesfield, then follow signs to Wildboarclough, A53/54/537 from Buxton to Cat and Fiddle then left just by Peak View tea room, signed to Wildboarclough. The Macclesfield and Buxton routes converge at the Stanley Arms. From Congleton, A54 to Allgreave, then follow signs to Wildboarclough and up the valley to the Stanley Arms. **Parking at the pub only with permission from the landlord.** Alternative parking at Clough House picnic site, GR. SJ 986698.

The walk

Stanley Arms to Forest Chapel

From the pub go right and at the T-junction follow the road signed to Wildboarclough. Go down the road for about 200 yards/metres and then bear right at the road junction, following the signs for Macclesfield Forest and Forest Chapel. Just past the 'Quiet Lane' signs, there's a rough track on the right, complete with a Prohibition of Driving sign. Turn right here and make your way steeply up the track for about 540 yards/½km, until you top the rise and there

before you is the little settlement of Forest Chapel. *Chapel House Farm is to the right, the little church of St. Stephen's is right in front of you. Just to the left is the former school and school-master's house. If you have time, do go into the church, which is a lovely little place. The church was built in 1673, presumably as a Chapel of Ease, as the nearest parish church would be many miles away. It is recorded that, for some reason it remained un-consecrated until the 18th century. The church was extensively rebuilt in 1834 as the date stone above the porch testifies. An unusual feature of the church is that it retains the ancient custom of 'rush-*

St Stephen's church, Forest Chapel

bearing'. The ceremony takes place annually on the first Sunday after 12th August. This dates back to a time when churches generally had earth floors and these were periodically strewn with 'rushes' to give a sweeter smell. The first reference to this at Forest Chapel is in the 18th century, but it is highly likely that it was normal practice from the time the church was built.

Forest Chapel to Shuttlingsloe

From the church go up the road to the junction and there turn sharp left. The lane climbs out of the hamlet, soon giving views down Wildboarclough, towards Shuttlingsloe and eastwards to where the Cat and Fiddle Inn can be seen, perched on the ridge top. Follow the lane down to a T-junction and there turn right.

Stroll along this lane for about 550 yards/½km, to the entrance to Standing Stone car park. Just beyond the entrance there's another T-junction with the

Walk 29

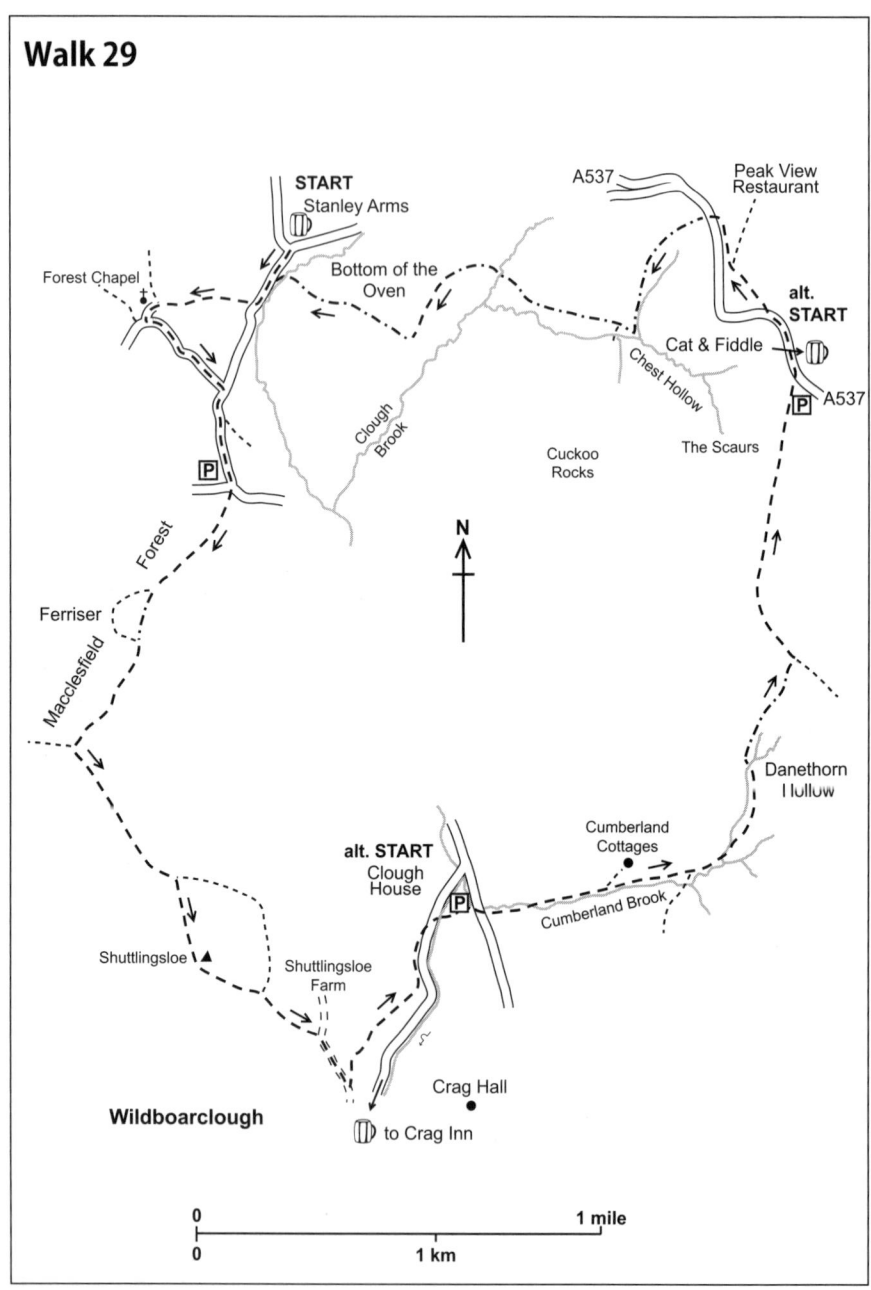

START
Stanley Arms

Forest Chapel

Bottom of the
Oven

A537

Peak View
Restaurant

alt.
START

Cat & Fiddle

Chest Hollow

A537

The Scaurs

Clough
Brook

Cuckoo
Rocks

N

P

Forest

Ferriser

Macclesfield

Danethorn
Hollow

alt. START
Clough
House

Cumberland
Cottages

P

Cumberland Brook

Shuttlingsloe

Shuttlingsloe
Farm

Crag Hall

Wildboarclough

to Crag Inn

0   1 mile

0   1 km

Walter Smith memorial stone just to your right. A bridleway leads straight ahead, signed to Shuttlingsloe. *The summit is hidden from view at this point, but there's a grand view down the valley and across towards Flash.* Go along the bridleway, which is a broad stony track with the forest to your right. Where the track bears right, there's a path leading off to the left, with a sign saying that it's for walkers only. *Judging by the tyre prints in the surface, clearly some people have reading difficulties! To the right, there's a view across to Tegg's Nose, down to the reservoirs and across to Jodrell Bank telescope.* Go along the path, which skirts the forest on the right and avoids the descent made by the stony track you were on earlier. To the left, the forest has been cleared. The path eventually drops down a short flight of steps to regain the track. Here go left.

Follow the track through the forest on a slightly rising course. *There are occasional glimpses of the reservoirs and Tegg's Nose to the right; one good spot even being provided with a seat.* After another short climb, the track levels out at a more open area. There's a kissing gate to the left, leading out onto open moorland.

The sign on the left tells you that you are now in Piggford Moor Nature Reserve and describes what you may see there. The view to the west is extensive, but it will get even better. Follow the stone paved path across the moor, eventually topping the rise, at which point, Shuttlingsloe comes into view for the first time. Very impressive it looks too. Cross the moor on a nearly level path, to another kissing gate and one of the ubiquitous Peak and Northern Footpath Society signs. Go through the gate and then right, alongside the wall, following the well-blazed route to Shuttlingsloe. One more 'interesting' stile and then a flight of stone steps leads up to the summit rocks. The path swings to the right to gain the summit, though it is clear that some cannot resist the challenge of a more direct final scramble.

The top of this miniature mountain is a gem. It has the usual trig point and a viewfinder. And what a view! Though this is not the highest point in Cheshire it must have the finest view in the county. This is particularly true westwards and southwards, where, on a clear day (as it was when I did the recce') you could see the Wrekin and the Shropshire hills, plus the Welsh hills from Llangollen northwards to the Clwydians. The nearer views are also impressive and there is a steep craggy drop towards Wildboarclough, where the next part of the route can be clearly seen.

Shuttlingsloe to Clough House

A sudden flurry of snow reminded me that I'd not done half of the walk, so I set off along the ridge in a westerly direction. At the end of the ridge, there's a rough path that descends a few rocky steps to a broader grassy path below and then bears left. Go down the steep path, over the stile and the stream and down to the lane leading to Shuttlingsloe Farm. *The imposing building on the far side of the valley is Crag Hall, a grade II listed building and the country seat of the Earls of Derby. The hall was built in 1796 by the then owner of Crag Mill.* Resist the temptation to carry on straight down the field. There's no right of way there. Go right, along the farm road and follow this down to a gate and cattle grid and there go sharp left along another track. There are no signs indicating that this is a footpath, but it is. You soon reach Bank Top and the path skirts to the right of the house and then past a substantial barn. Now the path runs along a well-built terrace that was obviously intended for vehicular use in the past. The broad grassy track runs firstly alongside a larch plantation and then through open fields, gradually descending until it reaches the valley road, almost at Clough House Farm.

Anyone who has started from the car park at Clough House should go left here and along the road for about 150 yard/metres to the car park entrance.

Shuttlingsloe from Clough House Farm

Clough House to the Cat and Fiddle

If you are starting from Clough House car park simply go out of the back of the car park, over the bridge and turn left up the lane to the T-junction.

If you have just come down Shuttlingsloe and have reached the valley road, go almost straight across the road and over the footbridge that spans Clough Brook. *This pleasant little brook has a nasty side to its character. After heavy rain it is prone to rise very rapidly. In 1989 there was a tremendous downpour and this generated a catastrophic flood, which claimed one life and swept away many bridges and large portions of the valley road. The Wildboarclough village website contains some graphic photos of the devastation. There are some particularly salutary shots of Clough House Farm and the wrecked bridge leading from the back of the car park.* A stile gives access to an indistinct field path. Bear left up the field, making for a gate in the top left hand corner, to the left of the barn (there's a signpost on the barn wall).

Go through the gate, into the farmyard and then right. *There were three dogs in the yard when I recce'd the walk. Two were wagging their tails, either being friendly or in anticipation of some 'fun'. The third dog was lying still, eyeing me up. Fortunately, all three were on chains so it was possible to go through the yard without being eaten alive. (If you are at all frightened of dogs you can avoid the farmyard by going to Clough House car park and then following the instructions at the start of this section).*

A gate leads out of the farmyard onto a lane (which comes out of the back of the car park). Go up the lane to the T-junction. At the T-junction, go straight ahead, through a gate and onto a rough track, signed to the Cat and Fiddle. Follow the track upwards. It soon dips to cross Cumberland Brook, where there is a footbridge. Continue up alongside the brook, pausing every now and then to look back at Shuttlingsloe, which looks very impressive from this angle. It's not known as Cheshire's Matterhorn for nothing. Soon the track is well above the stream, which is chattering away below in its fringe of woodland. The track forks. The route to the left leads up to Cumberland Cottage, which is now a bunkhouse particularly used by the Scout movement. The more obvious route carries on, following the trees and the stream upwards into Danethorn Hollow. Where the trees end you come into a much wilder landscape, hemmed in on three sides by hills and moorland. *Ahead and to your right you'll discern a terrace, which marks the continuation of the track you are on, making its way over to join the A54 near Sparbent. It was also the cart route leading up to Danethorn Colliery. This colliery was operating in the mid 19th century, exploiting a thin seam of low-grade coal. In 1880 it was operated by Messrs W & H Hand, but later maps show it as 'disused'. Looking up the valley, you can see the spoil heap ahead as a prominent conical mound. This marks the position of the main shaft. The first reference to coal working in this part of the world occurs in 1632 and small scale mining continued in some places until the 1920s and maybe even later, though not, apparently, at Danethorn.*

Just beyond a gate and stile and alongside a little waterfall, there's a three-way junction. Your route is the one on the left, signed as a footpath. This follows a small stream up a side clough. Actually, it would seem that the stream and the path are one and the same at times. The path is quite rough underfoot, but presents no difficulties. You pass a ruined building on your right. *This is the collapsed entrance to an adit that led into Danethorn Colliery. Whilst it's hard to believe, the path you are on was once a cart-track leading to this adit and used for collecting the coal and taking it down the valley.* A short way further on the path crosses the stream, just below another little waterfall. The path goes left, then curls round to the right to come alongside a ruined wall, above the waterfall.

A broad path leads up, over the moor to a gate. *It is worth pausing here and looking back at the view, which is extensive. Shuttlingsloe features prominently, as you would expect, but there's a grand vista, ranging from The Roaches across to Wales.* The path now dips to cross the headwaters of Cumberland Brook, here little more than a trickle, then rises again to reach the broad stony track that leads from Danebower Hollow to the Cat and Fiddle. Turn left here, having ascertained from the Peak and

Waterfall at Danethorn Hollow

Northern sign that you are on the right route. *The view from here is even more extensive than by the gate, but it is soon shut off by higher land to your left.* At a gate and stile the Cat and Fiddle comes into view ahead, and with it a wide view over to the north-west and eastwards. *Shining Tor, the highest point in Cheshire looms over the Cat and Fiddle. The Manchester conurbation can be seen and the hills at the back of Horwich. Eastwards, the view stretches to Kinder and the East Moors and there are glimpses of Mam Tor and Win Hill.* Stroll along the final few hundred yards/metres to the Cat and Fiddle. Cross the road with care. *There's a daily bus service from here to Buxton and Macclesfield.*

Cat and Fiddle to Stanley Arms

Walkers accessing this route by public transport will start from here. *Details of the Cat and Fiddle pub are in* **Walk 11** *of this book.*

From the Cat, walk alongside the A537 in the direction of Macclesfield, i.e. west. Keep on the verge; this is a busy road. In about 200 yards/metres, bear right along a roughly surfaced track. *This was the former coach road, before the A537 was built.* The old road climbs slightly then forks. Continue straight ahead, topping the rise and then descending towards the Peak View tearoom.

It's worth pausing to take in the extensive view from this point. Just before you reach the tearoom, go left and down to the main road. Cross the road and go over the stile signed as a permissive path.

Follow the obvious path, which is well waymarked and runs alongside a wall before bearing left and descending towards Chest Hollow. The path follows the course of a power line down into the valley, through a sea of reeds. Where the descent steepens, look left to the impressive valley head. *This is The Scaurs, a geological feature that's only visible from this path.*

The path now swings right, descending to reach the bottom of the clough. Ignore the little gate on the left, which leads into access land and continue ahead down the valley. The valley widens and the path bears right across rough grassland to a gate and stile. *Torgate Farm can be seen ahead and as the valley opens out still further, Shuttlingsloe comes into view and the Cuckoo Rocks just to your left.* The path heads for a gate and stile, waymarked with a blue bucket firmly fixed on one of the gateposts. Now the path bears right and crosses a culvert. Go up the hillside almost to the wall and then bear left, up a grassy cart track. As you top the rise, make for the wall ahead and there join a public right of way. *Looking over the wall, you can now see the Stanley Arms below. Unfortunately, there's no direct path to it from here.* Go left, alongside the wall to a gate. *Looking back up Chest Hollow you can see the Cat and Fiddle, perched on the ridge with the old and new roads winding up to it. Shining Tor dominates the scene in this direction, whilst ahead of you now is Shuttlingsloe.*

Go through the gate and bear slightly left in this next field, not heading for the obvious gate, but for the wall corner just left of it. There is a waymark, but it's not too obvious. At the wall corner, continue ahead with the wall on your right, to the end of the field and a gateway. Turn right immediately beyond the gateway, on a waymarked path heading up the field in a shallow depression. At the top of the field, go over the stile. *From here you can again see the Stanley Arms and you can also make out Forest Chapel and the lane leading up to it.*

Follow the wall on the left to a stile half way down the field. Go over this stile and then continue down beside the wall. *There's a notice on the signpost indicating that the path has been diverted at this point. Modern maps show the diversion, but older ones may still show the route as being across the field and through the farm at Bottom of the Oven.* Follow the diverted path down the side of the field to a gate at the bottom. Go through the gate and bear left, down to a footbridge over Tor Brook. A partly paved path leads from the bridge up to a gate that gives out onto the road. The Stanley Arms lies about 200 yards/metres to the right.

The Stanley Arms. 1178 ft/359 metres
Telephone 01260 252414. www.stanleyarms.com

The Stanley Arms is rightly known for its meals. It is situated at the head of Wildboarclough in the delightfully named, Bottom of the Oven. The pub is on the old road from Buxton to Macclesfield, but this route is well known and well used as a short cut by cars, so there's plenty of passing trade.

Prior to 1906 The Stanley Arms was a working farm and for many years it remained both a farm and public house. The original name of the pub was The Derby Arms, named after Lord Derby, but this was changed to the Stanley Arms before the Second World War. The pub is a Marston's house and so has a selection of real ales from the Marston's Brewery, including Marston's best bitter and the renowned Pedigree. There's also Guinness on draught.

The pub is 'rambler friendly' and the surrounding area of Macclesfield Forest and its associated reservoirs

Stanley Arms from Bottom of the Oven

has much to offer. The pub website claims that The Stanley Arms is one of the highest in the country, but this can't be correct. It's only the 12th highest in the Peak District, but that's irrelevant. It's still a grand pub.

Opening times
Open seven days a week from 1200.

Food is served: Monday to Friday from 1200 to 1430 and 1730 to 2100; Saturday from 1200 to 2100; Sunday from 1200 to 1900.

Walk 30: Wincle (The Wild Boar)

Start and finish	Gradbach car park. (GR. SJ 998662)
The route	Gradbach, Goosetree, Burntcliff Top, Heild End, A54, Wildboarclough, Clough Brook, Hammerton Knowl Farm, Wincle (Wild Boar), Hammerton Farm, Danebridge, Hangingstone Farm, Hanging Stone, (Lud's Church optional), Gradbach
Length	8.24 miles (13.25 km)
Ascent	1752 feet (534 metres)
Time	4¼ hours (exclusive of stops and any visit to Lud's Church)
Map	OS OL24 (White Peak)

Getting there

By bus. No bus service on A54. The Staffordshire Moorlands dial a ride service (Moorlands Connect) will call at Gradbach by prior arrangement.

By train. No station anywhere near.

By car. The Wild Boar is on the A54 Congleton-Buxton road, but the only parking is at the pub. You may be able to park there by prior arrangement with the landlord, but the best public parking is at Gradbach.

From Leek or Buxton use the A53 to just south of Flash Bar then through Flash village. Follow the lane and signs down to Gradbach car park. From Congleton use the A54 to Allgreave then right on the minor road to Gradbach. The car park at Gradbach is just in Staffordshire, signed to the right (a very sharp turn) down an even more minor lane.

The Walk

Gradbach to Wildboarclough

From the entrance to Gradbach car park turn right and go along the lane to the Youth Hostel. Skirt round the front of the hostel to locate a narrow bridge over

Walk 30

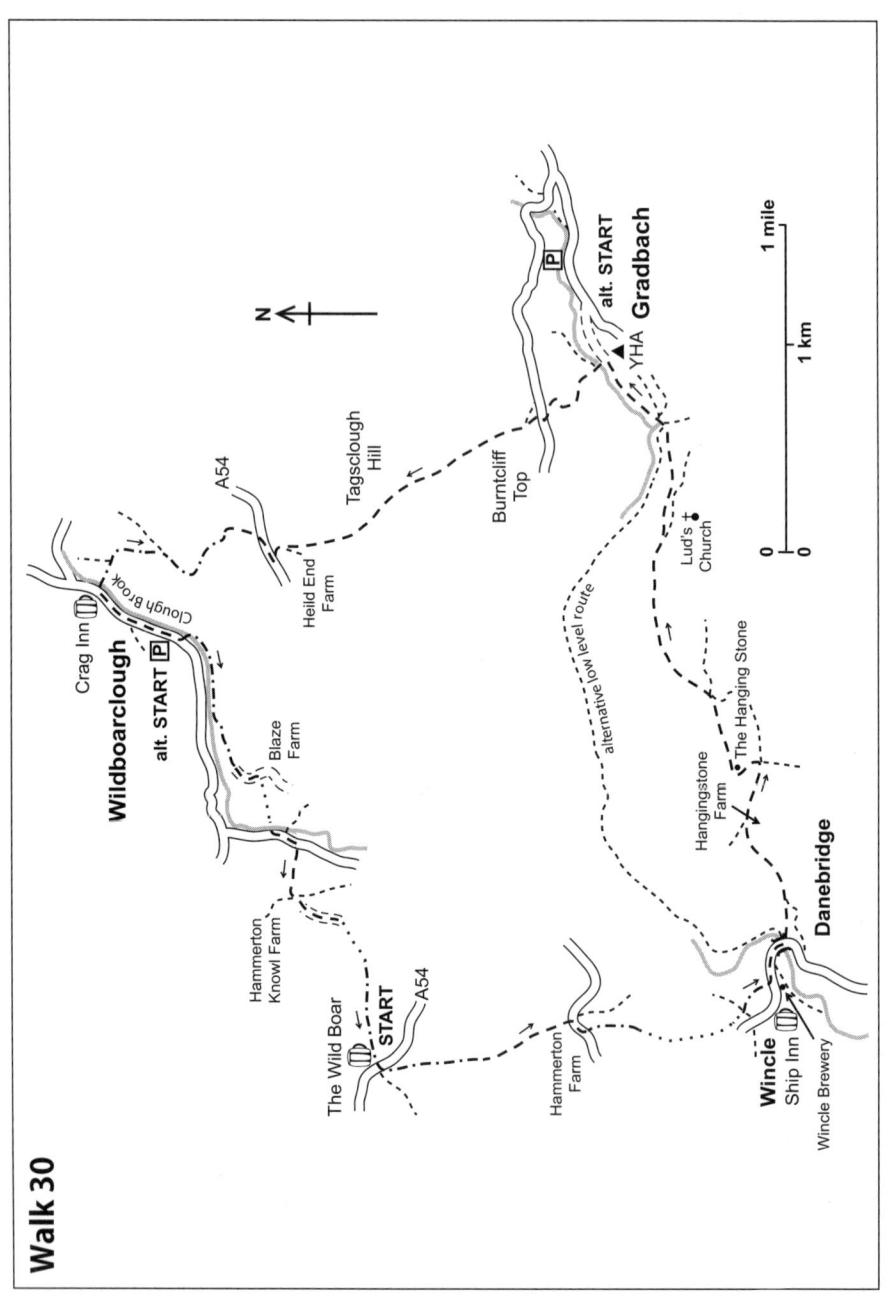

Wildboarclough

Crag Inn

Clough Brook

A54

alt. START P

Blaze Farm

Heild End Farm

Tagsclough Hill

Burntcliff Top

N

alt. START

Gradbach

YHA

Lud's Church

The Hanging Stone

alternative low level route

Hangingstone Farm

Danebridge

Hammerton Knowl Farm

The Wild Boar

START

A54

Hammerton Farm

Wincle

Ship Inn

Wincle Brewery

1 mile

1 km

0

0

the Dane. Cross the bridge, go up the steps and follow the waymarked path up past Goosetree, out onto the track up to Burntcliff Top where you cross the Flash-Allgreave road. Go straight across and once past the buildings, glance left. *The view is extensive, with Bosley Minn prominent and on a clear day you can see right across the Cheshire plain to the Clwydian range of hills in Wales.* The next mile is a delightful stroll on a good track, which according to the OS map is still a county highway, though only used as a footpath. *Keep admiring the view westwards. It becomes even more*

Gradbach youth hostel

extensive as you climb higher. Don't forget to look back as well to take in the panorama of the Roaches and Back Forest.

Continue along the track, climbing gently until higher land to the left eventually shuts out the view. As you top the rise there is a sudden view of Shuttlingsloe – the Cheshire Matterhorn, across the valley of Wildboarclough. There's also an interesting distant glimpse of traffic on the Cat and Fiddle road as it skirts the base of Shining Tor. Continue on the track, which now descends towards the A54 Congleton-Buxton road, joining the access to Heild End Farm en route. Where the track swings sharp left, go straight on, down a sketchy path to a stile onto the main road. Cross the road and go over another stile into fields. Bear right and go down the field, making for the right hand side of a clump of trees that shield a barn. There is no obvious path on the ground. The path skirts round the right hand side of the barn, then goes sharp left to a gate and stile. In this field, bear right, making for the right hand corner of the conifer plantation, passing through a gateway and another field en route. Follow the boundary fence of the wood to the field corner then go right, alongside the wall to locate a stile, at the end of the shelter belt of trees.

The path now develops into a walled lane, quite rough underfoot. This descends gently towards Wildboarclough. *The Crag Inn can be seen below, whilst the view ahead is still dominated by Shuttlingsloe, which looks ever more impressive.*

Where the track emerges into open fields, bear left (waymarked), making for a footbridge, which can be clearly seen ahead. Continue ahead to another footbridge and there turn left, alongside the stream. At the next way-marker

The view accross to Shuttlingsloe

post continue straight on beside the stream to a stile in the corner of the field. The stream is culverted at this point and so you emerge on the other side of the stile with the stream to your right – but not for long. Go down through the wood and cross the stream again, this time without the assistance of a bridge or culvert. Follow the stream down to a more substantial bridge, which spans Clough Brook and thus reach the road. Go left here and within a couple of bounds you are at The Crag Inn.

The Crag Inn. 889 ft/271 metres
Telephone 01260 227239. No Website

Although not one of the 'high' pubs, the Crag Inn is worth a mention. This cosy hostelry boasts open fires, a selection of real ales and traditional food.

The pub hosts an Octoberfest, which in 2012 showcased beers from the Wincle, Red Willow, Happy Valley and Bollington breweries. There have been repeated attempts in the recent past to close the pub and convert it to housing. So far this has not succeeded and the latest application was refused and the appeal dismissed in October 2012. Nevertheless this is a sign of the times where rural pubs are going out of business with monotonous regularity. The cry of 'use it or lose it' is apt.

Opening times
From 1100 to 2300.

The Crag Inn, Wildboarclough

Wildboarclough to The Wild Boar

From the Crag Inn, follow the road down beside the river for about 550 yards (½km), passing a lay-by. *(This offers a possible alternative starting point for the walk.)* Just past the lay-by go left, over a bridge and then immediately right at a footpath sign, to pick up a path beside the river. Follow this path, which is distinct at first but soon becomes less so as it reaches open fields. Keep close to the river for about 300 yards at which point the path bears away to the left, uphill to a wall. There's a waymark post here, but the route is obvious enough. Follow the wall as it bears round to the right and thus reach a farm. A couple of curious stiles take you into the farmyard and you skirt to the left of the buildings and onto the access driveway. Go up the driveway, negotiating the cattle grid or using the small gate provided and then pass Underbank Farm on your right. Just beyond the farm there's a small barn on the right, which is now one of the YHA's camping barns. A short distance beyond this a footpath sign directs you right, over a stile and into fields. *However, a sign beside the stile may tempt you to go further on along the driveway to Blaze Farm (200 yards/metres) where there's the promise of a tearoom!* Assuming you've not succumbed to the blandishments of Blaze Farm, go down the field, keeping towards the right hand side and so locate a stile in the bottom fence. *It should be noted that when this walk was recce'd there had been torrential rain the night before and the passage of this field was more reminiscent of the Somme battlefield in terms of the mud. A visit to Blaze Farm opens up the prospect of an alternative route avoiding the quagmire, but I'll leave you to work that one out for yourselves.*

Go down the next field, which was marginally less muddy, to a stile leading onto a footbridge over Clough Brook. A glance at the map will show that this is quite a complicated little crossing, because the footpath coincides with a ford that crosses the river diagonally and in so doing cuts across the line of the footpath. This could be interesting if the river is in spate, because just beyond the footbridge, the route of the track beyond the ford is obviously sometimes under water. Pick your times! Other than that, this is an idyllic spot and there's even a stone seat. Go up to the road and turn left, following the road up, round the corner to the wide entrance to the driveway to Hammerton Knowl Farm. *For some reason, the path is signed just beyond the driveway, but when the walk was recce'd the route was blocked by silage bales and temporary fencing. In any case, the only obvious reason for this route was to avoid the passage of a cattle grid, because just beyond the cattle grid there is a pedestrian gate through which the path emerges onto the driveway. On balance negotiating the cattle grid was the easier option.*

Go up the driveway, passing the 'farm worker's dwelling' on the right and then reaching a gate. The driveway continues; bearing away to the left, but the waymarked path goes straight up the hill on quite steep grass to a stile in the boundary hedge of the farm. Go over the stile and then straight on to reach the driveway again. Here there's a multiplicity of way-marks. *This makes one yearn for the continental habit of signposts that tell you where paths lead to, rather than our curious habit of merely telling you there's a path and leaving you to sort out where it goes.* Turn right and go into the farm yard, there bearing left past a ruined barn and out along another rough track. The track skirts Hammerton Knowl, which rises to your right. *To your left there's a fine view over towards the Roaches and looking back you can see the length of Wildboarclough and, of course, Shuttlingsloe.* Bowl along the track, admiring the view, but where the track begins to descend and swing right, leave it and go up the hill on the right to come to a fence. There's no footpath sign or waymark for this. If you reach a large trough on the right hand side of the track you've gone too far and should retrace your steps.

Follow the fence and wall, keeping it to your right and so reach a stile, thus proving that you are at least on a recognised footpath. Continue alongside the wall, which is now on your left, to a gateway. Here a tempting track leads away to the left, but this is not the route. Again there are no waymarks, but continue more or less straight ahead on a very indistinct path to a wall corner, where a more distinct path materialises. Follow this path to a large ladder stile on your left, by which time the Wild Boar pub is in view. Cross the ladder stile and make your way across the field towards the left hand end of the pub and thus reach a stile out onto the A54. Turn right for the pub.

The Wild Boar Inn. 1083 ft/330 metres
Telephone 01260 227219. No website

The Wild Boar is a 16th century coaching inn. It's a Robinson's house and as one would expect there's a range of that brewery's beers on offer, particularly Unicorn Best Bitter. The pub website describes it as "real ale, pulled with a proper head".

Like so many rural pubs, this one has expanded into food and an excellent job it makes of it too. Not only are there full-scale meals on offer, but also bar snacks. Hikers, ramblers, cyclists and motorcyclists are all welcome in this cosy Cheshire pub. There's even a campsite just behind the pub so you could do this walk, have a jolly good meal, chill out in the games room and then wander off to the camp site for a night's kip.

Opening times
Monday to Saturday: 1130 to 2300; Sundays: 1100 to 2300 (note that when the walk was recce'd the pub was certainly not open at lunchtime)

The Wild Boar Inn, Wincle

The Wild Boar to Danebridge
Directly opposite the pub is a gateway and stile with a footpath sign that has two direction arrows on it. You want the left hand path, but apart from the

first few yards (where there's a track), you'll be hard pressed to find it. Once at the end of the track, scan the field ahead of you and to the right of the clump of trees and you should spot a solitary way-mark post. Make for this and then continue ahead to pick up a line of hawthorns and then a clear farm track. Follow this track, which is metalled, down almost to Hammerton Farm. Here the track swings right, but a stile leads into a fine green lane that skirts the farm and emerges onto the road by the farm gate. The sign on the right says 'Beware of the dogs', but apart from the barking I came away intact.

Turn right at the road and go downhill for a short distance before turning left at the next footpath sign. *The construction of the stile leaves a good deal to be desired, but thankfully the field gate has a section for pedestrians – and it opens. Just make sure you lift your feet when going through the gate and not do as I did, trip on the bottom bar and almost fall flat on your face.* Negotiate the usual gateway morass and bear right, going down the field towards the stream and a well-hidden stile in the far right hand corner. There's no obvious path, but that should come as no surprise now. Go over the stile and almost at once go right, over a plank bridge. Go over a stile, bear left and up the bank into a field. The trodden path runs alongside the fence until forced upwards where the fence alters course. There you'll find another well-hidden stile. Go over this stile and down the next small field to a gate to the right of Mellor Knowl Farm. Cross the driveway, noting the fine old crane on the left, and go down the track to the right of the crane to another gate, leading into fields again.

Bear right and cross the field to a stile to the right of five large trees. Once over this, there's a multi-facetted footpath sign, but no cause for confusion, because your route is straight on, making for the wall corner. There's a very fine property on the right hand side of the path, also known as Mellor Knowl according to large scale maps. A stile in a non-existent fence leads to a steepening field, where you bear left to another stile at the bottom left. A further short descent and you are at a gate onto the road at Danebridge. The Ship Inn lies a little way up the hill to the right, but immediately opposite your gateway is the Wincle Brewery.

Wincle Brewery and The Ship Inn

Wincle Brewery
Telephone 01260 227777 or 01260 227555. www.winclebeer.co.uk
When the brewery was set up in 2008, the original intention was to brew on a part-time basis, but the business has expanded so much that it's a now a full-time job. The brewery produces some cracking beers with wonderful names,

usually with some local connotations. Their proud boast is that their beers are available in all the Peak District's youth hostels. Now where did I put that YHA application form?

The Ship Inn
Telephone 01260 227217. www.wincle.org.uk/ship_inn
The Ship Inn is a J W Lees house and a delightful country pub. The pub serves a range of real ales and both lunchtime and evening meals. Wherever possible, the meals use fresh, local produce. Booking is recommended. The pub is well sited for walks and walkers are made welcome, particularly in the tap room. On fine days, you can also enjoy the delights of the beer garden.

Opening times
Closed all day Mondays (except Bank Holidays when Sunday hours are kept). Lunchtimes: Tuesdays to Saturdays: 1200 to 1500 (last food orders 1430); Sundays: 1200 to 1600 (last food orders 1500). Evenings: Tuesdays to Thursdays: 1900 to 2300; Fridays: 1730 to 300; Saturdays: 1800 to 2300. Sunday evenings Closed.
Evening meals served Tuesdays to Saturdays from 1900, with last orders at 2045.

Danebridge to Gradbach
Cross the bridge over the Dane, noting how high the road is above the river. *The Dane has the reputation of being one of the fastest rising rivers in the country, being fed by a wide area of wild moorland, hence the need for this substantial bridge and approach embankment.* On the Staffordshire side of the bridge there's a footpath sign for Gradbach. Go left here and follow a wide track beside the river. After only a few yards there's a stile on the right and a signpost for a concession path to the Hanging Stone. *You have a choice. The route of the walk goes via the Hanging Stone, but a lot of climbing can be avoided by keeping on the riverside path, which is the Dane Valley Way. This route is not described in this book but you should have no trouble following it as it is well signed. If you do choose this option, skip the next 3 paragraphs.*

Go over the stile and up the steps alongside the tumbling stream. The path climbs through the wood, eventually joining a public footpath (waymarked), which trails in from the right. (*In the event of the concession path being closed you can get to this point from Danebridge simply by going a little further up the road into Staffordshire and picking up the path there.*)

Eventually the path emerges into open fields at a stile and the Hanging Stone is clearly in view ahead. Bear left across the field to a stile. *Your mind may be briefly distracted by the presence of a large solitary boulder in midfield, but you'll soon have bigger rocks to play with.* At the stile go right, making for Hangingstone Farm, but almost at once deviating left on a signed path which skirts the farm. This path emerges onto a track. *Here there is a confusing signpost that implies a right of way to Danebridge down the track, but there's also a very clear sign stating that there is no such right of way and the route is private.* Not of much consequence to you as your route lies along the track in the opposite direction, but every now and then there are reminder notices that the land on the left is private and there's no access. Clearly these strictures are not always followed, because there are paths leading off to the

The Hanging Stone

left, but best be on the safe side and follow the signs, which state quite clearly that there is a concession path to the Hanging Stone a little further on. You pass below the Hanging Stone and then, just before a gateway and cattle grid, there's a footpath sign on the left denoting the concession path. Interestingly, this is not as shown on the OS 1:25000 map, which quite clearly indicates that there's a public footpath up to the Hanging Stone. No matter. Turn left and go up the path, which soon brings you to the rock outcrop. *There's a plaque on this side of the rock in memory of Lt. Col. Brocklehurst (1888-1942) who died in active service in Burma in WWII. The plaque was erected by his brother in 1949. A flight of steps leads up the side of the rock and there's another plaque, this time commemorating Burke, a mastiff who was buried close by in 1874. The top of the rock is a fine vantage point, with views across to the Roaches, the Shropshire hills, the Wrekin, Bosley Minn, the Clwydians and then round to Croker Hill mast, Wildboarclough, Shuttlingsloe and Flash.*

From the Hanging Stone follow the waymarked path across the moor, soon reaching a substantial stile, which drops you into a deep hollow-way. Go left here and make your way steadily along, ignoring the path deviating off to the right towards the Roaches. Your path descends gently, soon reaching the first trees and then coming to a junction of paths beside a jumble of rocks. *If you've a yen to visit Lud's Church you need to go right here, but remember that you need to allow at least ½ hour to get there and back and do some exploration. For a description of Lud's Church* **see Walk 24.** If you are not visiting Lud's Church, carry on down the track following the route of **Walk 24**, soon reaching a footpath sign directing you left, down a rough flight of steps and a steep slope to a bridge.

Here anyone who took the Dane Valley Way alternative at Danebridge rejoins the route.

Cross the bridge and go up the path for a short distance, then go over a stone step stile on the left. Keep left along the track and so reach Gradbach Youth Hostel again, noting that it does food and drink on Saturdays and Sundays (presumably including Wincle Brewery products). You should need no further description to get you back to Gradbach car park from here.

Also from Sigma Leisure:

Best Pub Walks in the White Peak
30 Classic Peak District Rambles
Les Lumsden & Martin Smith

The 30 fabulous walks range from three to nine miles and ideal for family rambles. They start in such delightful Peak District villages as Ashford-in-the-Water, Alstonefield and Youlgreave, most of which are accessible by public transport — so that you can leave the car at home and savour the products on offer at the authors' favourite pubs.

Follow the recommendatios in this well-established — and completely updated — book for a superb variety of walks in splendid scenery and, after each walk, relax in a Peak District pub renowned for its welcome to walkers and for the quality of its Real Ale, often supplied by local independent brewers.

£9.99

Best Pub Walks in the Dark Peak
30 Classic Peak District Rambles
Les Lumsden & Martin Smith

A large area of Derbyshire is included in the Dark Peak, together with sections of East Cheshire, South Yorkshire and North Staffordshire, and the 30 rambles in this book are based on the very best parts of this wild and characterful region. The walks range from 3 to 11 miles and all start at or call at one of the many Peakland pubs in and around the picturesque villages of the Dark Peak.

Each walk includes information about the locality, yarns and legends of the area as well as general geographical description.

£7.95

Rocky Rambles in The Peak District 2nd Edition
Fred Broadhurst

"The Peak District has a dramatic story to tell and Fred Broadhurst is just the guide we need." – Aubrey Manning, presenter of the BBC TV series 'Earth Story'.

You don't have to be an expert or even an amateur geologist to enjoy these 'rocky rambles'! Where better than in and around the Peak District would you find geology right there beneath your feet - all you need to know is where to look.

The comprehensive glossary of terms, which covers the identification of Peak District Rocks, forms an invaluable supplement and provides 'at a glance' information for the reader.

£8.99

DARK PEAK HIKES
Off the Beaten Track

Dark Peak Hikes
Off the Beaten Track
Doug Brown

Here are 30 walks in the Dark Peak - the legendary northern part of the Peak District that covers some of the best hill country of Derbyshire, Yorkshire and Greater Manchester. Renowned for its unique peat ecology and striking gritstone scenery, the Dark Peak is a paradise for adventurous walkers intent on exploring the remoter parts of the moors.

Includes lots of helpful information for each walk – starting point, distance and estimated time, a general description including level of difficulty, and a very detailed route description.

£8.99

Peak District Walks starting from train stations
Peter Naldrett

Two types of train station walks are covered in this book: there are those from existing train stations that still have passengers bustling about them, and there are those from platforms that fell silent in the infamous closures of the 1960s. Whether you are wanting to reach your starting point via train or delve into the history of transport in the Peak District, this book has something for you. All the walks enjoy a fabulous route into some breath-taking countryside. Gorges, woodland, moors, farmland, rivers, glacial valleys and some tremendous hills are all included in this series of 20 walks, linked together by the transport routes that, today and in the past, dissected the Peak District. *£8.99*

A walking guide to the County Tops of Wales, the North of England and the Isle of Man
Howard Mann

There are many hill walking challenges in England and Wales, they include visiting the top of every one of the Lake District peaks or the summits of all the mountains over 2000 feet, but the one that is accessible to all, is to stand on the high point of a county or several counties. It is the option that is closest to home. Be it one of the historic counties or one of those which was created by the major local government reforms of 1974 and 1996, this book offers the casual walker a route to the summit of their chosen county and the committed hill walker challenges in some of the finest mountain terrain in the United Kingdom. Each chapter contains a brief history of the county, its geography and its high point and a detailed description and outline map of the route. *£8.99*

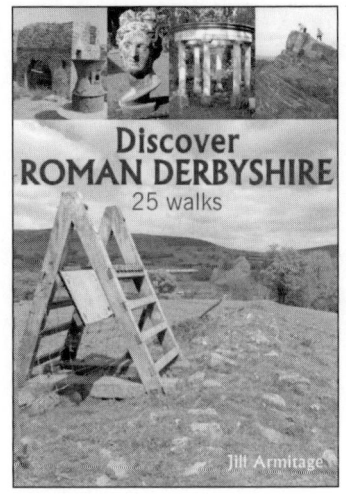

Discover Roman Derbyshire
25 walks
Jill Armitage

The Romans have been credited with giving Britain a network of roads that still has a profound effect on our road systems, so Discover Roman Derbyshire, 25 walks sets out to trace those roads on foot in the same manner that the Roman soldiers did when they occupied the region between the 1st and 5th centuries. The roads linked forts with their accompanying vici, busy trading centres where industry prospered similar to our present day towns. The walks not only include the roads, forts and vici, they also trace localities where finds have been discovered.

£8.99

Discover Celtic Derbyshire
25 walks
Jill Armitage

Discover Celtic Derbyshire follows the Portway from the key Celtic Hillfort of Mam Tor in North Derbyshire to the Derbyshire/Nottinghamshire border at Stapleford and the southern river ports. Along the route, you will encounter the hermitages and industries, visit tribal hillforts, those iconic symbols of the age, and through megalithic mysteries, ancient feasts and festivals, discover the lifestyle of these people the conquering Romans considered barbaric. They were not. They had their beliefs and their gods and the Roman conquest of Britain did not signal the immediate death of Celtic culture. That is why this area has a treasure trove of early curiosities and customs, showing that pre-history is not quite dead in this ancient heart of England. Of the 25 walks in this book, 15 are circular, however, the route of the ancient Portway has been divided into ten manageable walks ranging from 3½ -7 miles.

£8.99

Peak District Walking Natural History Walks
Christopher Mitchell

An updated 2nd Edition with 18 varied walks for all lovers of the great outdoors — and armchair ramblers too! Learn how to be a nature detective, a 'case notes' approach shows you what clues to look for and how to solve them. Detailed maps include animal tracks and signs, landscape features and everything you need for the perfect natural history walk. There are mysteries and puzzles to solve to add more fun for family walks — solutions supplied! Includes follow on material with an extensive Bibliography and 'Taking it Further' sections.

£8.99

Best Tea Shop Walks in the Peak District
Norman and June Buckley

A wonderful collection of easy-going walks that are ideal for families and all those who appreciate fine scenery with a touch of decadence in the shape of an afternoon tea or morning coffee —or both! The 26 walks are spread widely across the Peak District, including Lyme Park, Castleton, Miller's Dale, and The Roaches and — of course — such famous dales as Lathkill and Dovedale. Each walk has a handy summary so that you can choose the walks that are ideally suited to the interests and abilities of your party. The tea shops are just as diverse, ranging from the splendour of Chatsworth House to more basic locations. Each one welcomes ramblers and there is always a good choice of tempting goodies.

£8.99

Discovering Manchester
2nd Edition
Barry Worthington

This stylish walking guide doubles as a detailed account of the city's architecture, its history and tourism attractions. There are walks throughout Manchester including such major entertainment and cultural centres as the Bridgewater Hall, Urbis, the Museum of Science and Industry, the Lowry and many more. Explore the entire city – from the Corn Exchange to G-Mex, from the Cathedral to Affleck's Palace.

£10.99

Peak District Walking
On The Level
Norman Buckley

Some folk prefer easy walks, and sometimes there's just not time for an all-day romp. In either case, this is definitely a book to keep on your bookshelf. Norman Buckley has had considerable success with "On The Level" books for the Lake District and the Yorkshire Dales.

The walks are ideal for family outings and the precise instructions ensure that there's little chance of losing your way. Well-produced maps encourage everybody to try out the walks - all of which are well scattered across the Peak District.

£8.99